The Dynamics of War and Revolution

The Dynamics of War and Revolution

By Lawrence Dennis
Author of "Is Capitalism Doomed?"
and "The Coming American Fascism"

COPYRIGHT ©, 1940, BY THE WEEKLY FOREIGN LETTER

THIS BOOK HAS ENTERED THE PUBLIC DOMAIN IN THE UNITED STATES

WWW.EBOOK-DEPOSITORY.COM

Contents

INTRODUCTION	vii
DEFINITIONS: THEY MUST BE MADE BY THOSE WHO MAKE HISTORY	xv
MEANINGS OF KEY TERMS	xv

PART I: BACK TO FIRST PRINCIPLES

I. THE SOCIAL NEED OF PERMANENT REVOLUTION	3
II. THE VICTORS MAKE THE RULES	19
III. THE INTERNATIONAL JUNGLE	31

PART II: THE END OF THE CAPITALIST REVOLUTION

IV. THE INDUSTRIAL REVOLUTION—THE PROFITS OF NEW MONOPOLIES	43
V. THE FRONTIER—THE PROFITS OF FREE LAND	59
VI. RAPID POPULATION INCREASE—THE PROFITS OF CHEAP LABOR	77
VII. EASY WARS OF CONQUEST—BOWS AND ARROWS VERSUS THE MACHINE GUN	89
VIII. THE MASSES GO TO SCHOOL AND THE POLLS	109

PART III: THE NEW REVOLUTION. MARS, THE MIDWIFE

IX. NECESSITIES AND FRUSTRATIONS	119
X. WE FIGHT BECAUSE OF DEMOCRACY'S FAILURE	125
XI. FROM CAPITALIST TO SOCIALIST IMPERIALISM	131
XII. THE RETURN TO DISCIPLINE	143
XIII. POWER POLITICS	159
XIV. REALISM ENDS IN FOREIGN AFFAIRS WHEN THE PEOPLE RULE	169
XV. THE BLOODY FUTILITY OF FRUSTRATING THE STRONG	183
XVI. AFTER WAR, PYRAMID BUILDING	191
XVII. WE STAGNATE BECAUSE THERE IS NO COMMON WILL TO ACTION	205
XVIII. OUT OF WAR A NEW REVOLUTIONARY FOLK UNITY	211

Introduction

This book needs an introduction (1) to anticipate certain easy misconstructions of its major theses and, (2) to set the reader straight from the start as to the author's attitude and purposes.

First, let it be said that I am undertaking to explain rather than to advocate (1) the current decline and fall of capitalism and democracy; and (2) the new revolution which is worldwide and just beginning in this country. I do not seek to show what can or should be done (1) to save democracy and capitalism or (2) to stop the new revolution. I am concerned only over what can and should be done for the best interests of the American people, not of a system, during developments which I consider inevitable and already in progress.

Second, I argue that permanent social revolution is the only alternative to stagnation, pointing out that democracy, or capitalism on its economic side, was a great revolution and is fast becoming only a great legend. In so doing, I seek to explain the new revolution in various countries as a great and more or less inevitable process of social change the world over. I shall, therefore, probably be accused, though wrongly, of defending all revolutions and everything done in each one of them. I do not say that all revolutions are absolutely good. I say merely that any revolution that is big enough will end stagnation which is the essence of the social problem of today.

Third, as to war, I hold it probable that nothing can keep America out and that our going to war will prove futile for the purposes for which we shall fight because, in going to war against the Have-nots, we shall be lighting a world revolution abroad only thereby to bring about here the same revolution which I consider inevitable everywhere. I am in favor of the revolution here but deem the war way of bringing it about regrettable though inevitable in the present emotional attitude of the American people toward world events.

It will be easy to misunderstand or distort my position as to our going to war. It will seem to many that it is contradictory, at the same time, to disapprove of our entering the war, to approve of our going through with the new revolution and to say that we shall do so through entering the war. Obviously, from what I have to say, my personal preference would be to have the new revolution carried out here without our going to war in a futile effort to stop war abroad. What will be hard for many to understand about this book is that it is primarily my analysis of the situation and the near-future probabilities rather than a statement of my personal preferences. As I see no likelihood of my preferences being realized in the transition from capitalism to socialism, I do not devote a whole book to expounding them, as a detailed program, though I do not hesitate to express or suggest them from time to time in different connections. But my preferences are brought in only incidentally to the development of the book's main theses which are largely interpretative of actual trends and probable events.

The gravamen of the criticism against this book will probably be that it is defeatist, fatalistic, depressing, cynical, immoral, and lacking in faith in democracy and in the intelligence of the masses. All this boils down to the charge that the book is not utopian. To make the task of my critics as simple as possible, let me say categorically that I do not believe in democracy or the intelligence of the masses as my critics will generally use these terms. If democracy merited my believing in it or if the masses had social intelligence to which rational appeal could be made, we should not have fought the Civil War and the World War or be in the mess we have been in for the past ten years. If the masses had a social intelligence to which rational appeal could be made successfully, we should work out the new revolution in America without going to war. We should solve the problem of unemployment as quickly and as easily as we put two million soldiers in France in 1917-1918 to make the world safe for democracy. To suppose that an appeal to the intelligence of the masses to solve America's internal problems without going to war has any chance against an appeal to the emotions of the masses to go to war against foreigners is naive. I refuse to appeal to something I find no evidence of ever having existed. The argument against our fighting in Europe's wars can have appeal only for a small part of the elite capable of abstract reasoning. I shall be happy to be proved wrong in these conclusions. But, in my lack of faith in democracy, I can be proved wrong only by events, not by the words of my critics.

It will then be asked by many critics why, if I have so little faith in democracy and the intelligence of the masses, I write this book. The answer is that this book is addressed not to the masses but to the elite or to the ruling groups, actual and potential. It is the governing minority of wealth, prestige and power, economic and cultural, present and future, which determines whether, when, where, how, and whom we fight. The American people, of course, do not want to go to war at the moment. But neither have they wanted unemployment and huge relief deficits and taxes over the past ten years. What the people want and what they get are not always the same things. The trouble is that the masses do not understand and can never be made to understand clearly the implications of their desires.

If and when a majority of the elite or the ruling minority decide that the time has come for us to go to war, the masses will be made overnight to cry as lustily, sincerely, and innocently for war as a baby cries for milk. The elite, through their skilled medicine men, who manipulate the verbal symbols and moral concepts by which mass emotions are swayed and mass attitudes are created, can plunge us into war whenever they desire. The technique for doing this is the same as that explained in Pavlov's experiments in conditioned reflexes with the dog whose mouth was made to water every time he heard the sound of a certain bell, having been so conditioned by reason of being fed several times when the bell was rung. Science has given experts more skill, knowledge and instruments for manipulating the masses than the medicine men and witch doctors of old ever commanded. Universal education has made the masses susceptible to large-scale opinion and attitude manipulation such as would have been impossible in the days when only a few could read and write. In those days wars had to be fought by comparatively small numbers of specialized fighters, who could be brought under the command of one leader by the then available means of communication. Now, thanks to the progress of democracy, industrialism and science, to quote from our army's Industrial Mobilization Plan of 1936, "War is no longer simply a battle between armed forces in the field, it is a struggle in which each side strives to bring to bear against the enemy the coordinated power of every individual and every material resource at its command. The conflict extends from the soldiers in the most forward line to the humblest citizen in the remotest hamlet in the rear."

A simple proof of the people's lack of social intelligence as to war may be found in the almost total indifference of American public opinion, the newspapers and writers to the Industrial Mobilization Plan of the War and Navy Departments for the event of war. This plan would set up overnight a totalitarian economic dictatorship, supposedly, of course, for only the duration of the war. Do our papers and magazines discuss the implications of such a plan? Is the public interested in them? The answer to both questions is "Practically, no." Government officials give us long discourses on Secretary Hull's irrelevant free-trade ideas, on international cooperation, on the wickedness of foreign dictatorships and on what can or ought to be done about it. To the masses, one must preach either utopia or hate to be persuasive. But realistic plans laid by our army and navy to turn the United States into a totalitarian dictatorship on the outbreak of war are hardly mentioned in the public prints. Why is this so? The answer is that the vested interests of politicians and businessmen normally require the hoodwinking of the public, and that the public loves to be fooled about war by its statesmen as much as it loves to be fooled about life by the movies.

This book is not addressed, then, to those who will be stampeded into war like cattle into a corral but to all the elite, some of whom will lead the stampede and others of whom, like the author, will be swept along with the herd. It is written not as a pamphlet against, but as a guide to, what is going to happen. A book written with this purpose cannot be agreeably persuasive, because it must deal with unpleasant actualities and probabilities. To argue persuasively for or against American participation in war, one must make certain contrary-to-fact assumptions the basis of one's appeal. One of the many reasons for the breakdown of democracy is that, to be persuasive in propaganda or popular appeal, one has to be unrealistic, just as moving pictures have to be in order to command box-office appeal. It should need no explanation that while fictions or falsehoods may be successful for propaganda or box-office purposes, they are unsatisfactory for technical purposes. And this industrialized society of ours is an extremely technical affair. In a primitive society it made little difference what types of witchcraft the people believed in or practiced. But an industrialized civilization has to be run under rational control by an elite capable of a high order of rationality. Else we must get back, through a prolonged process of population decimation, to small communities which can be run successfully by witchcraft and the folklore about which Thurman Arnold writes with his tongue in his cheek.

Many critics will find it contradictory on my part, in a book which professes loyalty to rationality, to challenge eighteenth century rationalism and deny that the masses are susceptible to an appeal to reason. The explanation consists mainly of the paradox that eighteenth century rationalism was never entirely rational because never entirely true in its fundamental assumptions. The first requisite of rational centralized social control (which is now necessary and which eighteenth century rationalism held to be unnecessary by reason of the imputed rationality of mass behavior) is recognition that mass behavior and mass reactions are irrational. A rational manipulation of an irrational mass mind and irrational mass reactions must be the first objective of rational social control for any purpose. A theory or system of social control, politics or economics based on the assumed rationality of mass behavior is irrational because this assumption is untrue. It is doubtless rational for social control to use lies, as we did in war propaganda in 1917-1918 and as we shall doubtless do again, as instruments of mass manipulation. But it is not rational for the engineer to believe in and act on belief in lies. Successful technology requires empirical truth. Successful political democracy seemingly requires persuasive lies. Sometimes these lies are called idealism; the most favorable description of them to accord with the facts is to call them utopian factions or myths. But you cannot run a complex machine by myths and factions even of the law.

Many readers will, by reason of this book's frank recognition of the limitations and failures of democracy, assail the author as lacking in respect for the people or the dignity of man. This, of course, is entirely an issue of conflicting assumptions, not of facts versus assumptions. I assume that love of one's fellow men, respect for man and loyalty to one's kind are best expressed in attitudes, actions and institutions which best serve human welfare; and that the failure of democracy and capitalism to end unemployment condemns that system as inadequate for human welfare.

Others may, with equal validity, assume that it is better to have constitutional rights to do the physically impossible than it is to have work without such precious rights. I do not despise liberty, but I do not hold precious a liberty without its corresponding opportunity. I do not hold human rights cheap, but I would not give two straws for a legal right to do the impossible. A bill of rights which does not include the right to a job or an old age pension, but which is rather incompatible with this type of security, is today an absurd anachronism.

In his monumental study of history, Professor Toynbee says that "a civilization breaks down through a loss of harmony between its parts" and that "one source of disharmony between the institutions of which a society is composed is the introduction of new social forces, aptitudes, or emotions or ideas which the existing set of institutions was not originally intended to carry." And so he arrives at the conclusion that our Western civilization is struggling with the consequences of the introduction of two social forces, industrialism and democracy. Modern industrialism and democracy have developed conditions which only new forms of social organization can correct. To contradict successfully the foregoing statement it is necessary to show either that unemployment is a tolerable condition or that democracy can correct it. My critics are reminded that the burden of such proof lies on them and not on the challenger of democracy and capitalism.

Some readers may also, especially after we have gotten into a war which is called throughout this book a major mistake and misfortune for America, question the author's patriotism. Of course, this book is not the stuff to give the troops going overseas to kill with the idea they will thereby make the world safe for America, capitalism, imperialism or democracy. But, let it be recalled that the book was written well before the war and that it was written for an elite to ponder over during the war in preparation for its sequels. It will not imbue the masses with defeatism for the next war because it will never be read by the masses. If the masses could read and understand this book, we should not go to war for the Allies. The book cannot be blamed for contributing to defeat. It was written prior to our entering the war. It does not encourage civil disobedience. And it is too rational to appeal to the masses.

Far from trying to stop this war, I shall rather try to help it along once it becomes clear that the majority have been inveigled into wanting it. The best way to cure the American people of wanting to die for foreigners and utopian ideals is to let enough of them have the experience and then explain to the survivors what leaders and ideas were responsible for the futile adventure. Probably only a futile war can teach the American people the lessons of this book. If they want this form of instruction, I say as a good American and respecter of the will of the people "By all means let them have the education they so much desire."

*   *   *

A few words about the author may be in order at this point by way of clarifying his personal attitude towards this country's wars. In the summer of 1915 I paid my expenses, along with several hundreds of other young Americans, to attend the reserve officers' training camp which was the first Plattsburg camp experimentally inaugurated in that

Introduction

xiii

year by General Leonard Wood. I went to the first Plattsburg camp after we entered the war in 1917 and received a commission in August with the first graduating class. I served overseas as a lieutenant of infantry with the First Army Headquarters Regiment. I did not at any time during the entire course of the late world war believe in the war aims or idealism of the Allies or in our entering the war any more than I believed in or sympathized with the war aims of the central powers. In respect to that war I never ceased to be neutral in thought and feeling. As soon as we enter the next war I shall try to join up in any capacity in which I may be found useful. If I am found too old or incompetent for line duty, as is probable, as I am now 46 years old, I shall be delighted to serve my country with its war propaganda. I am just as ready to lie as to kill for my country. Any ethic which does not put a man's country above all else is a stench in my nostrils. I have for no foreign country any sympathy which would make it difficult for me to kill its nationals if ordered by my country to do so. My opposition to our entry into war is based solely on my ideas of American national interest.

This book has not been written with a view to keeping us out of war, for, as already indicated, I consider that a hopeless undertaking. It has been written in the belief that the disaster of our going to war for foreign interests and futile ideals is now rendered inevitable by the ideology and leadership to which we are now voluntarily self-subordinated, and by the exigencies of an economic impasse from which democracy cannot escape. This book has been written to prepare some of the elite against the day when a disillusioned America returns from a feckless foreign adventure, sadder and wiser. Then it will be possible to tell the American people the truth with every chance of being listened to and heeded. Then we can begin to purge this country of the ideology and leadership which will have been responsible for our having committed this blunder and suffered this disaster. The disaster will, almost certainly, not take the form of an American defeat. Our shores will be as safe at all times after our entry into war as they were at all times before, as far back as 181 3. The disaster will have been a futile sacrifice of American life to stop revolutionary change in Europe, futile because it will not have stopped but rather accelerated and extended to the lands of the Allies the revolution we shall have fought in the lands of the Germans and Russians. It will be our inglorious retreat from a revolutionary Europe without achievement of our war aims. These will have been the saving of democracy and the stopping of the wicked revolution abroad. Having fought in vain to stop the revolution in Europe we shall have to carry it out over here. This disillusioning experience will generate in Americans a hate of the ideology and leadership responsible for it. Such hate may give birth to a new American folk unity and dynamism.

If it should transpire shortly before or after the publication of this book that the war in Europe abruptly ends, that event by itself would in no way impair the validity of any of the theses here presented. For one thing, the war between the Haves and Have-nots would still go on; for another, the revolution also would go on; for a third, we should still be faced with the eventual alternatives of autarchy within this hemisphere or further attempts to interfere with or obstruct the revolution in other parts of the world. At the time of writing, the most likely and most imminent form of American interference seems to be that of joining the side of the Allies. Should this war enter another phase, the most likely forms of American intervention would take on other appropriate forms. The principles involved would, however, remain unchanged. And our long-run choices would also remain the same: to intervene or not to intervene.

Finally, this book has no concern with and makes no prediction as to the personal future of any of the dictators. What happens to them as individual leaders matters little. The revolution is important, not the personal fate of its leaders. This book makes the predictions that the revolution which, naturally, is most advanced in the Have-not countries and only incipient in the Have empires, the three great democracies, will spread over the territory of the Haves during the war, so that before its close, which may not be for a generation, the revolution, the world over, will have merged more or less into one great revolt of the Have-nots against the Haves.

It would be fatuous to try to forecast in detail the eventual developments of this titanic struggle between capitalism and socialism or between liberal democracy and totalitarian, authoritarian collectivism. But I am prepared to record definitely and stand on the prediction that capitalism is doomed and socialism will triumph.

Definitions
They Must Be Made By Those Who Make History

Meanings of Key Terms

The Elite
Revolution and Revolutionary
Dynamism

Democracy
Capitalism
Socialism

THE ELITE. Defining this term is like designating the fittest referred to in Darwin's law of the survival of the fittest. The in-elite are the people who run things. To describe them thus is not to say that one thinks they ought to run things or that one considers them morally or otherwise the best people or those most deserving to rule. The out-elite are those who might be running things if there occurred a shift in power. There can be no question as to who are the ins. I avoid use of the term ruling class because it carries certain regal connotations which are inappropriate in a republic and also as it might be thought to exclude that large class of economically powerful persons who never soil their hands with politics but who form part of the crowd running things. One cannot designate conclusively the future elite among the outs. One has to wait until they come into power. But one is justified in saying that there always is an out or potential elite which might become the in or actual elite in a change of circumstances. In the new revolution, the new elite will obviously be much in view and will be held to a higher or more definite degree of responsibility for what happens than the present elite. This always occurs in a major shift of power which focuses public attention on the facts of power and the personalities who hold power.

REVOLUTION AND REVOLUTIONARY. These terms are used simply to denote social change that is profound and widespread. By themselves, they do not refer to any particular kind of social change but to any and every sort of social change; or, in each instance used, to the particular type of change there under discussion. Thus, reference is constantly made to the capitalist as well as the socialist revolution; to the industrial revolution as well as to innumerable other varieties of revolution.

Unfortunately, most people think of revolution as a process of mob violence, disorder, anarchy and chaos. Mention of the French Revolution, for example, evokes to their minds lurid scenes in the streets of Paris and not the far-reaching social changes which constituted the substantial reality of the French Revolution. The fact is, the violent incidents of a great social revolution are to it about what the foam on the crest of the wave is to the rising tide.

This book is not a tract for revolution, or a diatribe against the present status quo. It is intended as a guide to the times which are nothing if not revolutionary, whether one likes the idea or not. It is not written for those who use the process of name-calling to make and unmake things to their liking. The purpose is to explain the end of one revolution and the beginning of another. If the purpose were to sell a specific variety of social revolution, whether capitalist or socialist, great care would be taken not to call what was being touted revolution, and to call its opposites or alternatives revolutionary. What was being advocated would be called evolution or progress or by some other popular term which, unlike revolution, encounters no sales resistance.

DYNAMISM AND DYNAMIC. These terms are used merely to indicate what makes the wheels of society go round. A driving force, so considered, is neither good nor bad. It is merely instrumental. In a given situation and moment it may produce what, according to the point of view, are deemed good or bad actions or results. The dynamism or dynamics of a society must be thought of simply as its vital energy, its power to go places and do things, good or evil.

DEMOCRACY AND CAPITALISM. These are companion terms. They describe two aspects of the same social system. Democracy may be called the political, and capitalism the economic, side of the system. Throughout this book the term democracy is used in the sense in which it is currently employed in popular speech. This usage is in keeping with the idea that definitions are not in themselves, as subjects of possible disagreement, worth arguing about and that words should be accepted and used in whatever sense they are generally current. Democracy, as the term is used in this book and in popular speech, refers to a certain pattern of ways and institutions which may be further identified by the phrases, parliamentary government, liberalism, a government of checks and balances,—all these terms meaning, among other things, a governmental system in which the rights of minorities to oppose the majority in certain approved ways is respected.

In my opinion, which I would not waste time trying to prove, an entirely different pattern of ways and institutions may with equal propriety and etymological correctness be termed democratic. Taking Lincoln's celebrated formulation "of the people, for the people and by the people" as being the essence of democracy, it may, I think, be fairly held that a socialist dictatorship of the most arbitrary sort, and one I personally might not care to live under, is as democratic as the government of Britain, America or France. The trouble is that we make it a *sine qua non* of democracy that it recognize certain minority rights which the socialist dictatorships deny.

In general, the American definition of democracy is merely government and society as we are used to them and like them. And, in this connection, we generally do not realize that the pattern we are used to, like and call democracy includes many other features, such as a perpetual land boom, which are not included in our idealistic definitions of democracy but which are part and parcel of our mental picture of the thing. Democracy may be abstractly defined, whenever a definition is demanded. But the people, in using the term, do not think of that abstract definition. They think instead of a complex of concrete realities of personal experience, one of which is a perpetual land boom and another of which is limitless opportunities for individuals to get rich quick.

In defining democracy, we Americans are apt to assume that nowhere can the people govern themselves unless they do so in the particular way we are used to and like. That is to say, we assume that wherever the people may be governed in a radically different way, their government cannot be of the people, by the people and for the people. I consider these assumptions and this definition of democracy wholly incorrect, etymologically, historically and rationally. But I do not consider the inaccuracy of such a definition of democracy a matter worth arguing about. I use the word only as we are accustomed to hearing it used. There are more important errors to clear up than those of popular definition. I am willing, then, to restrict the application of the term democracy to social systems the American people consider democratic. I am the more willing to do this because the systems we say are not democratic are not claimed by their supporters to be democratic. The Russian communists for a time attempted under the Trojan horse policy of the Popular Front to masquerade under the cloak of democracy. But now the communist wolves no longer seek to go about in sheep's clothing. Communists, Fascists and Nazis now leave the term democracy to the capitalist powers. So be it, then, for all purposes of definition.

It has always seemed to me that, in any objective sense of the term, all governments and societies everywhere in the world today, above the level of the tribal stage of culture, have to be democratic. That is to say, they must be governments more or less of the people, by the people and for the people. It would seem to me that the more arbitrarily and violently a people are governed today, the more dependent their government must be on continuous sanction by the will of a substantial majority. Otherwise, such a government would be overthrown overnight by an almost spontaneous revolt of the dissatisfied majority. It seems to me silly to say that the people cannot make an uprising because the dictator commands several million uniformed, disciplined and armed men. It is precisely because of the existence of large mass armies of soldiers and party legionaries that the dictator must enjoy continuous popularity in order to survive. A people's army must be assumed to share the feelings of the people. To say that the people's army or the popular party legion suppresses the will of the people at the command of the dictator does not make sense. Who coerces the millions of armed soldiers and legionaries? It is absurd to ask a realist to believe that a single man could survive twenty-four hours as dictator if the majority of his armed forces thought he should be ousted. This is especially true in a non-supernaturalist and materialist age and regime. The feeling of a majority of a people's army can never long be different from the feeling of the majority of the unarmed people of which they are a part. There may be some plausibility to saying that a Hitler or Stalin hypnotizes his armed millions with his personality and words. But surely it is implausible to say that he terrorizes them with physical force, since the physical force at his command is entirely in the hands of the popular army or party legions. The simplest proof of the inherent democracy of all dictatorships, using the term democracy this time in its etymological sense and not in the sense in which it is employed currently and throughout this book, is to be found in the importance given by the dictatorships to propaganda. The dictators may deceive the people but it is nonsense to talk about a small clique of leaders terrorizing with force millions of armed men. Neither Pitt, Napoleon nor even Disraeli or Gladstone went to the same great pains as the present-day dictators in selling their policies to the people for the simple reason that there was then far less democracy. The masses then were largely uninterested in politics. In those days only a small mercenary army had arms. But as I have already made clear, I do not in the least mind reserving the term democracy exclusively for systems which tolerate minority political opposition.

Where my use of terms like democracy and socialism will encounter most criticism and contradiction will be in connections I shall now try to explain. In general, when I talk about democracy, capitalism or socialism I refer to what is actual rather than to what is the ideal. Most readers will be entirely content with my calling the United States, Great Britain and the self-governing British colonies, France, the low countries, the Scandinavian countries and Switzerland democracies, and with my not calling the dictatorships democracies. They would be annoyed if I did otherwise. But they will be furious with me for linking certain conditions like chronic unemployment or resort to deficits and war, with democracy. In general, their view as to the correct use of terms like democracy is as follows: Everything they like about America must be identified with democracy and everything they dislike in dictatorships must be associated with dictatorship; nothing good must be mentioned in connection with dictatorships; nothing bad in connection with democracy.

I shall be told that the United States is not a perfect democracy and that democracy is not to blame for our failure to solve unemployment. Yet if one uses terms in this way, intellectual discourse about social problems becomes impossible. It may be fair for me to say that when my children behave as I want them to they are true to their name, family tradition and home training and that when they behave otherwise they are not good Dennises. The fact remains, however, that no matter what my children do, they are always my children. Similarly, no matter what crimes I may commit here or abroad, I can never cease to be a native of this country. The nation can terminate my citizenship or my life but it cannot ever alter the facts of my birth here or my American ancestry. It would be easy to say that Americans never commit crimes nor get smallpox by making it a law that an American ceases to be an American by committing a crime or getting smallpox. In the same way it can be made a matter of definition that nothing bad can be called democratic or attributed to democracy. To insist that democracy be discussed only in terms of its ideals and of such realities as accord with them is to make realistic discussion wholly impossible.

The Nazis cannot say that concentration camps are alien to their system and Americans cannot say that chronic unemployment is alien to our system. Facts are normative.

SOCIALISM. It is in applying the term socialism to the systems actually in operation in Germany, Russia and Italy that I invite some of the most violent criticism I shall receive. Believers in democracy and capitalism all want to have the system discussed in terms of its ideals and contrary-to-fact assumptions, but they are used to having to account for its realities. After all, democracy and capitalism have existed now for many years as a system both of ideals and working institutions. But socialism, up to the Russian Revolution, has never existed in a national way except as a system of ideals. Hence believers in socialism and persons well informed about the subject have applied the term socialism solely to the theory or ideals of socialism. In this book I never mean utopian socialism when I use the term socialism, unless I so qualify it. When one has before one's eyes socialism in practice, why talk about socialism in theory as opposed to or different from socialism in action? I am not interested in Bellamy's, Norman Thomas's, Ramsay McDonald's or Caspar Milquetoast's brand of socialism. I am interested in socialism only as an operating fact, whether in the degree found in Russia or in the New Deal.

Many American socialists will say that Russia and Germany do not have socialism, meaning their variety, which is unimportant. The observation is like the statement of those of one Christian sect that another Christian sect is not Christian. After all, if most of one hundred and eighty million Russians or eighty million Germans call what they have socialism, this fact is more important for purposes of definition than the opinion of a handful of American or British idealists who are politically insignificant, but who believe theirs to be the only genuine variety of socialism. The definitions of the doers are more important than the definitions of the talkers. I adhere to the definitions of socialism embodied in the deeds of foreign socialists in power and not to the verbal and academic definitions of socialism made by American socialists not in power. This I do not only because actions speak louder than words but also because there is no widely current and accepted definition of socialism among the American people.

If socialism is to be a useful term and concept, it must be broad and elastic in meaning. It must apply to realities as well as to ideals, to real situations as well as to utopias. No definition of socialism in the abstract can be valid as against a definition of something in action called socialism by those in command. G. D. H. Cole, in a pamphlet published in October 1938 entitled *Socialism in Evolution*, tried without success to formulate a definition of socialism and admitted his failure by saying "As I see it, this idea of human fellowship is the root idea of socialism." With this the followers of Stalin, Hitler and Mussolini would all agree.

Socialism as a term or a concept must, if it is to be a useful tool of thought and discussion, apply to trends as well as working systems. More public ownership in displacement of private ownership, more public control in substitution for private control of industry, trade and agriculture, more progressive taxation aimed at the equalization of fortunes and income and in general more collectivism and less individualism, must all be considered socialist trends. Briefly, socialism is a relative and not an absolute term. In political practice, as distinguished from political theory, there are no absolutes. To say that anything is not socialism because it does not conform to the standards of some absolute is absurd, just as it would be absurd to say that there are no democracies because there are none conforming to any given set of standards. Most thinking about democracy or socialism is wrong in this respect. It is assumed that there are certain abstract standards defining democracy or socialism and that any given system called by its exponents a democracy or a socialist society must be judged by these standards and accordingly pronounced to be or not to be the real thing.

One's thinking should run the other way round. America and England are examples setting the present standards of democracy as a system in operation. Russia and Germany are examples setting the present standards of socialism as a system in operation. To say that America is not a democracy or that Russia and Germany are not socialistic because they do not measure up to one's own standards for both terms is merely to show conceit. Definitions must be made by those who make history, for a definition which has no historical basis is not different from a dream. One great trouble with the social sciences in the democracies today is the habit of seeking escape from facts in the processes of definition.

Many believers in utopian socialism insist that it must be democratic. I am inclined to conclude from recent and current experiments that socialism is incompatible with democracy in the sense we commonly use the latter term. But on this point I keep an open mind. When I can be shown democratic socialism in operation I shall believe it possible. Until then I shall not say that it is impossible. But, while conceding the possibility in the future of a democratic socialism, I shall insist that a non-democratic or non-parliamentary socialism be recognized as the only working model of socialism we have in the world today. To say that an undemocratic socialism is not socialism is sillier than saying that an American convict in the penitentiary is not an American or that a businessman who fails to make money is not a businessman. Anyone has the right to say that his brand of socialism in theory or as an ideal is preferable to another brand of socialism in operation. But no one has the right to say that the idealist has a monopoly on a term like socialism or democracy.

I concede the idealist's right to apply any term he chooses to his unrealized dream but not to deny the same right to the realist to apply any term he chooses to his realized accomplishment. I grant Norman Thomas's right to call himself a socialist but not to deny to Hitler or Stalin the right to call themselves socialists. For me, democracy and socialism are primarily historical and not moral or ethical terms. An unrealized dream or ideal may be an historical event quite as much as a realized achievement. Therefore, utopian socialism has a place in the history of ideas and cultural forces. But it must not be overlooked or denied that those who make history also have the right to make definitions and that every reality has its corresponding idea though every idea does not necessarily have its corresponding reality. In other words, Hitler's definition of socialism is as valid as that of Leon Blum or Norman Thomas.

COMMUNISM, FASCISM AND NAZISM. As for these terms, there should be no question as to definition: First, because each is authoritatively defined by its official governmental exponent; second, because, in this book these terms are little used and never as important elements in any statement. In the theory of this book communism (Russian style), Fascism, and Nazism are merely different national variants of socialism. And all these variants combine many of the features of capitalism, laissez-faire and the free market with socialism, state capitalism and planning.

In the United States it is obvious that we shall not have a Russian, Italian or German, but an American brand of national socialism. What we call it is of little importance. As for the question what will it be like, the most important and informative answer that can be given at present is that it will be a permanent revolution.

And so this book is about the new revolution in the United States

Definitions   xxiii

as a process of change already begun rather than about some dream of a new American utopia. One cannot talk realistically about a new order to be realized years hence either here or anywhere else. One can, however, talk realistically about a current process of change.

In linking together Russian communism, Italian Fascism and German Nazism and in declaring that the New Deal is a movement in the same general direction, I do not say or imply that these different national phases of the same world-wide revolution of socialism are entirely alike. Still less do I imply that they are friendly to each other. In this there is nothing contradictory. Capitalistic and democratic countries have fought each other in the past and, in all probability, socialistic countries will fight each other in the future. People fight because of their similarities more often than because of their dissimilarities. There is for the time being a natural tendency among the capitalist great powers to combine against and resist the socialist great powers, because the latter are challenging the status quo.

The world-wide revolution of socialism, however, is greater than this conflict and will go on during, and in spite of, and after these wars just as the capitalist revolution of the eighteenth and nineteenth centuries went on through the inter-capitalist wars of that era. One can follow intelligently the new revolution, though not the day-to-day military and diplomatic moves of the leading contestants.

Fascism and Nazism differ from communism mainly in the manner of coming into operation. A vital element of the Fascist and Nazi way of coming to power was the taking of the big businessmen and middle classes into the socialist camp without resistance and, even, with enthusiasm on their part for a revolutionary movement which they lacked the social intelligence to understand. Bringing about socialism through the deception of the industrialists and middle classes in Germany was the alternative to bringing it about through civil war. This achievement was partly the result of guile on the part of the Fascist and Nazi leaders whose thought was steeped in radical socialist ideology, and partly the result of the inherent naivete of the industrialists and middle classes who were easily made to believe that Fascist and Nazi radicals would avert communism and preserve capitalism. Back in 1933 and 1934 I was one of the few writing Americans who saw that both Fascism and Nazism had to end in an extreme form of socialism by reason of the pressures of inevitable trends in social change. I derided the interpretations of Fascism and Nazism made equally by the conservatives and the communists at that time. Incidentally, it is to be remarked that American communists and fellow travelers, who are as unsophisticated in politics as Wall Streeters or Mrs. Roosevelt, helped both Mussolini and Hitler no end in the early days by denouncing them as capitalist stooges. My book, *The Coming American Fascism,* was treated by many leftist critics as wholly irrelevant to Fascism because it did not accord with the then orthodox Moscow interpretation of this new phenomenon. On this point, the orthodox line of Union Square and the Union League Club was the same. Both of these areas, incidentally, are as remote from reality as they are from America in their political opinions.

To me, in 1933-1936, as now, the idea then being advanced on Park Avenue and lower Third Avenue that the demagogue of a popular national socialist movement with a private army of the people under his orders could be the Charlie McCarthy of big businessmen was utterly preposterous. I have known intimately too many big businessmen to have any uncertainty as to the role they would be playing in any Charlie McCarthy act with a Hitler. Businessmen are socially the least intelligent and creative members of our ruling classes. Without their legal, spiritual and advertising advisers at their elbows, they are less articulate than the average taxi driver or longshoreman, and they make much less sense. I am firmly convinced that the chief reason for Charlie McCarthy's popularity is that so many millions of Americans who have to go through life as stooges enjoy hearing for a few minutes a week one of their kind talk back as they have the will but not the wit to do themselves.

The instruments of power are guns and propaganda. Whoever commands these commands money. Why should a political regime enjoying a monopoly of propaganda and guns take orders from men who have nothing but money? Money can never have more power than guns and propaganda give it. Property rights derive from guns and propaganda, not guns and propaganda from property rights. Once a propertyless elite of political demagogy capture the instruments of guns and propaganda, i.e., the state, the formerly propertied elite enjoy property rights only on the sufferance and conditions fixed by the new holders of the perennial instruments of power, arms and idea propagating machinery. The notion that a socialist Caesar could be given orders by a man with nothing but pieces of paper called property always seemed to me absurd. I have no doubt that it now seems equally absurd to Herr Thyssen.

The Fascist-Nazi method of transition from capitalism to socialism was obviously more humane for the capitalists and business executives and far better for the community than the communist way of sudden liquidation of one system with its managing personnel, and inauguration of the successor system without adequate experts. It is better to make socialist commissars of industry of the capitalist industrialists than to make corpses of them, both for their sakes and for society's sake, which can use them better alive than dead. Thus the socialist state is given time to train its personnel under experts while the latter are able to end their lives in service and in comfort.

The fact that the Fascist-Nazi detour around communist liquidation had to be made by means of deception of the capitalists is merely another proof of the unworkability of democracy and the political genius of Mussolini and Hitler. If industrial democracy were feasible, the industrialists of capitalism would cooperate in the working out of solutions for unemployment and progressive socialization of industry without necessity for Fascist deception, the communist firing squad or our getting into a world war to get socialism via the Industrial Mobilization Plan.

A repetition of the Hitler formula in the United States seems unlikely for several reasons. One reason is that capitalists are now on to it. The American capitalist fly probably cannot be kidded into walking into the Fascist spider's parlor as a refuge against communism. When Hitler came to power the "best" society in Germany, as elsewhere, regarded Mussolini as a savior of capitalism and Hitler as a promising model of the same leadership. The losers are always wrong. But it would now be futile for any aspiring American national socialist to pass the hat among the American plutocracy unless he offered promise of such reaction that he could not possibly secure a popular following. Contrary to the apparent belief of the Republican party sponsors of reactionary stooges, no political movement anywhere today can long succeed as the ostensible cause of the rich versus the poor. Hitler was able to exploit with guile the gullibility of the "best" people, and with the utmost sincerity the patriotism of the nationalists who wanted to see Versailles avenged. The anti-communist line got the capitalists, the anti-Versailles line got the army and the nationalists, the anti-Semitic line got the masses as well as the classes while, at the same time, sugar-coating the initial pill of anticapitalism. Marx said that anti-Semitism was the socialism of fools, by which he probably meant that only fools would fail to understand that anti-Semitism was usually a manifestation of selective anticapitalism.

A second reason the Hitler formula will not work in the United States is that we have no counterpart of the treaty of Versailles which a demagogic leader can use to line up the veterans and patriots who want a respectable and conventional reason to go places and do things. To work up nationalist fever in America one has to invoke some alien nationalism. One must either wave the Union jack or else emote over the oppression of some foreign minority. The most dynamic nationalism we have in this country, of course, is that of the Jews, which is international. Americans have yet to become a nation.

The most important thing to understand about revolution is that it never comes in any two countries in the same way. In this book I hazard the opinion that it will come in an entirely original and unforseeable way. It will come, most likely, under leadership of the returned soldiers and the new wartime bureaucracy in charge of industrial mobilization, all, or most of whom, will face after the war the alternatives of heading up a new revolution or an old bread line. The things the leaders say to win mass support will have no long-run importance. They will be significant only as indications of the type of propaganda needed at the moment to catch the masses. It may be good minor tactics to call the socialism they are inaugurating antisocialism. What the resulting system eventually turns out to be will be wholly determined by the imperatives of the situation and only to a very slight extent by the wishes of either the leaders or the masses. If the leaders are, as they are likely to be, inspired geniuses, they will understand the demands of the situation and will adopt the necessary measures to meet them. It is with forecasting these exigencies of the near future on the basis of current conditions and trends that this book is chiefly concerned. The two needs of tomorrow's revolutionary leadership are first, understanding of the situation and second, a will to meet it. Hitler's revolutionary genius has consisted in understanding since the war, as no liberal democratic leaders anywhere have understood, that capitalism is doomed, and in having always a will to do concrete things about it. Given an understanding of the situation and a will to action, plans and their execution follow as matters of course. Whatever else it may be, the result is action which is the only cure for stagnation.

Part I. Back to First Principles

Chapter I. The Social Need of Permanent Revolution

Chapter II. The Victors Make the Rules

Chapter III. The International Jungle

Chapter I
The Social Need of Permanent Revolution

The revolution is dead! Long live the revolution! As the world swaps revolutions and imperialisms, those of capitalism for those of socialism, it is time for Americans to take new bearings. For doing this they will find little guidance in Herbert Spencer or Karl Marx. Heraclitus and Machiavelli are much more up to date. Change and power are today's facts. To cope with them we must think in terms of social dynamics and not of social statics. The latter-day liberals hoped to stabilize the dynamism of the industrial revolution and the frontier which are now over. The Marxists caught the equally chimerical vision of a classless society of workers from which the state would have withered away, leaving the ideals of laissez-faire to flourish in the garden of liberty completely rid of the noxious weeds of private capitalism.

The realist of today dreams no such dreams. He seeks to ride, not to stop, the mounting wave of revolutionary change and power politics. His main hope is to succeed in doing this without going under. In his more sanguine moments he may also hope to some extent to shape the pattern of change. Thinking patriotically he cherishes these aspirations for his nation and kind. The intellectual problem is to understand, not contradict; the emotional problem, to feel with and not resent the rising tide of change and power. The practical problem is how personally and nationally to survive. The order of the day for us should be the preservation of the American people. It should not be the preservation of institutions and customs at the expense of human lives or welfare. We must save ourselves amid the processes of war and revolution. We cannot save ourselves by trying to save everybody else or by seeking to preserve doomed institutions.

Much of our present confusion is due to a failure or refusal to recognize the social necessity of dynamism. Democracy, since the end of its revolution, has developed a conservatism that hopes to render the dynamic static and the status quo perpetual. The system now in peril is private capitalism on its economic side and parliamentary democracy or government by the play of minority-group pressures on its political side. In both phases it was formerly dynamic, expansive and revolutionary. It is no longer. The end of growth is the beginning of death. The war phase of 1914-1919 has been reopened.

This, more truly than the last, is a war to make the world safe for democracy, or for the economic system on the continued functioning of which the British Isles and the capitalistic plutocracy everywhere abjectly depend for survival. The worldwide collapse of international capitalism would reduce the British Isles and those who live mainly on the fruits of ownership the world over to a situation fully as painful as that of today's Jewish refugees. America, therefore, is being groomed for another war to save this system. Such a war, to succeed for the democracies, would have to roll back the rising tide of socialist change and restore the dynamism of a revolutionary nineteenth century capitalism. The real question is not whether the new revolution of the Have-nots ought to be stopped and the old revolution of the Haves revived but whether these accomplishments are possible under present circumstances.

In grappling with this problem of the hour the first fact to be considered is that continuous and revolutionary social change is the prime requisite of a highly organized industrial society. By revolutionary is not meant revolutionary of any particular sort but, quite simply, social change of any kind that is rapid, drastic and widespread and, most important of all, that involves expansion and growth.

Liberal critics of the Nazi-Soviet alliance make a great deal of the current deviations of these two revolutions from their original lines of doctrine and direction. No reproach of a revolution could be sillier than that it had been guilty of change. The fact that so many liberals and radicals are shocked by the change of direction manifested by Russian socialism merely shows them ignorant of the nature and function of revolution. Their idea of social revolution has been essentially pietistic and static. The American liberal and radical idea of the Russian Revolution was essentially like the pietist's idea of heaven, something sweet and static. Some liberals were actually saying with unconcealed relief in early 1938 that the Russian Revolution was about over, meaning that the socialist status quo in Russia had been about established. How absurd! The Russian Revolution, of course, though started in 1917, did not touch eighty percent of the population of Russia, the peasants, until the collectivization of the farms beginning in the early thirties. And its expansive imperialism has just begun with the conquests of Poland and Finland.

Actually, there is just one thing a revolution has consistently to maintain in order to survive, and that is change. The nature of the change does not matter. The appropriate accompanying rationalizations will naturally change along with everything else. The deviations of German socialism from *Mein Kampf* or of Russian socialism from *Das Kapital* are as natural as the deviations of modern capitalism from the theory of Adam Smith's *Wealth of Nations.* The only consistent feature of the capitalist revolution of the past hundred and fifty years has been continuous change, which is the only law of any and every social revolution.

The function of revolution is not to get people anywhere in particular and especially not to keep them anywhere once it has got them there. The function of revolution is simply to keep them moving on with a purpose and a hope which will change as they move. Not to understand this is not to know history. Capitalism and democracy ran on the dynamism of the commercial and industrial revolution, frontier settlement, exploitation of virgin natural resources, rapid population growth, easy capitalist-imperialist wars of conquest and the continuous broadening of public instruction and the suffrage. In all these processes the one element of consistency is—change. The only important fact about them for us today is that, as processes of change, they are now about over. Capitalism has entered upon transition from dynamism to legend. This process is one of stagnation which is being broken by war and the new revolution of socialism.

The statement that the dynamic function of change is neither good nor bad but just to keep things moving may shock many who like to think of social change as improvement or progress. Whether any given pattern or phase of social change is improvement and progress must, in the very nature of things, always be wholly a matter of a value judgment, and, consequently, the subject of wide divergence of opinion. The leaders of every revolution or phase of social change, naturally, call it good, improvement, progress, etc. Their followers, participating in such change will, of course, agree, while a great many others immediately affected by such change or observing it from a distance, either in time or space, will disagree. Thus, today, the majority of people in the democracies are emphatically of the conviction that both the Russian and German revolutions are mainly bad. With such value judgments we have, in this discussion, no concern.

We are concerned here merely with the following broad generalizations about revolutionary change: First, that continuous revolution is a permanent social necessity to avert stagnation. It is not said that stagnation is good or bad or that stagnation is worse than change. It is merely said that revolutionary change is the only alternative to stagnation. So, to any one who might say that he would prefer any degree of stagnation to the Nazi, communist or any other revolution, I have nothing to say in contradiction. The second generalization is that any revolution of sufficient quantitative degree will avert stagnation; or that, for this purpose, one revolution is as good as another, provided it is revolutionary enough. In making this statement I do not say that, so far as my preferences go—which are not involved here—one revolution is as good as another. Nor do I say that the reader should not mind what kind of revolution the country has so long as it has enough of one to get out of stagnation. I merely say that, for the purpose of ending stagnation, any revolution that is big enough will do.

It is important to establish the foregoing points clearly in one's thinking for the purpose of realistic analysis of the present situation, the essence of which is stagnation, except as modified by war. Let me try briefly to explain. In the first place, human nature or human behavior in large groups tends to social inertia or stagnation rather than to social dynamism. This is confirmed by history and current observation of savage or primitive communities. Society since the beginning of recorded history, has needed war and the prophecy and creative urges of the abnormal, the social deviates, the unbalanced or the crazy men of destiny to take it out and keep it out of stagnation. Peter the Hermit started the end of the Dark Ages by inciting the people of Europe to go off to the wars of the crusades. The fifteenth and sixteenth century reformers and discoverers, another crazy lot, continued the revolution. The merchants and inventors of the eighteenth and nineteenth centuries brought it down to our day. Now a new crop of Caesars is leading us out of stagnation along the path of revolution. Society does not tend to dynamism but to stagnation. The wise men and social scientists of the democracies have not understood this. Lenin, Mussolini and Hitler have understood it.

In the second place, ethical and rational idea patterns in the democracies tend to be utopian and static rather than dynamic. The average American believes that the American Revolution in 1776-1785 was to be our last revolution. His idea of revolution is that, if it is of the right sort, it will end a bad situation and create a good situation which will thenceforth become stabilized and permanent. Thereafter, something he calls "normal" becomes permanently established. To this "normal," a sound society is supposed always to be getting back. I have never seen this happen, of course, and have only seen the country get into new and worse messes one after the other. But, even in the midst of this most explosive and revolutionary phase of modern history, people still talk about getting back to normal as the country shoots down the rapids to the precipice of a second world war in this generation.

The American who talks of getting back to normal will usually tell you that he believes in evolution rather than revolution. This bromidic preference he owes largely to the influence of the befuddled sociological thinking of Herbert Spencer and a long line of liberals of the nineteenth century who decided to apply Darwin's law of the survival of the fittest or natural selection to social change. To say that, in natural history, the fittest survive is a tautology. It merely amounts to saying that what is fittest to survive survives. You don't know what is fit to survive until it has survived. Then you know it was fit to survive because it survived. But Spencer and his school transmuted this blinding flash of the obvious into moral law by wishful thinking. Social change, according to them, was a process in which the best survived. Fittest and best, of course, were synonyms. Best, in liberal discourse, always means what the person using the term likes best. Now the liberals understood that in revolutionary change what they liked best might not always happen. So they decided they preferred evolutionary change, à la Darwin, for in such slow and long-drawn-out change, they figured they couldn't lose. Since what they liked was best or fittest, it was bound to survive. They had Darwin's discovery for that. Their idea of Darwin's thesis was that it meant the inevitability of progress in the sense of improvement or betterment. Under evolution things just had to grow bigger and better in every way. Obviously, there is nothing in Darwin to support such wishful thinking. There is no more ethics, morals or aesthetics in natural selection or the survival of the fittest than there is in the jungle, where the principle can be seen at work in its most fundamental form.

Another error of the people who think they prefer evolution to revolution is that they usually don't stop to consider how slow evolution in natural history really is and how much faster social change has to be in any society of which they would care to be members. The evolutionary change Darwin observed and wrote about in natural history occurs with a slowness that, in social change, would be total stagnation. As a matter of fact, considered relatively to social dynamics, evolution in the jungle is dismal stagnation. Some reader may remark that there would appear to be nothing stagnant about a bee hive, an anthill or a tiger chasing, catching and eating a deer. Yet from any social viewpoint all that is utter stagnation. For tens or hundreds of thousands of years the same species of ants or bees have been doing identically the same things, and with the same instruments and in the same way; the same species of tigers have been chasing, catching and eating with the same biological equipment and the same technique the same species of deer. Over a million years or more the tigers have no doubt grown a little longer and sharper teeth, a little broader jaws and a little stronger paws while the deer have grown a little lighter and fleeter legs. But for tens of thousands of years, they have been doing the same things in the same ways. That is evolution.

The difference between evolutionary and revolutionary change is mainly one of speed. People who think they would like an evolutionary rate of change simply do not understand the meaning of the terms they use or the dynamic requisites of the society they know and prefer.

The importance of clearly understanding the dynamic and purely unmoral function of change cannot be exaggerated at a time like this when the major problem is stagnation. America's problem of unemployment could be solved by rebuilding America or going to war with Japan. The war with Japan is the more likely. Why? The answer is that our social philosophy recognizes a need for national defense but not for social dynamism. We do not need to fight Japan for national security. Such a war would not serve our national interests. But the people are conditioned to react in certain ways to the mystic words "national defense" etc. like Pavlov's dog in the experiment. So all that is necessary to get us into war with Japan is to tinkle day in and day out in the people's ears the sound of certain symbolic words to which they respond by wanting to fight and to identify Japan always with the sound of those words.

One can drone daily in the people's ears the fact that we have ten million unemployed and they feel no emotional response because they have not been conditioned to regard stagnation as something bad or to consider revolutionary change, its alternative, as something good.

There are thirty-five million Americans who need government assistance and billions of dollars of un-utilized American productive plant capacity. There are not ten thousand Americans in the entire Far East or a billion dollars of American money invested there. But it is impossible to stimulate Americans to action over the thirty-five million Americans needing relief or the billions of wasting American capital in this country, while it will be the easiest thing in the world to launch Americans into a futile five or ten year war which will cost billions over negligible American interests in the Orient. A good part of the explanation is that our folklore contains no recognition of the continuous necessity of revolutionary social change but does make national honor and national defense verbal symbols with which the people can be moved like puppets into any wild adventure.

Rauschning, in his *Revolution of Nihilism,* has made a best seller of the discovery that the essence of German and Russian socialism is dynamism, meaning chiefly the will to power and the use of power for social expansion and change of a revolutionary nature. To most readers, the mere statement of these creative characteristics comes as a terrible indictment. It is not strange that democracies which shudder at virility and power have declining birth rates. By failing to see that liberal democracy and capitalism, as well as all other great systems, religious, political, dynastic or republican of the past were great revolutions while they flourished or until they declined, Dr. Rauschning falls short of being the profound philosopher needed to carry off his essay in current social prophecy. His failure to see that any complex society requires the dynamism of continuous revolutionary expansion and change invalidates many of his conclusions.

At heart, Rauschning is a pious, Protestant monarchist and landed Junker. He is attached to three major hierarchies of God's anointed: the court, the church and the army. This faith is no ground for reproach. But it is a reproach to his knowledge that he does not recognize that Christianity, every monarchy, every landed aristocracy and every military caste arose out of revolution and that no one of them ever flourished as a static institution. The Roman Catholic church, for instance, has always insisted on its destiny as the Church Militant until it becomes the Church Triumphant. It has accordingly remained evangelical, ever carrying on the propaganda of the faith and maintaining foreign missions to revolutionize the heathen from the faiths and ways of their fathers to those of the Church. The Protestant sects have followed the same philosophy. Both in origin and early development, they were dynamic agencies of political and economic revolution. The Protestant Reformation, after all, was just one big political revolution which gave birth to modern nationalism and the types of wars it has made inevitable. As for the monarchs and their landed retainers throughout Europe, they never kept the peace or left their neighbors tranquil over any lengthy period during the past two thousand years.

Stalin and Hitler have created few revolutionary or military precedents not to be found in the annals of Europe's great monarchs like Charlemagne, Henry the Eighth, Elizabeth, Peter the Great, Louis the Fourteenth, Charles the Fifth, Frederick the Great or Napoleon. Henry the Eighth attacked the Roman church by nationalizing the English church and Elizabeth attacked the institution of property by commissioning English pirates to prey on Spanish shipping though she brazenly denied it in official replies to Spanish protests. The idea is now being advanced in polite British and French circles that a restoration of the monarchy in the several states of a dismembered Germany might usher in a welcome era of relief from the assaults on established institutions and the wars of the new socialist, Have-not dictators.

Rauschning has plenty of ground for criticizing the Nazi and Soviet dynamics which he miscalls nihilism. But he fails to offer a substitute dynamism or to recognize that a lack of dynamism was the reason for the collapse of the Weimar Republic or that revolutionary dynamism is the only alternative to stagnation.

Only a primitive people such as a community of savages, shepherds or nomads can be comparatively static. Possibly men would be happier living in more static and less dynamic societies. Be that as it may, let it be clearly understood that the industrialized millions of our great urbanized states today must either live on a new dynamism or die either in stagnation or in some adventure of desperation brought on by hunger. The present world is not ripe for the simple life. It could be made so only by the decimation of two thirds of the present population.

A new life of Woodrow Wilson, on the title page, fittingly calls him "the disciple of revolution" But his revolution, unlike that of Lenin, never came off, largely because, unlike Lenin's revolution, it sought to reverse the dynamic current of social change, ever flowing towards closer economic integration. Wilson's revolutionary ideology called for atomization in Europe under the glittering formula of self-determination. For a revolution today, and probably for a revolution in any period, that was wrong. Great revolutions are epics of social unification and never of social atomization. Capitalism was an attempt to unify the world under the rule of the British fleet and the Bank of England. The political and economic disintegration of Europe may well come as a sequel of a prolonged war. But if it does, it will come as a part of a return to the Dark Ages, and not as a revolution. The British and French, in fighting for the dismemberment of Germany and the Balkanization of Europe, are not fighting for a revolutionary idealism, in 1940 any more than in 1914-1918. Their prior wars revolutionized, created and unified.

The first practical result of Wilson's attempt at an internationalist world revolution was, as already remarked, the Balkanization of Europe, which Stalin and Hitler are now undoing. The next result was to commit the League of Nations to the maintenance of an impossible status quo. Out of this commitment grew a whole series of international misadventures, culminating in the Anglo-French war declaration of September 3, 1939 all aimed at the prevention of social unification by Japan, Italy and Germany. This policy amounts to an undertaking to reverse the historical and revolutionary processes of imperial expansion, thus far the only formula of large-scale social unification that has ever worked.

The Wilsonian revolution of international idealism was one of destruction, not creation. Lenin, Mussolini and Hitler have all made creative revolutions in their own countries. A creative revolution in one of the democracies in this century remains to be made. The Wilsonian revolution of destruction liquidated such workable social integrations as the Austro-Hungarian empire and the German empire, the first of which was decrepit when dissolved by the international idealists. But the internationalists could destroy better than they could build. They replaced these nineteenth century political integrations, having an obvious economic raison d'être, with no workable twentieth century substitute. Since the war, all that democracy has created of historic importance has been a sterile and suicidal internationalism, the dying gasp of the commercial and industrial revolutions which were democracy and capitalism in flower. Since the war, capitalism's only enduring creation has been unemployment.

Because the dynamic function of revolutionary change is so little understood nowadays, we hear on every side unrealistic comparisons between the democracies and dictatorships. Thus we are told that the difference between the two is that democracy is traditional and peaceful while dictatorship is revolutionary and warlike, as well as most unnatural. These dichotomies remind one of the classical example of the textbooks on formal logic: "The difference between a horse and a cow is that a horse has a head and a cow has a tail." Democracy or capitalism, as a matter of fact and not of definition, was never anything but the commercial and industrial revolution, with its accompaniments of extremely rapid population growth, frontier settlement and easy imperialist wars. These historical processes have been transmuted into a lot of abstract concepts, mostly now contrary to fact, which go under such names as ethics, law, political and social science, economics or just plain common sense. The characteristic fallacy of all liberal ideology is the assumption that a brief pattern of expansion and change was able to establish norms, ethical and aesthetic, for all time and that these norms constitute a body of truth wholly divorced from the limitations of time and space.

The simple historical fact, as will be shown more amply in succeeding chapters, is that capitalism or democracy was essentially one big, long revolution which is now over for the same reason that the offspring of one pair of breeders never proliferate until they cover the face of the globe. The liberal ideologists would have us believe that the new revolution of socialism is an orgy of blood and anarchy bursting upon the idyll of democratic peace, traditionalism and stability. The tradition of democracy is revolution; its essence, change and expansion; its characteristic incidents, territorial aggrandizement and easy wars. Democracy, when it flourished, i.e., when it was revolutionary, militant and successfully imperialistic, never respected the rights of the weak except as it suited capitalist or nationalist interests. Examples: the British conquest and the two and a half century long oppression of the Irish, the African slave trade, the extinction of the Indians in North America to make it safe for white democracy, the opium war on China, the conquest of India, the conquest of the Boer Republic etc., etc. What we are now witnessing is just the end of one revolution and the beginning of another, the new revolution being one of a non-commercial elite and the old revolution having been one of a merchant class elite.

BRITAIN, THE WORLD'S PREMIER REVOLUTIONIST SINCE THE FALL OF ROME

We affect horror over the thought that certain foreigners are spreading a new sort of world revolution. We forget that for centuries —the process can be dated back to the sinking of the Spanish Armada in 1588—England spread the world revolution of commercialism and industrialism. Beneficent or maleficent, as one's point of view may cause one to regard it, the transition from a world of economically self-contained communities to a world organized on the principle of the international division of labor was always revolutionary and intermittently bloody.

First came in England the enclosure of land, following the early successes of British piracy and foreign trade. In this way a self-respecting and self-sufficient British peasantry was converted into the submerged proletariat of the British slums. In the rising factory system the new wage slaves worked twelve and fourteen hours a day, while children of ten were driven to Work twelve hours a day six days a week. This English industrial revolution was forced upon its victims by means of the constable's arms and the landlord's economic pressure, which drove commercial settlers on the land to urban squalor and factory jobs to earn the rent money there to exist. It was not a matter of consent but coercion, a historical fact which wholly invalidates one of the most popular rationalizations of democracy, that of economic freedom. This rationalization is based on the fiction of freedom of contract, according to which the worker only a few days from starvation bargains freely with the employer having the means to employ or shut down and live comfortably for an indefinite period.

The British world revolution was imposed by coercion with the aid of a world monopoly of sea power, maritime shipping, banking and industry. Thus Clive conquered India to force upon its teeming millions the British commercial revolution. Thus our Commodore Perry, with diplomacy and without violence but with men of war at hand in Yeddo Bay forced on Japan the same revolution. The simple fact is that the Anglo-Saxons, during the past three and a half centuries since Elizabeth, have been the greatest propagandists and militant protagonists of world revolution since the Moslems and the Romans.

Revolution, in the light of history though not of liberal doctrine, has to be thought of as an instrument as well as an incident of imperialism. Marxism erroneously made socialist revolution the antithesis of imperialism. Stalin is effectively correcting this error. To subjugate another people you must first revolutionize them. That, in the imperial process, is far more important than defeating any number of times their armed forces in pitched battle. Subject peoples are never fully conquered until revolutionized to the ways of the conqueror. This may mean learning Latin or English, making the sign of the cross or turning one's face toward Mecca, adopting Roman law or the English law merchant, using the sterling bill of exchange instead of rational barter as people have done for thousands of years, or wearing Manchester prints instead of far more beautiful homespun.

Stalin cannot be a successful Pan-Slav imperialist, or Hitler a successful Pan-German imperialist, without using some brand of world revolution, exactly as did the British, the Moslems or the Romans, as an instrument of imperial policy. The Japanese failure in China is due to their incomprehension of the necessity for the use of a new formula of imperialism. Their industrial and British-aping liberal intelligentsia, industrial plutocracy and naval apprentices of the English imagined that they could imitate what had been the British technique of conquest in India, little realizing that the revolution is rapidly driving Britain out of India. With equal obtuseness the Japanese sought, by selling exports below cost at a reasonable wage for labor, to emulate British foreign-trade success, won along much sounder lines. This temporary success won on a falling Japanese standard of living cannot last.

Stalin and Hitler, whether they personally succeed and survive, or not, are both using, with local adaptations, the twentieth century formula of socialism for imperialist and industrial expansion. This formula the Japanese may readily adopt, using it in alliance with China exactly as Germany will use it in alliance with Russia. The capitalist formula of imperialism will no longer work in large countries like China or India, nor will it pay in many lesser colonies. Imperialism, however, is not dead. Germany, Russia and Japan are aggressively imperialistic and must so continue. But the new formula cannot be that of Cobden and Pitt.

Revolution, expansion and imperialism make up a social behavior pattern essential for highly integrated industrial civilizations. The chief reasons are what Stuart Chase has called technological imperatives. Our principal social need is not adjustments and lubricants but drive. Our enemy is not friction but stagnation. The unemployment and public deficit figures are eloquent in proof of this.

The necessary drive for a complex society such as ours must be generated by a combination of an expansive ideology and technology. Call it a combination of faith and economic planning if you will. These essential dynamisms are a scheme of values people are willing to die for and a pattern of change and expansion they are able to make work. Just now everyone professes an eagerness to die for dear old democracy but nobody demonstrates an ability to make it work, i.e., to create full employment without war. The values of democracy and capitalism are no longer credible because their mechanics are no longer workable. Material values must be materialized. Dying for impossible ideals or vain hopes is an old human custom and one of Mother Nature's most efficient means of population control.

The collapse of the industrial revolution as a capitalistic dynamism —it is, of course, an animating force for socialism—leaves democracy and capitalism with only the temporary and final dynamism of suicidal war. As we shall have occasion to point out, the type of easy and lucrative warfare—guns versus tomahawks or superior versus inferior technology—of imperialist and frontier conquest on which alone democracy and capitalism can flourish, ended with the Boer and Spanish-American wars. Those were the last wars to be won by democracy. The World War was democracy's first attempt at suicide. It was not entirely successful, producing at first only Soviet Russia, then later the great depression; and out of the latter German national socialism. The present attempt of the democracies at self-destruction has every chance of being one hundred per cent successful. The Haves can win from the Have-nots only during a certain and now departed phase of world trade, industrial change, population growth and frontier settlement in which the victorious Haves can exploit the labor and markets of the defeated or submerged Have-nots. Today that is no longer possible. If the American and British Haves, the world's premier capitalists and democracy lovers, cannot exploit profitably the labor and markets of their Have-nots at home but must support them in idleness out of the surplus of the Haves, how can these same Haves expect to derive benefit from a victory over the proletarian nations of Germany, Japan and Russia? Today any major war fought by democracy and capitalism must be suicidal for the system and good for either socialism or chaos or both.

The need of a modern industrialized society for an ideology and a technology which are both extremely revolutionary, like those of democracy and capitalism in the nineteenth century, grows more acute every hour. During the late eighteenth and nineteenth centuries capitalism ran on the revolutionary idea of free trade and on the revolutionary technology of the new inventions of steam, electricity and the transition to power production and railway transportation. The ideology justified and motivated expansion. The technological changes facilitated it.

Yesterday the ideology of capitalism called for booms. Today it calls for retrenchment in order to balance the budget. The doctrinary imperatives of the system now demand public economy at a time when there is no likelihood of a compensatory expansion in private investment. The profit incentives growing out of nineteenth century expansion are lacking in present-day stagnation. Therefore, sound liberal principles are anachronisms, the following of which under present conditions would be nationally suicidal.

The only formula now feasible for a necessary amount of activity, other than that of war, which the democracies cannot hope to win, must consist in a raising of living standards and pyramid building. By pyramid building, which will be discussed more fully in Chapter XVI, is meant housing and public-works construction which cannot be financed or paid for in a capitalistically sound manner. But more luxuries and leisure for the working classes or more non-reproductive public works would be downright waste and immorality in terms of the ethics of our American system. Our ideology could rationalize the building of the railways in the nineteenth century and the building of highways for the automobiles of the middle classes in the twentieth century. It could even, as late as 1929, rationalize the building of now half empty office buildings. All this could be justified on the basis of profit expectancy. But industrial expansion and economic acceleration along the only lines now physically possible must be pronounced morally wrong and prove institutionally impractical under our present American system.

The problem now confronting us, then, is essentially spiritual and technical. It is one of why (ideology) and how (technology) shall we keep busy. Our democracy can no longer find moral reasons or an institutional setup for full employment, as it did in the nineteenth century. This is not a matter of opinion but of fact. It can be contradicted only by deeds, not words. No amount of explanation of what might be done if only a great many other things were done first is relevant to the statements just made. Democracy is pronounced the favorite of the overwhelming majority of the people. It is in power. It is not being obstructed by foreign foes. If it fails, there can be only one verdict: it cannot deliver the goods. That must be the verdict of the past ten years and must remain the verdict until it is changed by the employment figures.

This failure of democracy and capitalism really antedates 1929. It goes back of 1913 and may be considered as one of the causes of the World War. Thus came the World War which provided the dynamic formula for five years. Next came the phony private credit inflation of the twenties to finance consumer expenditures not warranted by the prevailing level of consumer incomes and to permit capital investments which had no possibility of ever yielding a profit, as subsequent experience demonstrated. This second phase of capitalist breakdown ended in the collapse of 1929. The formula of the third phase, or that of the thirties, has been equally phony. It has consisted of an inflation of public credit to finance more consumption and public investment than can be permanently sustained in this manner or eventually liquidated along sound capitalistic lines. The fourth and final formula of the forties is to be that of a grand fling of public credit inflation to fight a war against the consequences of our failures and follies. But war will not end these consequences. It will only intensify the causes.

An industrialized, urbanized and highly integrated modern society cannot tolerate indefinitely large-scale unemployment such as is now chronic in democratic America under peace. Nor can it effectuate without revolution and anarchy the relapse of a third of the population into subsistence peasanthood or workhouse urban concentrations on permanent relief. In the depressed areas in England there are men of forty who have never known steady employment during their entire lifetimes, the basic industries of their communities, textiles, coal or shipbuilding, having gone into chronic decline right after the war. There can be no security for property without security of employment. Democracy has no remedy for the farmer and the unemployed except deficits and doles. It has no alternative to stagnation except suicidal war. These statements can be refuted only by performances, not by explanations of what would happen if only certain things were done which are not done.

One great trouble with the leaders in the democracies is that because they, themselves, find it so easy and comfortable to survive under stagnation, they somehow feel that the underprivileged will be able to do likewise, especially with a little assistance from the privileged. The leaders of the privileged, obviously, do not like this situation. But they lose no weight over it. And they definitely consider it preferable to any sort of revolutionary change which might disturb their present comfort. Democratic and capitalist leadership in America, Britain and France today has just one real peacetime concern, to stabilize stagnation. Thus they hope to avert revolution. Meanwhile most of our leaders are cherishing the idea of a temporary take-out war. History, however, proves that action is easier to sell than stagnation. That, of course, is precisely why the take-out war for democracy is so popular in high political, financial and intellectual quarters.

From another war we stand to gain much in disillusionment and reeducation if, as seems practically certain, we suffer enough in consequence. The last world war, though it created Soviet Russia and the great depression of the thirties, still failed to teach the democracies very much. Thanks to the American military and economic rescue, they did not suffer enough. In the anger and bitterness of our next postwar frustration we shall finally be able to liquidate the present leadership and ideology responsible for sending in 1917 and in the forties the flower of American youth to die on European battlefields for unworthy interests and unattainable ideals. Out of this holocaust of American blood and suffering should arise a new American ideology and leadership.

The social Frankenstein created by the nineteenth century capitalism and democracy has to go on at an ever accelerating speed of revolutionary change or else collapse. An urban industrialized population cannot turn pastoral or nomadic to save relief taxes on the wealthy and survive. Now the necessary industrial acceleration can be kept up only in war or pyramid building. The necessary dynamism is no longer to be found in the expansive processes of the eighteenth and nineteenth centuries. So, for the solvent of our illusions and the source of a new faith we turn, in the tradition of the ages, to war, to holy war abroad to be followed by class war at home. Thus will disappear our ideological and institutional anachronisms and thus may arise new patterns of thought and ways appropriate to a world which has changed since the foundations of our present culture were laid.

Generalizing broadly and summarizing briefly, it may be said that the more highly organized the society, the more dynamism it needs; and the greater the necessary dynamism for minimum operating velocity, the more revolutionary and expansive that dynamism must be.

Chapter II
The Victors Make the Rules

Thus far we have outlined for further elaboration an analysis of the present and a view of the future which to many will seem most unpleasant. Perhaps the first point to make clear about this analysis and view is that the bases are facts and logical deductions from such facts rather than ethics or preferences. An ethical analysis of the world situation today can only serve to rouse righteous indignation for a holy war. It cannot throw light on practical ways to peaceful solutions. The easiest way to attack a social interpretation is to invoke morality against it. Showing that it is repugnant to prevailing ethical prepossessions is naively thought somehow to make it untrue. As right always prevails in the end, because whatever prevails thereby becomes right, the general reasoning which underlies the ethical attack on realism is that if it is contrary to current ethics it must be contrary to fact. The fallacy consists of not recognizing that ethics change like every other social institution. One simply cannot discuss the changing facts of a dynamic society in terms of the dogmas of a static morality. Saying that a revolution is immoral amounts to saying that it is immoral to change old for new morals. If George Washington had lost, he would have been hanged as a traitor and ever afterwards so spoken of in British history. As he won, his treason has become, even in British history, a great Anglo-Saxon tradition. British ambassador to Washington, Lord Lothian, correctly, though cleverly, called George Washington the founder of the modern British Empire.

Taking an ethical view of social facts makes it possible to eliminate from the frame of reference of one's social thinking anything that displeases. Such elimination may take the intellectually dishonest form of calling the unwelcome fact or future probability temporary or abnormal. Social change, of course, is one long story of so-called abnormal behavior. Pointing out these facts about the use of ethics as an adjunct to wishful thinking is not an attack on morality or a demand for an unmoral social philosophy. A social philosophy has to be ethical. Its first concern is with what ought to be. But the implications and consequences of a given ethic can and should be periodically tested by the criteria of reality. That examination is one of the major tasks of this book. Value choices, as such, cannot be validated or invalidated by scientific observation and logical inference. But their practical effects and probable consequences can be so determined, and should be.

In short, ethics cannot be proved good or bad but they can be proved workable or unworkable and they can be changed. Some facts, however, cannot be changed. When an ethic runs up against a fact that cannot be changed, the ethic has to be changed. If we cannot bring back the frontier, the industrial revolution or the average family of seven children of Puritan days, we must change the political, ethical and economic norms of those days for norms appropriate to the changed facts of today. Ethics are good or bad according to given criteria. The criteria should include current realities. The big point to keep in mind is that an ethic does not have to be possible, whereas an action does. We can try disastrously and often suicidally to live by no longer possible moral rules or we can make our ethics ht the facts of our changed situation. A nation can make an ethic of a war to make the world safe for democracy or a war to conquer a piece of territory, like Texas and California, the Boer Republic or Poland. An individual can make an ethic of getting rich quick. The realization or nonrealization of any one of these ethics is a matter of fact and not of ethics. The difference between making the world safe for democracy in 1917 or 1940 and making Texas safe in 1849 for Jacksonian Democrats and slavery is not ethical but practical.

This book, far from lacking moral premises, is written on the basis of certain definite ethical assumptions. Its purposes are highly ethical. Its method aims to be scientific and logical, not ethical. The governing assumptions in this respect are the following:

First, facts are normative, that is to say, facts should determine rules, being paramount to rules. A rule which contradicts a fact is nonsense.

Second, ethics should be made consistent with realities which cannot be reconciled to given ethics. Ethics, of course, do not have to be realizable, but they should be. Impractical social ethics should be discarded.

Third, ideals should be attainable. Frequently they are not, but they ought to be, where national policies are concerned. Which is to say, nations should not pursue, especially with arms, unattainable ideals.

Fourth, laws should be enforceable, which is to say, unenforceable laws ought to be repealed or not enacted.

Fifth, social institutions should be workable; institutions should be scrapped when found unworkable.

Sixth, suicide is morally wrong. Therefore, any ethic which imposes upon a nation self-mutilation or self-destruction is to be rejected out of hand as unethical. If a nation is asked to destroy itself for right, justice, truth, democracy, liberty or something else whether abstractly or concretely described, the answer is not that these abstractions are wrong but that suicide is wrong. Sometimes, it may be added, also, that a given national suicide will not advance any of the ideals which are invoked to justify it.

The above propositions are not unmoral since they are statements of what, in the opinion of the author, ought to be believed or done. But they apply scientific or nonmoral tests to the implications and probable consequences of morals.

Bismarck once said that politics is the science of the possible. Ethics is clearly the science of the desirable which, literally, can mean anything, possible or impossible. In determining what is possible and what may prove suicidal for a nation, ethical criteria are of no use whatever. The issue is one of fact. Scientific observation and logical inference can demonstrate fairly well what is actual, possible and probable. They cannot prove what is morally right or wrong. They can show what is but not what ought to be. Attempting the impossible or committing suicide may be deemed morally right or morally wrong in given circumstances for an individual or a nation, according to the ethical standards used. Japanese ethics sometimes impose suicide on the individual.

Turning for the moment from the abstract to the concrete we may remark that if a man says that America should join Britain and France in their crusade to make the world safe and good, or however the crusade may be described in moral terms, he expresses a purely ethical opinion. Ask him why and he will probably give a reply something like this: "Because democracy and the American way are worth fighting and dying for." Now it is wholly irrelevant to this moral judgment to show that Americans cannot preserve these ethical values by fighting and dying in Europe. The facts are that the world is not safe and good and cannot be made so by an American expeditionary force in Europe. But the people who want to fight against dictatorship and for democracy are not usually concerned with what is possible or probable. They are concerned with what they call right and wrong, and they want to do something about their feeling of concern, and the thing they feel like doing is fighting. These people were wholly uninterested in practical ways and means of preventing dictatorship and preserving democracy such as were constantly advanced and discussed during the twenties. The only propaganda the democracies are successful with is that creating a will to fight. The only times the idealists and moralists of twentieth century democracy are potent and creative are when they are advocating a war for democracy, as in 1917 and 1940. Then what they create is destruction. When the destruction is over they are unable to create their ideal social order.

In another age and with a different conditioning the people now eager to fight for democracy would have been as ready to fight for the Prophet of Allah or for Saint Iago and the Holy Cross, the dying cry of thousands of Spanish adventurers who fell in the Spanish conquest of the Americas. These adventurers in search of gold and glory, in the name of the gospel, of course, were as little interested in the fulfillment of the ethics of Jesus as most people who are today ready to die for democracy are interested in the realization of the spiritual values of democracy, whatever these may be. More recently in certain lands the masses have been conditioned to want to fight and die for the dictatorship of the proletariat.

What moves the people who talk passionately about fighting and dying for a symbol or an abstraction is simply an inner compulsion to suffer, to fight and to die. These sadistic and masochistic drives are important social forces which should be wisely controlled by political leadership. Their symbols and rationalizations are interesting, necessary, but relatively unimportant because they are easily changed. Giving vent to these impulses is a great human experience, an end in itself, an ethic or an ultimate spiritual value. As Nietzsche so profoundly remarked "A good war justifies any cause." Anything a people say they are fighting for is their ethic, and so is fighting for it. The ethic of fighting is usually more real than the ethical value supposedly being fought for. Thus, what most people want who desire to fight for democracy is not democracy but war. They stand to get the war and lose democracy, all of which will matter little to most of them.

The stock market and business indexes, rising on war hopes and falling on peace fears, give a fairly conclusive and objective measure of what the people really want. The Gallup polls and current statements indicating the desire of the majority to keep America out of war merely reflect the ethic that it is wrong to want war. The shy young virgin who goes to her first rendezvous with a notorious Casanova affords a perfect example of the ambivalence of human desires. Nature cries out in her for one experience while conventional ethics make her deny that she is moved by her suppressed desire. So, in respect to war, the American people, conditioned with certain ethical attitudes toward war, profess a strong aversion to it, while moving unerringly in that direction under the irresistible impulse of their mass desire for war. As these lines were being written the arms embargo was repealed. The American people were then hastening to their rendezvous with Mars, strong in the moral conviction that they were proof against his seductive wiles.

The fact is, contrary to a current ethical doctrine of this, though not of every past and current, culture, people normally love suffering, war and danger. Momentarily, this normal desire is heightened by the subconscious awareness that war offers the only escape from the stagnation of the past decade. If people did not love to fight they would not do it so often, now twice in one generation. Savages fight most of the time. In industrialized society the orgies and rituals of suffering and death have to be limited to periodical large wars. The more privileged, of course, are able at any time to seek danger and death in mountain climbing, hunting wild game or the more democratic sport of reckless automobile driving which yearly kills more Americans than the late world war. What sold the Wars of the Roses, i.e., the wars between the House of Lancaster and York, was not a love of roses or a love of those two dynasties. It was a love of war. The same love will sell a war for democracy and capitalism, not a love of either of these abstractions or the systems which they denote. The war's the thing, not the symbol for which it happens to be fought.

The foregoing is neither a disparagement of war nor of the usually meaningless symbols for which people fight. In the ethical philosophy of this book war is not wrong in the abstract or in the absolute. War is right or wrong relatively to the ideals and interests of a given nation in a given instance. Some people, of course, take the view that war is wrong relatively to the ideals and interests of mankind or humanity. For religious or transcendental purposes, this is a perfectly good ethic. For practical purposes it is not, because for practical purposes mankind has to be considered and dealt with as divided into nations and classes. There are many communities in the world, but there is no one all embracing community of mankind, except as an abstract concept. According to the ethics of this book, a war in which we might be engaged would be immoral and wrong only if and because it did not seem likely to serve the interests of the American people as a whole.

A nation, according to this book, does wrong relatively to its interests if it lights a war for the impossible. For that nation, such a war constitutes fighting for fighting's sake which is on the lowest level of the animal kingdom and not a good national ethic. War for food, territory or war of the kinds the democracies used to fight makes sense. Our fighting the Indians and the Mexicans to take their lands was a good kind of war, that is good for us as a people since we got rid of the Indians and got their lands. A war for utopia is a bad war for anybody simply because there is no such place as utopia.

It is interesting that the American people almost unanimously approve the war of the Allies for the impossible and with equal unanimity disapprove the German war to conquer Poland which was not only possible but extremely easy and logical for the Germans, just as was our war for the conquest of Mexico. Before 1914 the democracies fought for the attainable. Since 1914 they have been fighting for the unattainable. Can a system survive that has become synonymous with the quest for the impossible and resistance to the inevitable?

It is nowhere said in this book that democracy or the American way of the nineteenth century are not good ethical values. It is merely pointed out that these values are no longer realizable and that a war between the democracies and the dictatorships will hasten their total disappearance rather than assure the perpetuation of democracy and its values. As memories, of course, they will live on. Saying all this is no assault on democracy or American ways of the nineteenth century. All honor to their memory, but let us have the facts about their present feasibility. Telling an old man that he is no longer young and to be his age is in no sense an insult either to his age or his youth. Americans as a people are not senile; it is their nineteenth century polity and economy which are in late maturity. Civilizations come and go but the peoples who live through them go on through the ages. As Jacques Maritain poetically phrases it "Worlds which have risen in heroism lie down in fatigue for new heroisms and new suffering come in their turn and bring the dawn of another day."

Present confusion of thought about these vital problems is largely due to the influence of three important factors in American culture: The first is wishful thinking, a national habit encouraged largely by our amazing luck as a young nation growing up rapidly in one of the richest territories ever given a great people to develop. The second is our Puritan tradition, which, among other things, makes us always tend to equate morality with self-interest and desire. The third is our extreme legal-mindedness, which is partly the result of the preponderance of lawyers in the ranks of our cultural leaders, 70 per cent of our legislators being attorneys, and partly a direct heritage of eighteenth century rationalism. The latter is really the parent of present-day American legalism. Our legal priesthood, which we owe to the Protestant Reformation and the eighteenth century French rationalists, has taken over the functions and the technique of exploiting myths for the purposes of social control formerly monopolized by the priests of the Roman church and other great cults of the past.

And so it happens, in an essentially technological and economic age, we have most of our social thinking done by men with the minds of priests; not by men with the mentality of engineers and executives who live by getting things done, but by lawyers and teachers who live by talking and writing about how things should be done—and devising ways of keeping things from being done, or excusing their not having been done. Having spent the past century mechanizing society, we refuse to treat it as a mechanism which has to have dynamism and scientific adjustments.

Few people ever stop to think how useful ethics can be to wishful thinking. To make an ethic of a wish or an interest is to make it override the obstacles of physical reality. One would not use that ethical approach on a broken-down machine. When one's automobile breaks down, one does not send for a faith healer or pray over it. But when our industrial machine starts hitting on only four or five of its eight cylinders, businessmen and politicians begin praying over it and telling us that the remedy is a revival of confidence or faith in America. What the machine needs is gas—the fuel and not the talking kind. The ethical approach to a conflict of interests may also serve to bamboozle a great many simple-minded people into giving you your way against their best interests. During the late world war our farmers did not say, "Let's have a war to raise wages." Our bankers and investors did not say, "Let's have a war to raise interest rates, security prices and land values." Our industrialists did not say, "Let's have a war to raise sales and profits." Puritan influences made such frankness impossible just as it inhibits a security owner from saying that he hopes a peace rumor which puts stock prices down is unfounded.

Selfish interests alone could never have got us into the late war, nor can they, unaided by ethics, get us into a war today or tomorrow. Had the issues of the late world war been debated in purely nonethical terms, America would not have entered the war. The resulting peace would never have been one of negotiation, like the peace of Vienna in 1815, rather than one of dictation. And it might have lasted as long as the unmorally made peace of Vienna. The peace of Versailles was history's greatest diplomatic failure because it was also history's greatest triumph of the ethical approach to the solution of international problems. At Vienna it was honestly and unmorally recognized that Europe's peace must always depend on the right kind of balance of power. At Versailles it was assumed that Europe's peace could be made secure by platitudes and promises on pieces of paper. This assumption was rendered mandatory by the moral and contrary to fact propaganda which the victorious Allies had had to use to win the war, one of the fruits of the spread of democracy. The victors at Vienna in 1815 could be realists and act more intelligently in making peace than the victors at Versailles in 1919 because they had been able to fight the war with the aid of fewer lies and of less morality and hypocrisy.

Then, after the war and its culminating follies of the peace, we entered upon a decade of financial and economic follies for the successful perpetration of which certain highly ethical assumptions were indispensable. We lent some seven billion dollars to foreigners while raising higher and higher tariff and immigration barriers which made repayment practically impossible. This absurdity could have been obscured as well as it was only by a fog of pietistic internationalism. According to the moral "line" the borrowers were honorable, the contracts valid and the process of capital exports sanctified by centuries of British precedent. Like most of our recent and current ethical prepossessions, these moral arguments in favor of foreign loans were based on irrelevant facts and oblivious of relevant facts. In this case the only relevant fact, that of the impossibility of making the necessary transfer of loan repayments from foreign currencies to dollars was either ignored or flatly denied by our economists who, as usual, talked morality and refused to face unpleasant facts. Our social scientists and cultural leaders were practically unanimous in glorifying and rationalizing the follies of postwar international finance, almost wholly on moral grounds, since the processes did not bear scrutiny on scientific grounds. During this same hectic period, speculative greed was inflating American security prices to preposterous heights. But any realist who, on purely accounting principles, dared to question the soundness of such values was most effectively crushed by the only argument that was unanswerable—except in terms of the rather difficult analysis of this book—the appeal to morality: To question the soundness of market values was to show a lack of faith in America and its constructive political and business leaders, its Hardings, Coolidges, Hoovers, Mellons, Mitchells, Wiggins and Youngs. Leveling this charge at a critic of the American way of the twenties was like the good old Puritan custom of charging a person with witchcraft. Saying "Don't sell America short" was the never failing ethical technique.

When Prohibition, a recognized experiment in moral betterment, was being debated and adopted, the argument that it was unenforceable carried no weight. The reasons were the ethical approach and the Puritan tradition. The practical issues again were befogged in a cloud of righteousness, thanks to the Anti-Saloon League, an aggregation of fanatical pietists. Drunkenness was bad and sobriety was good. That was enough. To say that the law could not be enforced was to insult our good American law abiding tradition. Once the issue can be resolved into one of morals, any opposition on practical grounds can easily be shouted down. The only trick to the Puritan legalistic technique is that of getting your ethical major premise accepted. The rest has to follow like night the day. Use of this technique is hastening America into war.

The conflict or issue over what shall be our rules, our ethical norms, our laws and our taxes, our rights and our duties is essentially one of naked power. It can be settled with ballots or bullets, by compromise and give and take or by war, but not by law. A clear understanding of this obvious and inescapable fact will do more than anything else to avert civil war and international war. Our Civil War was the result primarily of both sides taking a stand on the Constitution, law and ethics, and, in so doing, refusing to recognize that the other side had an equally good case in ethics, law and theory, as the other side in every important class or international conflict always has. If the basic assumption of the legalists had been true, the Supreme Court would have resolved peacefully the issues over which the states fought in 1860-1865. The Supreme Court did decide in the Dred Scott decision that slaves were property everywhere but the North refused to accept a decision that did not harmonize with the exigencies of a growing industrialism. When classes within a nation or nations within the society of nations become deadlocked over what shall be the rules or the rule in a given question at issue, the alternatives are compromise or war. Those who try to force acceptance of their legal or moral theory are merely making civil or international war inevitable in cases in which men are willing on both sides to fight.

Few peoples are able to grasp the comparatively simple truth that class conflicts and international wars are contests not under rules but over rules. In domestic politics our industrialists have long taken tariff subsidies for granted. Now many of them regard subsidies for farmers, doles for the unemployed and large pensions for the aged as highly unethical examples of class legislation. Class legislation they are, but we have never been without class legislation. The theory of a government and scheme of social organization which favors no class and is impartial towards all classes is without basis in history or logic.

Whatever a majority has the power to cause to be enacted into law becomes legal and ethical under any practical theory of government. Why say in respect of any new proposal which the majority or any substantial minority may advocate that it would be illegal or unethical? Anything can be made legal and ethical by due process of law. Every government is, and can never be anything else but, a government of laws. Any feasible form of administration can be legalized. That of Russia or Germany is just as legal as that of the United States or Switzerland. Law is a manifestation of political power and is as valid as that power is effective. For a thing to be lawful in Bangkok or Berlin it does not have to accord with American ideas of what is lawful. The only sound argument against a piece of legislation is an appeal to the interests of the majority, not an appeal to the ethics of the minority. This, essentially, is why the current socialist and collectivist trend is inevitable and irresistible. It is based on appeal to majority interest. The majority, of course, must learn its interest by experience rather than inductive reasoning. The attitude of the majority towards its interests must be emotionally conditioned rather than rationally inculcated. The majority must get its idea of national interest through propaganda rather than an appeal to reason which can be made effectively only to the elite minority. The mass majority will always find eventually an elite minority to harmonize the interests of the majority with those of such a minority and to supply rational leadership to the majority. It may be rationally argued by the Haves or any other minority that a certain measure detrimental or destructive to their interests will also result harmfully to the interests of the Have-nots or the majority. But it is nonsense for the Haves to say that the Have-nots do not have the right to do whatever they please in constitutional and legal form. The strictly nonethical, nonlegal approach to these problems and conflicts will, in the long run, prove best under modern conditions for all minority interests, as well as for peace.

Thanks largely to the influence of the legal and ethical doctrinaries, most of the members of our privileged minorities today still think that the masses are sufficiently conditioned by some religious faith to make them obey indefinitely the ethical mandates of the ruling class. To a limited and ever decreasing extent this is true. But the extent to which it is now true does not make it a safe rule over an indefinite future for the Haves and the privileged minorities.

CHAPTER III
The International Jungle

In international relations the ethical problem is even simpler and the logic of the factual situation more obvious than in the class and minority-group struggle within nations. The two groups of forces causing conflict in the world today are classes or pressure groups within nations and nations within the society of nations. Classes within a nation like those of labor, agriculture or the aged pension seekers can by coalition and logrolling become momentary majorities for the purpose of securing class legislation. They can also become a triumphant revolutionary majority. This is actually happening today to a greater extent than is commonly perceived due to the subtleties of democratic lobbying and logrolling. The Have-nots are already running a fairly obvious revolution in America by means of progressive taxation on the rich and subsidies to the poor farmers and unemployed. Most of the time, however, social classes do not constitute a sovereign political majority for broad political power purposes. Nations, on the other hand, are sovereign all the time, that is, to the extent of what is physically possible for them to do. For the purpose of making decisions they are unquestionably and always sovereign. Else they are not nations. This being true, nothing could be more provocative of war and less conducive to peace than the legal or ethical approach to any international difference. This is the central point of the present chapter.

The popular notion is that the way to prevent war is to invoke law and morality. The contention here is that that is precisely the way to get a war started. The appeal to law or ethics in international differences is simply an attempt to impose upon another nation an alien theory of law and justice. In international affairs the appeal to law and ethics always brings down the house at home. Abroad it inflames public opinion equally but to an exactly opposite conviction and impulse.

In 1915 Mr. Wilson made the bad decision of refusing on good moral grounds recognition to a bad president and government of Mexico. This act inaugurated a new era of righteousness in American foreign policy. It started the chain of events in our relations with Mexico, the latest link of which is the expropriation of two hundred million dollars worth of our property in that country. This ideology got us into the World War; it got us into several bloody interventions in Haiti, Nicaragua and Mexico; it has made Mexico unsafe for American lives and property; and it is by way of getting us into a second world war within one generation. But these melancholy experiences in no way affect the faith of our present ruling classes and government officials in this normative or legalistic theory of international relations. And why should experience invalidate a theory which transcends mundane realities and rests firmly grounded on principles which, being morally right, do not have to be historically or otherwise right?

The ethical or legal theory underlying this tendency of our government since the beginning of the Wilsonian era revolves around unreal concepts of the nature and functions of what is called international law. This theory is ideal but contrary to fact. A strong case can be made out for the contention that what goes by the name of international law is not law inasmuch as it lacks most of the essential attributes of law, such as certainty, uniformity and enforceability. But, for practical purposes, there would be little point to such an argument. If, by common consent, people call something international law, the sensible attitude to take towards such usage of words is to accept it. Those who talk about international law are consistent in one respect and inconsistent in many others. What they refer to as international law always means the same body of rules, which makes their use of the general term consistent; but what they refer to is always a selection from this body of rules which can be matched by another wholly contradictory or inconsistent selection from the same body of rules, which makes their use of the term international law most confusing. International law always means the same thing or the same body of rules; only these rules are often mutually contradictory.

If our Secretary of State says that Proposition A is international law and the Foreign Offices of London, Berlin or Moscow say that the exact opposite or something wholly inconsistent with A is international law, the probabilities are that each is entirely correct. The thing to understand about international law is not how to reconcile its contradictions, for that is impossible, but merely to know their respective sources in international law. This allows the priesthood to discuss facts and interest conflicts in a language the laity cannot understand. The use of this language in no way facilitates understanding of, or promotes agreement about, the real things in dispute. But it does assure the legal priesthood prestige, power and a meal ticket. It is like the game of scriptural or Marxist exegesis. No religious argument can ever be settled by reference to the Bible. No Marxist argument can ever be settled by appeals to the writings of Marx. No international dispute can ever be settled by reference to international law, except where all parties are willing to accept one particular set of rules and canon of interpretation. And, if all parties are that much in agreement, there is likely to be no dispute which will not be settled by mutual concessions wholly aside from legal rules.

One invaluable key to an understanding of international law is realization of the fact that anything relating to several nations is ipso facto international. Therefore, if one group of nations says that cotton is not contraband and another group says that it is, or if two groups of nations uphold any two mutually contradictory propositions, it must be recognized that the fact that they do so makes each of these propositions good international law. Secretary Hull, in protesting against the action of the Russian government in refusing to release to the American owners the German prize, the ship "City of Flint," invoked as good international law a ruling of the Supreme Court releasing under similar circumstances the British ship "Appam," a German prize during the war. Secretary Hull was correct in citing anything the Supreme Court has ever held affecting international disputes as good international law. And so would any other nation be in citing anything held by its courts affecting international disputes as good international law. Our Supreme Court, of course, has repeatedly reversed itself in making new rulings. An American Secretary of State invoking one selection from that interesting bundle of contradictions called international law as the basis of an argument and moral appeal would never dream of admitting that the opposite thesis could be sustained with equally good authority by another selection from that storehouse of dissenting opinion, dogma and precedent called international law.

There are a few minor exceptions to the general rule that there are no universally accepted international rules. These exceptions are mainly rules of diplomatic immunities, precedence and protocol. The chief reason these particular rules happen to enjoy practically universal acceptance is that they involve almost no conflicts of vital interests. They are accepted for the same general reasons that people ordinarily take their place in a line and do not fight over who goes first through a revolving door. Such generally observed rules of behavior in no way establish a basis for hoping that all forms of competition and conflict between individuals can be eliminated by observance of the same etiquette.

Then there are the fairly numerous examples of arbitration, over five thousand in all, in which nations have agreed to pacific settlement of a dispute in accordance with some prearranged formula of procedure and subject to certain mutually agreeable rules. In such cases international law and the lawyers go to town in a big way, simply because in these particular instances both nations would rather concede everything in dispute than fight. The only problem in such cases is for the lawyers and the protocol to save the faces of all concerned by working out a formula of final settlement along more dignified lines than those of simple horse trading. The result is a great victory for international law and fat fees for many international lawyers.

Thus, in the case of our Alabama claims against Britain, arbitration provided an excellent ritual for a compromise whereby the British paid us fifteen and a half million dollars for losses suffered by our shipping as a result of the British having allowed Confederate privateers to be fitted out in and depart from British ports during the Civil War. That was a grievance over which we should never have gone to war with Britain but through which Britain might have lost much more than fifteen and a half million dollars worth of American good will. Two dictatorships would have disposed of this difficulty by a simple negotiation and some arbitrary settlement. In this manner the German minority problems in the Italian Tyrol and the Baltic states have been summarily disposed of without recourse to legal principles or formulas of settlement. For democracies some international judicial procedure would have been necessary for the disposal of these issues. The fact that Germany and Italy settled a long standing difference by summary action does not prove that all future disputes between these two countries can be settled in that way. Why assume that because two nations settled a minor difference by arbitration they can dispose of all disputes in the same manner? The assumption is obviously unreasonable and contrary to experience, yet it is basic to most of the current claims for international law.

The following simple generalizations about international law will make its limitations clear:

First, it is not a body of codified law.

Second, with certain exceptions affecting mainly diplomatic immunities and protocol, it is not a body of universally accepted rules.

Third, international law is a body of miscellaneous principles, rules, doctrines, precedents and agreements to be found in a long line of state papers, treaties, textbooks, articles, arbitral and court decisions and public utterances of statesmen and supposed authorities.

Fourth, the elements of this corpus of so-called international law are largely contradictory, mutually exclusive and inconsistent propositions as to international rights and duties. A given rule or set of rules may have been accepted by a given group of nations and even used by them in a specific past period and situation thus becoming international law. Yet, in the changed circumstances of today all or most of the same nations may reject those rules without ever having formally proclaimed repudiation of them. Hence the utter meaninglessness of the term international law in the sense of being positive law.

It can be seriously argued that thinking of international problems in terms of the words, definitions and abstractions which make up international law instead of in terms of the current realities of experience is wholly bad for peaceful settlement of international differences. If there were universal agreement as to the norms and concepts or if there were just one body of norms, international law might serve as a useful instrument for the examination of conflicting claims. But, as there is no such agreement, dragging what is called international law or a bunch of legalistic contradictions into an international dispute usually makes matters worse by adding an argument over words to an argument over things, thus increasing the heat but affording no additional light. It also confuses the relevancies of the present with the irrelevancies of the past.

The fact is that the chief utility of international law today is as a tool of propaganda and dialectics for home use. It creates the requisite moral justification in the minds of the people of the home government for the demands of that government and any war those demands may render inevitable. Dr. Goebbels invokes international law quite as often and quite as effectively for the persuasion of his own people as President Roosevelt does for the persuasion of his own people. But neither persuades the people of the other by an appeal to international law, hence its futility for peaceful purposes. From the point of view of a neutral, wars are fought between right and right, not between right and wrong. The chief utility of international law is to put one nation in the right and the other in the wrong, hence it is of no use for purposes either of neutrality or the prevention of war. It goes without saying that once a nation goes to war its people believe that they are right and their adversaries wrong. But this view serves only the ends of waging war, not the ends of maintaining neutrality or averting war. The point just argued is advanced somewhat more guardedly in a book entitled *Nationalism* by a study group of the Royal Institute of International Affairs, as may be seen from the following quotation: "May not the function of the public conscience be, not to influence national policy but to provide a moral basis for policies determined on purely national grounds?"

To pit one ethic against an opposite ethic is ipso facto to commit to war the people and the force factors behind each of the opposing ethics. People who link ethics with peace, as is the current practice, are simply oblivious of the facts of history. So far as nations are concerned, and it happens to be nations and not angels that we are talking about, the best definition of an ethic is something the people are willing to fight for. And ethics are not only what nations fight for but what makes them fight.

The truth is that every nation has made a supreme ethic of war and no nation has ever really made a supreme ethic of peace. The proof is simple: Every nation is ready voluntarily to make the supreme sacrifice for war. What great or small nation in modern times has ever voluntarily, or otherwise than under foreign military compulsion, made a really great sacrifice for peace? Christianity bids men make a supreme sacrifice for peace by turning the other cheek. What nation observes this Christian ethic? It would be contrary to the ethics of nationalism for a nation, voluntarily, to make a supreme sacrifice for peace. And that, fundamentally, is why we have wars. The point is that, so far as nations are concerned, it is not so much ethics they fight for as it is ethics that makes them fight. National ethics make wars; they do not prevent wars. And the only type of ethics that could keep one nation out of war, the Christian ethic of turning the other cheek, for example, is wholly incompatible with nationalism. A universal international system of ethics which would prevent all nations from making war is virtually a contradiction in terms. Nations would not be nations if they lacked the means and willingness on occasion to make war.

So, paradoxical as it may sound, those who cherish the ethic of averting wars in the world in which we live in, should strive to keep ethics, morality and international law out of diplomacy and international relations as much as possible. If peace through war is desired, talk law and justice; if peace through compromise is desired, talk facts. Ethics are not an easy basis for concession. The one thing nations cannot gracefully compromise on is moral principle. Material interests, on the contrary, are easy subjects of compromise. The peace ideology of our postwar internationalists has concentrated on law and morality and refused to talk realistically economic and political facts, such, for example, as, tariffs, immigration barriers, access to raw materials, redistribution of colonies and raw materials, the distribution of the world's gold, the means of transferring international payments and the other innumerable bread-and-butter realities of life. This emphasis on law and ethics coupled with a disregard for the material problems of the struggle for existence has culminated in another war, which, if it is to make sense, must be a world war, within a generation of the last world war. This culmination surely bears out the thesis of these two chapters: that social ethics for this world, especially in relation to national problems, should be consistent with facts.

Not only have ethical abstractions been used since Wilson to confuse political and economic realities, but now Christianity, as an ethical ideology, is being pressed into the service of warmongering. Miss Dorothy Thompson in one of her columns during the early days of the second Anglo-German war of this century actually made this conflict one of Christian versus anti-Christian values. It may be fair to say that many of the values of German and Russian national socialism are not only not Christian but anti-Christian. But the same can be said with equal truth of many of the dominant values of the capitalism and imperialism of Britain, America and France. To call any conflict of class interests within a nation or of national interests within the society of nations of the present-day, a war between Christianity and anti-Christianity is a sheer confusion of terms. No class or nation today is waging class or international war mainly, if at all, for objectives which by any stretch of the imagination can be called Christian. For one thing, truly Christian objectives are not pursued by means of class or international war. The simple historical and philosophical facts are that Christ never issued a call to class or national war. Those who are now summoning their fellow men to fight for British, French or American imperialism in the name of Christ are pious frauds. The call to fight for Caesar should not be made in the name of God, except where the two can be combined as happened in ancient Rome or present-day Japan. If the system calls for the separation of church and state, God and the church should not be mobilized for every war. But they are.

Individuals can take refuge in religious escape; nations cannot. The individual can flee into the wilderness and live on locusts and wild honey. The nation, the community or the social class cannot renounce the world, and escape from it to a religious asylum there to live a life of devout contemplation and prayer supported by the working and sinning community outside. The tens of millions of people crowded into a small area like that of the British Isles or Germany cannot take seriously a religious ethic, the practice of which would mean starvation for millions of them. Specifically, they cannot reject discipline as regimentation, a war for feeding places as immoral or a program of socialization at home and aggrandizement abroad as selfish. And to say, as do many internationalists, that the overpopulated nations, poor in land, food and raw materials, are able to buy all they need is the rankest intellectual dishonesty when it is known that the world is ruled by autarchy and policies of tariff and immigration exclusiveness. For one nation to invoke against another Christian ethics which no nation can possibly practice and remain a nation is the height of inconsistency. And it is an inconsistency which no Christian ethic prescribes.

The saddest commentary on the invocation of ethics, especially those of Christianity, in connection with current conflicts is that the motive is usually selfish and bellicose, hence highly unchristian. Our wealthy conservatives do not plead for Christian charity, nor do they go and sell all that they have and give to the poor as Christ bade the rich young ruler do. They invoke Christian ethics for the protection of the money changers or to support the class interest of the rich against the class interest of the poor. Our militant liberals do not invoke the ethic of the Prince of Peace, the ethic of good will to men and peace on earth, but seek only to pit the Cross against the swastika or the hammer and sickle. The appeals to ethics are made in support of unchristian interests and unchristian acts in defense or furtherance of those interests. They are made in cases where an appeal to facts would not be convincing and where the action sought is against the best interests of those to whom the appeal is made, as well, of course, as against the most fundamental Christian ethic.

In conclusion, this book up to this point argues that good social ethics must be good social mechanics and dynamics, which is to say that they must work. Social ethics must change with social facts. Those who would oppose facts with ethics will learn to their sorrow that power is paramount to preference and that might which prevails thereby always becomes right.

Part II. The End of the Capitalist Revolution

Chapter IV. The Industrial Revolution—The Profits of New Monopolies

Chapter V. The Frontier—The Profits of Free Land

Chapter VI. Rapid Population Increase—The Profits of Cheap Labor

Chapter VII. Easy Wars of Conquest—Bows and Arrows versus the Machine Gun

Chapter VIII. The Masses go to School and the Polls

Chapter IV
The Industrial Revolution

Part Two of this book is an autopsy of the capitalist revolution. This chapter is an autopsy of the industrial revolution as a capitalistic dynamic. That page of history calls for neither a funeral oration nor an indictment. The prevailing opinion that, on the whole, the industrial revolution did far more good than harm to mankind, is not here controverted. Our interest in the process is confined mainly to establishing one fact and drawing certain inferences: the fact that, as a constructive force for private capitalism, the industrial revolution is now over. Technological change continues. But such change is neither dynamic nor constructive for capitalism any longer. The great capitalist democracies are already industrialized. Further industrial or technological change in them will go on but will not prove helpful to capitalism as a source of increased total demand.

The first and, perhaps, the most important of the five major reasons why the capitalist revolution of the past three hundred years is over is considered in this chapter. While the industrial revolution is over as a capitalistic dynamic in America and the British Empire, it is in its infancy in Russia. There it is not proving a constructive force for world capitalism. In the first place, Russia's going socialist after the World War robbed capitalism of what might have been its last frontier and one the exploitation of which might have prolonged the life of world capitalism for several decades. In the second place, Germany's going national socialist in 1933 closed to capitalism the backward and unindustrialized areas of southern and eastern Europe. The industrial revolution in the twentieth century moves eastward from the Atlantic across Europe and westward under Japanese leadership across Asia,— but, in both movements, under the banners of socialism. Therefore, for vast areas of backward Europe and more backward Asia, the industrial revolution is just beginning, but not as a dynamic force for capitalism. No matter who wins or what happens next in China, British and American capitalists there are on the way out. This is why our fighting Japan for the open door in China or for Chinese national sovereignty will be a folly on a par with our entry into the last world war.

In certain backward areas of the United States the industrial revolution is still in progress. But, alas for capitalism, the industrialization of one area at the expense of another has not a dynamic or beneficial net effect on the capitalist system. The rapid industrialization of the South accompanied by a corresponding de-industrialization in the North and the East is not good for American business as a whole. Industries moving from New England to the South in search of lower production costs create some additional prosperity in the South at a Grade B level of living standards, but in so doing, seal the doom of prosperity in many New England regions at a Grade A level of living standards. This is the industrial revolution for the South, perhaps, but not for America as a whole. This is not the sort of industrial revolution on which nineteenth century capitalism flourished.

During the nineteenth century the industrialization of one region, whether in England or New England or even in Germany, invariably facilitated and accelerated industrialization in other regions all over the world. Thus, the rise of steel, machine and tool industries in Birmingham and Sheffield, England not only meant industrialization and higher living standards there but also contributed to identically the same processes in America and other far-off lands which were thus enabled to start new industries and build new railways with British machinery and steel rails. Today, however, the rise of the largest steel mill in the British Empire out in India does not stimulate railway or factory construction back in England. It means less steel production and fewer jobs in England, fewer English steel exports and less cargo for British bottoms. Momentarily certain British capitalists may receive dividends from the Tata works in India, the largest steel mill in the British Empire, while British workers lose jobs as a result of the expansion of the Indian steel industry. But, as soon as the Indians go nationalistic and do to British capital what the Mexicans have recently done to British and American capital invested in Mexican oil fields, the British investors in India will be out of dividends just as thousands of British workers have been put permanently out of jobs as a result of these investments. As a process of technological change and as a mighty dynamic of socialism, the industrial revolution is still going on. But as a capitalist dynamic it is over.

There can be no doubt that the industrial revolution is the chief factor responsible since 1917 for the survival and success of socialism in Russia. As it may be possible for industrialization to go on in Russia for another century before that country attains the industrial maturity and saturation with factories and machinery now reached in Britain and the United States, there is no immediate occasion for worry about the adequacy of Soviet dynamics. The population factor, also, is especially dynamic in Russia and favorable to the success of socialism. The Russian birth rate is twice that of the democracies. Moscow has three times as many births each year as Chicago, a city of about the same size. As the death rate is falling rapidly due to improved hygiene and better living standards, the rate of population increase in Russia today is about four times what it is in the United States. In the decade 1940-1950 our annual net increase in population will average about 700,000 while that of Russia will be between 3,400,000 and 4,000,000. The question arises: Can socialism work without an industrial revolution and rapid population increase, both of which dynamics are necessarily temporary? While this question need not worry Russian socialists for several generations, it is of vital concern to Americans, Englishmen and Frenchmen as well as Germans.

It may well be that war and religion are the only ultimate and enduring social dynamisms. Those here listed on which nineteenth century capitalism and democracy ran are all necessarily temporary. Wars, of course, are included in that list. But the nineteenth century wars of democracy were never totalitarian wars. They were also mostly easy wars which the democrats and capitalists had fought for them by mercenary armies largely, and always with firearms usually against the natives who fought with tomahawks or bows and arrows. Easy wars for one side are obviously temporary. Today at least one of the yellow peoples is as well armed as the whites.

Actually, capitalism, by itself, was never really dynamic. Profit seeking by individuals may be considered dynamic, but it can only occur in a situation in which a combination of dynamic forces, such as the frontier and easy wars of conquest, make the winning of large profits possible for the lucky. It is not a dynamism like war which can be practiced anywhere, anytime, by any people. Ireland's fight against England over the past three hundred and fifty years is an example of perennial, profitless and dynamic warfare with economic resources for warfare at a minimum on one side and at a maximum on the other side. Profit seeking is not today a dynamic force in the interior of China under communist war lords and brigands. Nor was it anywhere in the world a dynamic force for thousands of years in the past; for instance, not anywhere in Europe between the fall of Rome and the opening of the Renaissance a thousand years later. The profits dynamism inheres in the nature of a special situation, not in human nature as we have been taught by the classical economists. Living on the hunt was a dynamic way of life for the North American Indian a century ago. But, for this way of life to be possible for a group, there must be available an adequate supply of game. The real source of this particular dynamism is the game supply, not an innate love of the chase. The fact that capitalism is not in itself dynamic is an important new discovery. It has taken the necessity for relief and pump priming deficits running each year into the billions over a period of ten consecutive years in the most richly favored of all capitalist countries to reveal this truth. Before the depression, even the Marxists considered capitalism as inherently dynamic though doomed to smash up in a head-on collision with a more dynamic working class revolution. Actually it is coming to grief in no such heroic manner. It is slowly dying of pernicious anemia and waiting for a major war collapse to administer the *coup de grace.*

The driving forces of nineteenth century capitalism, all listed on the page preceding this chapter, are now making a success of socialism in Russia. Capitalism cannot run without these driving forces; socialism can run equally well with them; and their availability does not depend on whether a nation is capitalist or socialist. It will be known a century hence, when the frontier and the industrial revolution will be over in Russia, whether socialism can run without this particular blend of fuel, or whether it will be able to run on an entirely new source of power, say brotherly love. Nothing in the Russian experiment with socialism so far warrants such a hope.

Inasmuch as continuity in social change has to be maintained if chaos is to be averted, it is desirable to understand what has made the social wheels go round in the past and what may and may not make them turn in the near future. As just observed, neither capitalism nor socialism is by itself dynamic. The trouble with most of our social thinking is that, being done in terms of eighteenth century rationalism, it takes dynamism for granted and assumes that the chief social problems are those of knowing what you want and how to get it. The chief social problem is that of generating and unifying the social will that creates activity, change and what we have been wont to call progress. Differences in the availability and effectiveness of dynamic forces are not matters of mass preference but largely of historical necessity. The Russians by going socialist did not create the expansive forces which are now carrying them forward. They merely provided those forces with a new and more efficient vehicle. The same forces made a success of capitalism in America during the nineteenth century: the frontier, population growth, the industrial revolution, extension of public instruction and the suffrage.

Socialists and liberal reformers with socialist leanings have generally confused our problems quite as much as the reactionaries or the defenders of things as they are. Neither the socialist nor the capitalist has been willing to recognize that his system depends absolutely on certain social dynamisms which are not peculiar to the system but which are peculiar only to given countries at given times and in given military, economic and population phases. Both socialist and capitalist doctrinaries think in terms of an ideological system rather than a factual situation. Saying this is an indictment neither of capitalism nor of socialism. It is merely a plea for realism in analyzing both.

It explains nothing to say that capitalism is a profit system or that socialism is a welfare system. What we need to know is why a society can be operated on the profit motive in one situation and phase and not in another. Capitalism did far more for welfare in its heyday in America and England than socialism has done since the war in Russia. But this fact proves nothing about the comparative availability of capitalism and socialism for use in Russia or Eastern Europe, or even the United States, today. To get at the roots of these problems we have to think things, not words; we must think events, not abstractions.

The industrial revolution was a series of events in time and space. We cannot think realistically of capitalism and democracy without thinking concretely of the events which constituted the industrial revolution. It was a continuation of the commercial revolution which began about the opening of the seventeenth century when the first English colony was founded at Jamestown and when more or less continuous trade relations with the East were established by the British. The piracy of the Elizabethan era provided working capital for the ensuing and more respectable ventures of trade and colonization. The entire movement stretched from the beginning of the seventeenth to the beginning of the twentieth centuries. It may be traced still further back to the Crusades and then to the Renaissance or to the beginning of the fifteenth century, which marked the rise of new interests, tastes, and economic demands resulting in the creation of the modern state, new religions, science, the voyages of discovery and the development of trade routes and relations.

With the commercial and agricultural revolution in England in the seventeenth century also went political and social revolution. (The agricultural revolution introduced rotation of crops and a more efficient land utilization which made possible population increase by enlarging the food supply.) Cromwell's revolution of 1649 and the Glorious Revolution of 1688, which liquidated the Stuarts and divine right of kings and established the supremacy of the shopkeeper, i.e., of parliamentary democracy, were the great events of the political revolution of the seventeenth century. This new regime was revolutionary only as long as it was expansive, which was up to the turn of the century forty years ago. Technological change still goes on in America, but it is no longer expansive for the industrial system as a whole.

Between 1720 and 1760 British exports doubled and between 1760 and 1795 they doubled again. French exports increased fivefold between 1715 and 1789. The big idea was international division of labor; the big incentive, the possibilities of making fabulous profits. The battle for the inauguration of the factory system was won in the eighteenth century with the inclosure of the land. The battle for free trade was not won until the repeal of the last corn laws in the middle of the nineteenth century, by which time England had ceased exporting and started importing food. The great revolutionary tract of this movement was Adam Smith's *Wealth of Nations*, published in 1775.

It was a revolution, the transition from feudalism to industrialism; from pastoral and inefficient agricultural production and small handicraft production in the home for strictly local or regional consumption to mass production in specialized plants for a world market; from serfdom to contract labor; from barter to money and credit. The details may be omitted on the assumption that they are well enough known to every reader for the purpose of following intelligently the argument of this book.

Liberal economists and historians have never been entirely happy over the application of the term revolution to this bright era of a young and healthy capitalism. But, as Professor Bonn, writing in the *Encyclopaedia of Social Sciences* on the industrial revolution says, "A revolution which continued for a hundred and fifty years may well seem to need a new label. Yet, despite all hesitation, the term stands and no better one has been devised." Tawney said that the material appearance of England changed "more profoundly than at any other time since the epoch of the last geological changes."

This chapter underlines a few generally overlooked points about the industrial revolution. The first, as already indicated, is that, as a constructive or dynamic force for capitalism, it is over. The second is that its essence was revolutionary change. The third is that it was change by growth or continuous expansion, which means that it had to be a transient phase in the history of any country in which it occurred. This means that these expansive processes cannot be revived. The fourth is that, on the economic side, the most important characteristic of the industrial revolution for capitalistic purposes, after that of continuous expansion, was monopoly.

Summarizing briefly, the end of the industrial revolution for capitalism means the end of a phase of change, growth and monopoly. No features of capitalism have been more laboriously understated or glossed over than those just mentioned. Malthus and Sismondi were among the few influential theorists of the early nineteenth century to give the expansion aspect serious consideration. Liberal thinkers of the nineteenth century generally refused to discuss social problems in their entirety or to envisage society as an organic whole. Their respective fields of inquiry were definitely circumscribed by artificial boundaries of definition. One still hears intelligent people speak of keeping politics out of economics or government out of business, a wish one would rationally expect only burglars or criminals to entertain. The social sciences of the nineteenth century were built around the individual and not around society. What was studied, discussed and explained was the individual, his desires, motives and behavior, considered in detachment from the living social organism and the moving social drama of which the individual is never more than one, and usually an extremely minor, actor. For these theorists, society and the state were nuisances, like droughts and epidemics, with which the individual had to contend and over which he had to triumph.

Growth in geometrical progression and monopoly were two features of the industrial revolution and two requisites of capitalism, and possibly also of socialism, which liberal theorists simply refused to examine in a scientific manner. Explanation of the reason growth by geometrical progression must always be temporary is left for the chapter on population. That this sort of growth was the essence of capitalism, was recognized by few thinkers except the Marxists during the nineteenth century. This is understandable. A man courting a beautiful young maiden does not discourse to her on the brevity of youth and beauty and the inevitability of old age and death. Liberal thinkers were engaged mainly in courting, not in scientifically examining, the system from which they expected and received so many favors.

The Marxists, who, for moral reasons, were denouncing and not wooing business, quickly got off their most devastating criticism of the system on to one of their many moral tangents. One of these led to the inevitability of the overthrow of the system by the victimized workers, a point which seemed increasingly untenable as the standard of living of the alleged victims steadily rose throughout the nineteenth century. Another Marxist tangent led to an equally chimerical concept of a classless, stateless society. Now it becomes evident that what is wrong with capitalism is not its abuse of the workers or the workers' resentment against the system, but the simple fact that it is running down, to the sorrow of the workers quite as much as the bosses. Eventually working class resentment against the capitalist and managing classes may develop, but only if and because, in the breakdown of the system, the latter oppose change. The trouble with the industrial revolution is not that it made millionaires but that it now fails to create enough jobs. As a capitalist dynamic, it is over. The liberal theory that capitalism would go on forever growing bigger and better is to be blamed only for being wrong as a forecast.

Statistical measurements of the changes wrought by the industrial revolution in recent times could be multiplied ad infinitum, as for example, the following: At the beginning of the Civil War we had only thirty thousand miles of railways against 260,000 miles today. At the turn of the century we had only a hundred thousand miles of surfaced highways against some 900,000 miles today. In 1850 we manufactured products of a value of only about a billion dollars as against seventy billion for the banner year of 1929. During the past two generations output per worker in industry has increased three and one third times from 1870 to 1930 and real wages have more than doubled. But the broad facts of industrial change do not need to be proved or illustrated. What we are interested in is the process as a past dynamism and a future possibility.

Business-cycle theory has been spun now for a full century on the basis of the implied assumption that the phases of boom, collapse, depression and recovery constituted a perennial sequence like the four seasons of the year. It was explained with some degree of success why one phase succeeded another. But it was not found possible to time these occurrences. The chief value of this research and theorizing was to furnish assurance that as we had always recovered before we should always recover again, especially this time.

The trouble with the business-cycle theory during the industrial revolution was that it failed to see the tide for the waves. It assumed that a tide which kept rising for a century was as permanent as the Gulf Stream. In terms of geological time, even the Gulf Stream and the present seasonal variations of the weather are not permanent. In relation to the millions of years man is on the earth, the past century or two is but a brief moment, hence the utter absurdity of most textbook talk about what is normal, natural or economic in reference to social phenomena, the basis of such talk being only the history of a mere century and that century being the most abnormal one since the beginning of history. Projecting upward moving trend lines of past statistical series into the future for an indefinite period is not science but hokum. The impossibility of perpetual growth or expansion is one of the most easily verified laws of science. The one point which all business-cycle theories should have stressed was omitted or inadequately stated in all of them, namely, that nineteenth century growth curves of capitalistic institutions and statistical series could not long be maintained.

During the postwar period economists have sought to get around certain iron laws of physics and mathematics by arguing that the industrial revolution could be indefinitely prolonged and stabilized as an evolutionary process. This was to be achieved without necessity for continuous population increase by means of the simple expedients of raising living standards and introducing new inventions and techniques all the time. Thus Professor E. L. Bogart, writing as late as 1935 in his *Economic History of the American People* said, "The new technology, based upon the use of electricity, the internal combustion engine, the radio and the airplane, is inaugurating economic and social changes even more momentous than those introduced by the inventions of the steam engine one hundred and fifty years ago."

The catch in generalizations like those of Professor Bogart's is that they are inadequately correlated with the entire social process. Steam, electricity, the railroad and steam driven factory, automobile and all the allied inventions and industries went with an era of expansion and activity in which unemployment was virtually unknown. Inventions were not dynamic by themselves but only in conjunction with population growth and the frontier. The only real test of the dynamism or momentousness of industrial change is that of total economic activity. If activity and employment at present peacetime levels remain stationary or decline, no matter how revolutionary inventions and technological changes may seem, it is idle to call them momentous or dynamic. An invention which enabled man to harness unlimited motive power from the sun or the cracking of the atom might soon create such a crisis of unemployment that extreme socialism would have to be adopted almost overnight.

The simple truth is that, for capitalistic purposes, technological change used to be dynamic in the era of the frontier and rapid population growth, but is no longer because these last named factors are no longer dynamic. Today, so far as stimulating business expansion is concerned, industrial changes are no more dynamic than changing crossties or steel rails on a railroad. In industrial maturity large corporations, which produce most of our manufactures, are able to take care of technological change as a matter of routine out of reserves set aside out of earnings. As for entirely new products, they now tend to replace old products and to result in no net increase in consumption or production. Thus, to cite an important case in point, the production of petroleum for light, power, heat and transportation now takes less labor than did formerly the production of coal and agricultural fuel for draft animals. This last item alone absorbed the output of twenty-five million acres now unneeded. Electric refrigeration displaced ice and thousands of icemen. The talking pictures displaced hundreds of theaters and disemployed thousands of actors and musicians. Television may displace the talking picture theaters. But, and this is most important—the railroads a century ago did not displace the horse as the automobile has done since 1900. The factory ended homecraft industries, but gave rise to far more employment than it terminated in the home.

The classical economic doctrine, valid up to a few years ago, that labor displaced by new machinery, always found new employment as a result of the investment of the additional savings effected by the new machinery, rested on the assumption that banks and capitalists would never fail to keep funds or idle bank reserves fully employed and, by such failure, lose interest. In theory this was true only because in practice there was always a demand in excess of supply so far as savings were concerned. During the industrial revolution capitalists did not hoard and banks did not carry colossal surplus reserves as at present. The nineteenth century theorists stated or implied that there was no hoarding because of an innate human aversion to hoarding.

The Industrial Revolution

This, obviously, was not true, as the rich in the East have for thousands of years hoarded their wealth in idle gold, silver and precious stones. Whether the rich hoard or not in no way depends on their personal preferences as between keeping money hoarded in gold and precious stones and putting it out at interest. It depends entirely on whether the objective conditions of the period provide sufficient investment incentives. Liberal economists basing their theory on the experience of the most abnormal century and a half in all history assumed that investment incentives and attractive interest rates were perpetually normal conditions. Actually, they were, in the nineteenth century, normal conditions only because of the phenomenally abnormal character of that brief era.

One big reason there was no hoarding and there was an industrial revolution during the nineteenth century was that, in those abnormal times, almost every new industry became to some extent a monopoly. Now if there is anything an orthodox economist abhors, it is monopoly. The economists spend most of their time trying to prove that monopoly is bad for business and businessmen spend most of their time trying to achieve monopoly or failing in business because they are unsuccessful in achieving it.

There is more hypocrisy about monopoly than any other subject in the whole field of economics. For practical purposes, monopoly may be defined as the enjoyment of a situation in which competition need not be feared. If three automobile makers share more or less equally two thirds of the automobile sales in this country over a long period of time without ever engaging in cutthroat price competition, it may fairly be said that each of the three shares a monopoly and fears no competition from the makers of the remaining third of the cars sold or from each other. If an individual opens a restaurant in a community having twice as many restaurants as it needs, he cannot be called a monopolist unless, perchance, his cooking happens to be so much more popular than that of any of his competitors that he need not fear competition. In that case, he becomes a monopolist.

Monopoly is not a legal but a factual situation. A railroad may have a legal monopoly to furnish transportation where there is not enough traffic to make profitable operation possible, the case in innumerable railway lines in America today. Whether a franchise holder has a real monopoly or not, depends entirely on the facts of operation and not on the legal charter alone. During the nineteenth century not only American railways but also textile mills both in Manchester, England,

and Manchester, New Hampshire, enjoyed for decades on end virtual monopolies solely by reason of the expansion processes of that phase of economic history. Today the railway and textile industries in both England and the United States are permanently depressed industries though they are more efficiently conducted now than ever. Today many new industries are arising, some of which, like aluminum or agricultural machinery, quickly acquire a monopoly situation and enjoy monopoly profits and prosperity, while millions of their consumers are on relief. But such prosperity is offset—in the cyclical downswings more than offset—by the lack of profits and prosperity in such major basic industries as agriculture, the railroads, the textile trades and coal mining all of which are in permanent decline as profit makers. The net result is chronic depression, except as mitigated by pump priming. Broadly speaking, most of the service industries, certainly the railroads, are prosperous only during those brief periods of peak industrial production.

Those who argue that the industrial revolution can go on forever in an evolutionary form also fall back on another fallacy of classical economics, that of consumer sovereignty. According to this hoary fallacy, goods and services are produced for a profit in response to consumer needs and demands. The fallacy makes the consumer sovereign. His demand is supposed to regulate or determine the quantity and kinds of output. The inventory explanation of business slumps and rallies rests on the same error. According to this particular refinement, business slumps because inventories, or stocks of merchandise in warehouse and on the shelves, grow too large, wherefore orders for more goods are temporarily curtailed; and business revives because inventories grow too small, wherefore new orders begin to be placed to replenish depleted stocks. Actually, of course, inventories are never either too large or too small in the absolute, but only relatively to current demand. This, in turn, rises in measure as inventories are expanded and declines as inventories are allowed to shrink by reason of the curtailment of new orders. The inventory explanation, therefore, is largely a piece of circuitous reasoning.

If the notion of consumer sovereignty were true, there would be no long depressions. Consumer needs and wants are limitless. Therefore, capitalists, producers and merchants would continuously expand production and thereby create purchasing power to pay for all that was produced. The only limit to total production would be that of potential productive capacity. And potential productive capacity would steadily increase by reason of the continuous reinvestment of the savings of the profit makers and by reason of new inventions and new sources of raw materials. This is the way it happens in storybook capitalism. According to the storybooks, the only reasons it does not so work out in practice are numerous devils like government interference, institutional frictions and persons and groups lacking in good will. Barring the interferences of these devils, production and consumption would go on expanding in an ever widening circle. According to Say's law, production necessarily creates the purchasing power to pay for what is produced. Hence there can be no overproduction or underconsumption due to the mechanics of the system.

Why does it not really work that way? Or why does the industrial revolution not go on forever? The answer, of course, is that the major premise of consumer sovereignty is 100 per cent false. Producer demand, not consumer demand, is sovereign. The producers decide what, when and how much to produce, including the volume of construction and producer goods activity such as new plants, office buildings, etc. In other words, volume and rate of reinvestment of profits and savings determine swings in consumer demand. Producers and investors determine swings in the volume and velocity of the flow of consumer purchasing power. Booms are made by producer and investor optimism and ended by producer and investor pessimism. Consumer needs and desires have no more to do with the up- and downswings than sunspots. When producers decide to curtail production, consumer purchasing power declines and thus arise good reasons to cut production and employment and wages still further. The process is reversed by a change in producer and investor psychology. The producer decisions, as everyone knows, are governed mainly by changes in expectations of profit.

It may be asked why, if capitalists could keep up the boom merely by maintaining expenditures for new capital goods and larger inventories, they do not do so since they would thus keep up consumer purchasing power, sales to consumers and profits. The answer is fairly simple and has been most clearly stated by the Marxists: It is compound interest or the continuous reinvestment of profits. For the system to work, the accumulation of private income yielding wealth in geometrical progression must be fairly continuous. This, obviously, is a mathematical and a physical impossibility over any long period. That it went on long enough to enable a school of theorists to make it a norm of their system is one of the peculiarities of the past hundred and fifty years. The explanation is to be found in two sets of factors. The first, already mentioned and to be discussed further in connection with the frontier and population growth, was that of an unprecedented expansion of the physical factors of labor, land and producer's goods in geometrical progression during this abnormal nineteenth century. The second part of the explanation was that constant and large losses by unlucky investors and business enterprisers during that era kept down the rate of capital accumulation, while, at the same time, perfectly fantastic profits from lucky strikes and rising land values provided enough incentives to new investment to offset the discouragement of the large losses.

Capitalism, or the process of continuous investment of savings in new profit-seeking enterprises, might work in a perfectly static economy and population if current losses on business operations and ventures always equaled current savings and profits and if, on this basis, incentives to new investment and enterprise proved ample. Thus, each year, the write-off would equal the write-up and there would be no compound interest or geometrical-progression problem. But, as a practical matter, and as we now have ample opportunity to observe, it cannot work out this way unless the winners are allowed to keep the winnings and unless the winnings are, in many cases, sensationally large. Today progressive taxation on incomes makes it impossible for the big winners to keep more than a small part of their winnings, if they win, or, when they lose, to deduct their losses from their winnings of a prior or later period. Either a company or an individual may make a net profit over a period of ten years but actually, as a result of taxation on income, be a net loser, if it has alternating years of large losses and large profits.

In consequence of the reduced number of chances of making a killing and of the certainty, if and when one is made, of having to pay most of it out in progressive taxation, wealthy investors and large enterprisers are now seeking investments and operations which present a minimum of risk. Among the results, naturally, are increased hoarding and unemployment. Hoarding may take the form of larger surplus cash reserves of banks or larger purchases of government and high-grade bonds refunded at ever lower rates of interest, or of the simple holding of more cash by individuals.

Positive evidence that industrial expansion as a capitalist dynamic is over may best be found in the fact that since 1929 capitalism in

America has been unable to get a single boom started except on fear of inflation. The first was the short-lived spurt of 1933 which was generated by the devaluation of the dollar. The second and more substantial one came in late 1936 and early 1937 as a result of the payment of the bonus and unusually heavy deficit spending by the federal government. The third began in mid-1938 on a rescue increase in public spending for relief and rearmament following the 1937 slump caused by a drop in deficit spending from the 1936 peak. The fourth came in 1939 on the outbreak of war in Europe. No one of these four spurts was in any sense a capital goods or investment boom. No one of them was generated by expectations of profits from industrial expansion. Each was caused by fear of inflation. As a capitalistic dynamism, then, the industrial revolution is over. Therefore, public investment or pyramid building must supplement or completely supplant profit-seeking private investment.

Chapter V
The Frontier
The Profits of Free Lands

The frontier was to Americans what the empire was to the British. The two dynamisms were as alike as two peas. Dynamism, of course, is not the wheels but what makes them go round. The British, having a monarchy and caste system, made an *ism* of the empire. We made *isms* of our Constitution and federal system. But neither was dynamic in the sense just defined. Our founding fathers and their immediate successors sought to create in our political institutions and ideology brakes (checks and balances) rather than driving force. Of the latter they saw enough and too much in our frontiersmen and expansionists, who brought on the War of 1812 in the hope of taking Canada and who fought the Mexican War of 1848 for Texas and California. The British ruling classes had their brakes in the monarchy and the caste system, so they tried to make their empire, as a political *ism* or a spiritual value, as dynamic as possible.

The American frontier and the British Empire also have this in common: As historical processes, they are both over. As a place the American frontier ceased to exist about 1890, whereas the British Empire, as a place, still exists, having taken in some 800,000 square miles of German colonies as recently as the close of the World War. This acquisition of territory, unlike previous acquisitions, added nothing to British prosperity. As an historical process, the British Empire ended not long after the passing of the American frontier. The Boer War and the death of Queen Victoria at the turn of the century marked rather definitely the close of the British Empire as an expansive process. The conquest of the Boer Republic was the last profitable stroke of British imperialism. Empire is a process of expansion by conquest, not just the place so acquired. It is a matter not so much of being in the red on the map as of being in the black on the yearly balance sheet of international payments.

The socially important fact about an empire is getting it and, about a frontier, getting rid of it. The two processes amount to the same thing. Getting rid of the American frontier amounted to getting the

American empire. Being republicans and Puritans, we could not well call ours an empire. We had no emperor. Besides, our governing, though not ruling, imperialists, the Eastern plutocracy, felt that the less said about their ownership and power, the better. They were interested in the take, not the glory. They wanted to rule indirectly and anonymously. Their principal device for ruling eventually, along in the eighties, came to be the modern corporation which has been called by the French, with their genius for logical definition, the *société anonyme*.

Briefly, so far as empire is concerned, it is the growth, not the existence, the getting, not the keeping that is historically significant and socially dynamic. A nation grows great by winning an empire. It cannot remain great merely by keeping one. Indeed, once it stops growing it will start decaying. This is clearly proved by Spain and Portugal both of which went into decline once they ceased to increase their imperial holdings. Mankind is destined to live by toil and struggle, not by absentee ownership. When a nation becomes stagnant to the extent of seeking to live securely on the income of foreign spoils won at the point of the sword in its more adventurous days, invoking world morality for the peaceful enjoyment of its earlier loot, that nation is ripe for destruction by younger social organisms whose people are more eager to live dangerously and more willing to die gloriously.

What we now call capitalism, democracy and Americanism was simply the nineteenth century formula of empire building as it worked in this country. Here the process was often called pioneering; its locus, the frontier. But the process, not the place, is the thing. Now that empire building along the lines of the nineteenth century formula is over, both for the British and ourselves, capitalism and democracy are over as we knew them in that past era. It is as simple as that. We may yet expand territorially by taking Canada, the Caribbean Islands, Mexico and Central America. Such expansion may prove necessary to our national security in this hemisphere. But it is unlikely to provide a social dynamism equal to that of the nineteenth century empire building. Unlike the Have-nots, we shall not expand because we are land hungry. Hunger is dynamic. In the twentieth century, unlike the nineteenth, no profit is to be made out of increasing available supplies of raw materials and foodstuffs. Profit making is dynamic. But, to be dynamic, it has first to be possible. The conditions creating this possibility are the primary dynamisms of capitalism.

The historical function of the frontier was to provide opportunities, incentives and escapes for individuals. Thus private enterprise, parliamentary democracy, liberal freedom and tolerance were made possible. Our problem today is self-preservation as a people. The solution must be sought in collective organization, not individual escape—to a better place, job or business. Our most influential thinkers today see this to be a problem of preserving a system which went with former opportunities, incentives and escapes. But no amount of fighting against Germans, Japanese or other foreign devils can possibly preserve what has already ceased to exist.

What actually is at stake is not America but the British Empire—British prestige, power and possessions all over the world. It is their tough luck as a people that by increasing the population of the British Isles in the pursuit of industrial and financial profits far beyond their insular means of subsistence they have made their self-preservation dependent on either (1) the perpetuation of a world system of free trade and international division of labor which was possible only in a frontier, empire building era, now over with no hope of restoration; or (2) the speedy emigration of half the population of these now inadequate isles. It is a confusion of issues to equate the defense of the American people with the perpetuation of an impossible world system of money and trade and of British imperial expansion and hegemony on the continent of Europe.

The American people can preserve themselves and their present continental possessions. But they cannot preserve either the American or the British systems of the nineteenth century, except as memories. These systems were the American frontier and the British Empire. It is not Hitler and Stalin who are making it impossible to turn back the clock.

It was Professor F. J. Turner's great contribution to American social thought to give clear formulation to the now rather obvious idea that the creation of a new civilization is essentially a series of historical events rather than a collection of abstract definitions. He expressed the idea very well when, in an article in the *Atlantic Monthly* of February, 1903 on "Contributions of the West to American Democracy," he said "Political thought in the period of the French Revolution tended to treat democracy as an absolute system applicable to all times and to all peoples, a system that was to be created by the act of the people themselves on philosophical principles. Ever since that era, (in 1939 as much as in 1903) there has been an inclination on the part of writers on democracy to emphasize the analytical and theoretical treatment to the neglect of the underlying factors of historical development." Professor Turner had launched his really epochal thesis, though in an extremely mild form, in a paper he had read in July 1893 at Chicago before the meeting of the American Historical Association on "The Significance of the Frontier in American History." Probably most of the army of students who have since read and written on Professor Turner's great thesis have missed the force of his tradition-shattering idea.

Oversimplifying it one may say, Americanism is the frontier. It is not the Constitution or the federal system. Nor is it any mere system of ideas or collection of words. It is the events and experiences, the historical process, of the frontier. Professor Turner's thesis is usually stated somewhat inadequately as follows: For the first time in history, a highly civilized people found themselves living on the edge of a limitless expanse of free land available for settlement and the development of whatever type of culture they desired, largely untrammeled by most of the heritages and restraints of older and more congested societies. But he really said a good deal more, as we can appreciate better now than in 1893, when he told American historians that, "The existence of free land, its continuous recession and the advance of American settlement westward, explain American development."

In a particularly lyrical passage, Professor Turner said, "This perennial rebirth, this fluidity of American life, this expansion westward with its new opportunities, its continuous touch with the simplicity of primitive society, furnish the forces dominating American character." And again, "The growth of nationalism and the evolution of American political institutions were dependent on the advance of the Frontier." Americanism was a process rather than a principle. The principles were determined and validated by the events of the process. Even that most essential of social principles, social unity, was, in eighteenth and nineteenth century America, the product of the experiences of the frontier. On this subject Professor Turner writes, "The effect of the Indian frontier as a consolidating agent in our history is important. From the close of the seventeenth century various intercolonial congresses have been called to treat with Indians and to establish common measures of defense. Particularism was strongest in colonies with no Indian frontier. The frontier stretched along the western border like a cord of union. The Indian was a common danger, demanding united action."

Free land and lavish gifts of natural resources to exploit were the frontier's contribution to the success of private enterprise. The railways, of course, are the classic example of private enterprises being subsidized in their inauguration by colossal grants of public lands which were subsequently sold at huge profits by the operating companies. In the absence of these contributions today, we find the railroads bankrupt, pump priming deficits necessary and class conflict irrepressible. Capitalistic or private enterprise has always needed subsidies or something for nothing, like free lands and a perpetual land boom, to stimulate it to a necessary amount of activity. There is now a lack of risk capital seeking new ventures, notwithstanding the glut of savings and near zero money rates. The chief reason is that the day of rising land values and an abundance of windfall profits from the frontier is over. Even in the oil industry, in which wealth literally gushes from the ground, the incentives to extensive new investment are today comparatively small. Oil prices for most producing areas are unremuneratively low relatively to exploration costs and production uncertainties. Competition in some fields is so keen and monopoly in others so abusive that venture capital is not attracted in large volume into this bonanza industry, the chief need of which for the moment is curtailment of flow in already producing areas. Briefly, even the oil industry is no longer dynamic.

During the frontier era, even agriculture was dynamic. Now it is on relief. During the frontier era, a farmer did not have to be a good businessman or an efficient producer to attain a competence in his old age and leave a modest estate. Today farmers are getting two to three times as much out of a given piece of land or with a given amount of human labor as they got a generation ago. Yet the farmers are relief problem No. 2. The more efficient in production they become, the worse off they are. Formerly a farmer had merely to acquire a large tract of land in his youth, pay off his mortgage by selling off part of the land at a big profit, pay taxes which were extremely low and raise enough for his current needs. The rise in land values constituted for the average American farmer up to 1920 a steady and rapid source of enrichment without effort or risk on his part. He enjoyed a foolproof prosperity due to a perpetual land boom. This

was the American way in agriculture. The story in terms of dollars and cents can be seen at a glance in the following figures from the

Decennial Censuses since 1840. Even during the drastic deflation following the Civil War farm land values rose.

THE AMERICAN LAND BOOM OF THE FRONTIER DAYS AND ITS POST-WAR DEFLATION

	1935	1930	1925	1920	1910	1900
Number of farms in the United States in thousands	6,812	6,288	6,371	6,448	6,361	5,737
Value of land and buildings in thousands	$32,858	$47,879	$40,467	$66,316	$34,801	$16,614
Average value per farm	$4,823	$7,614	$7,764	$10,284	$5,471	$2,896
Average value of land per acre	$31	$48	$53	$69	$39	$19
	1890	1880	1870	1860	1850	
Number of farms in the United States in thousands	4,564	4,008	2,659	2,044	1,449	
Value of land and buildings in thousands	$13,279	$10,197	$7,444	$6,645	$3,271	
Average value per farm	$2,909	$2,544	$2,749	$3,251	$2,258	
Average value of land per acre	$21	$19	$18	$16	$11	

The most dramatic and perhaps the most conclusive proof that the frontier as a Constructive force is over may be seen in the stationing of border guards along the highways leading into California and other western states to stop the inflow of American workers and their families who might become an added charge on already overburdened relief and old-age pension rolls. There have even been cases of what was tantamount to judicial deportation of American families from one state to the state from which they came. The day is fast approaching when jobless and indigent Americans will require permits and visas to migrate from one community where they are on relief to another where they will immediately have to go on relief. Let an American share cropper of the South whose ancestors may have lived in this country for ten generations back try to take the traditional American way out of his economic impasse and he will soon learn from border guards that the American way of freedom of migration is past history and not current reality.

A most essential feature of the frontier and of the social philosophy it bred was that of escape. Most of our immigrants came here in flight from distasteful conditions abroad. Most of the migrants from the East to the West were moved by the same desire to find escape. The frontier was the Promised Land of the escapists, whether Pilgrim Fathers, poor gentlemen settlers in Maryland, debtors released from imprisonment for debt who settled in Georgia or Mormons in search of an area in which they could have as many wives as they liked. Two essentials of escapism as a practiced philosophy are a frontier and a population small enough to allow of rapid growth and fluid migratory movements. Sir Henry Maine, a great philosopher of the law, made a thesis of the point that the rise of modern civilization marked a transition from status (serfdom) to contract. Taking a view of only the legal aspect of the change, one is apt to infer that it occurred mainly because people preferred freedom of contract to fixity of status. The fact is, what made the transition possible was the frontier, not mass preference. There is freedom of contract in a significant sense only to the extent that there is opportunity for contract.

Now that the frontier is over, all social philosophies of which escape forms an integral part are wholly anachronistic. Today there is no frontier and no escape to be found in migration, so far as large masses of people are concerned. This goes for American share croppers and unemployed quite as much as for Polish Jews or German industrial workers. Much of the prevailing confusion of thought about international problems stems from a failure to recognize that the days of escape ended with or shortly after the first world war of this century. The passage of the restrictive immigration law of 1923 by the American Congress did more than the treaty of Versailles to seal the doom of democracy and capitalism in Europe. In the midst of the second great war of this century, many people in the allied countries and America reason somewhat as follows:

War is terrible. For the Germans it must be more terrible than for the British because the Germans are poorer. Therefore, the Germans may be expected sooner or later to revolt and force their government to accept peace on the allied terms, because this would at once give them the blessings of peace.

The Germans cherished that expectation in November 1918. They were subsequently disillusioned, not by the rigors of reparations in

1919-1923, but by the cessation of foreign loans in 1929 and the ensuing and consequent collapse of capitalism in Central Europe. The German people now know that a peace on the terms of the Allies which would involve the smashing of German national socialism could not be followed by capitalistic prosperity, because they know that if capitalism does not work well enough in America to reduce unemployment under ten million, it would work much less well in Germany if imposed as an allied condition of peace. And the Germans know that the failure of a peace on the terms of the Allies to yield prosperity to Germany would be due not so much to the rancor of the Allies as to the breakdown of their economic system which is another way of saying the end of the frontier.

The common people in America and England are somewhat less well aware of the facts of the world situation of capitalism, as the superior wealth of these democracies permits them to take better care of the unemployed and farmers by means of relief and doles, than is possible in poor countries like Germany. Popular faith in democracy and capitalism in America depends mainly on the size and duration of relief for the unemployed and the farmers. A philosophy of escape is still possible only because and as long as WPA can take the place of the frontier. The new American frontier is on the Treasury steps; the new American pioneers are the ham and eggers.

All social philosophies built around escape for persons and personal property have, during the past twenty years, receded further and further into the realm of the impractical. They are now more impractical throughout the world generally than they ever were before in all the two thousand years since the death of Julius Caesar. As late as the period from the nineties to 1914 and from 1919 to 1924, labor displaced in Europe by reason of the adoption of higher tariffs in America could easily migrate to this country to find employment in the booming new industries under tariff protection. Today there is no escape anywhere from the adverse effects of economic nationalism. There is no escape in free trade any more than there is in a flight to Mars, for free trade as we shall see further on is impossible. The plight of the political refugees during the past five years furnishes the most poignant proof of the end of the frontier and with it of all avenues of escape. Russia, the one country still with a frontier and an industrial revolution in progress, has not offered to take the political refugees. Socialism in action, unlike capitalism, is not a formula of individual escape or compatible with the practice of escapism. The Christian religion, which during the Dark Ages could always offer in its far-flung institutional centers sanctuary to fugitives from persecution other than its own, and from the world, is now wholly unable to open its doors anywhere to the political refugees of Europe. It has no temporal power or significant political influence as a social philosophy of otherworldly escape. The world is moving towards national socialisms and regional economies and away from formulas of escape. The one great area, Russia, in which escapism would still be most feasible, is a leader in the new quest after national self-sufficiency and socialist autarchy, or in the escape from escape.

It is in fashion these days to say that the end of the geographical frontier still leaves a limitless frontier of unsatisfied human wants and undiscovered inventions as a perennial source of opportunities and incentives to keep capitalism going. This argument, if it is to be dignified by that name, consists largely of a play on words and a confusion of thought. The frontier of need and discovery, so-called, is purely nominal, or a matter of giving the name of something that was real to something that is nothing but an unreal dream. The refutation of this argument is substantially the same as that made on pages 54-55 of the argument based on the alleged sovereignty of the consumer. If consumer desire instead of producer greed were the dynamic force under capitalism, the argument based on an assumed limitless frontier of needs, discoveries and technological changes would be entirely valid. In the processes of exploiting for private gain a rapidly growing supply of land and people, human needs did *happen* to get satisfied in increased volume. But this result was purely an incidental and, in no sense a dynamic or causative, factor in these processes. As long as supplies of land, labor and natural resources becoming available for exploitation were rapidly increasing, there was a constant shortage of capital, machinery, housing, transportation facilities and means of subsistence for the workers. This shortage constituted a real industrial frontier. It was a frontier of need, not luxury. Capitalism needs a frontier of scarcity which will keep interest rates high and profit margins wide. It cannot flourish on a frontier of industrial abundance in which interest rates would drop to zero and incentives to private investment would virtually disappear.

The cheerful optimists who talk so glibly about new horizons for capitalism, always fail to mention its most important new frontier of the past twenty or thirty years, namely, *that of rising distribution costs.* One, of course, understands why business optimists overlook this particular frontier on which capitalism has been expanding so rapidly of late years. This is a type of business expansion business enterprise has relied on to an increasing extent for volume and profits, but it is not a type of growth businessmen or economists care to boast about. This development has really amounted to a growing substitution of luxuries for necessities.

The Twentieth Century Fund published in 1939 an illuminating four hundred page study by a committee of experts entitled "Does Distribution Cost Too Much?" It is hard to escape the conclusion that the answer is "Yes," though the committee does not definitely formulate it. The facts, however, are impressive. It was found that in 1929 of a total of sixty-six billion dollars paid by ultimate consumers, thirty-nine billion dollars or fifty-nine per cent represented costs of distribution. This percentage has been steadily rising for the past seventy years, the rate of increase being greatest during the past twenty years. Between 1870 and 1930 the number of workers engaged in distribution increased nine times while the number of those engaged in physical production, including, of course, the processes of manufacture, increased only three times.

This increase in distribution costs, of course, is by no means wholly bad from the point of view of welfare—the better the bottling of milk or packaging of bread, the more elaborate the facilities for refrigeration and distribution of fresh fruits and vegetables all winter long, the more facilities through which luxuries can be enjoyed by the masses, the better for general welfare. But while this trend may in large part mean higher living standards, it means disaster for private capitalism and it also means a lack of welfare for the victims of unemployment. The increase in distribution costs is due mainly to two important changes, the first of which has just been alluded to briefly, namely, that of a higher standard of living. The second change is that of increasing competition, as may be seen all over the countryside on sites where, within a stone's throw of each other, from two to a half dozen filling stations with identical facilities and products and each costing from twenty-five thousand dollars to one hundred thousand dollars to install compete with each other, though any one of the competitors could easily take care of all the business shared by the lot of them. It may also be seen where a half dozen milk wagons cover daily the same territory. Over a billion dollars of unnecessary and surplus filling-station equipment has been installed and is being operated. On the count of competition, increased distribution costs are proving fatal to private capitalism. On the count of increased luxury consumption necessitating more expensive distribution and servicing, the trend is also sure to prove fatal to the profits system, since profits require keeping down wages once a static phase is reached. Our distribution plant and industries are unprofitable as business enterprises except in boom years like 1929 and 1937.

The trouble now is that, in a mature phase of industrialization, the point has been reached where the productive plant of the nation has an output in excess of the subsistence necessities of labor and demands of further profitable industrialization. This, of course, is why good capitalists—practical businessmen and theorists—are ever crying out for a revival of foreign trade and foreign investment. Many naive New Dealers have argued that higher living standards as a result of higher wages and taxes and lower profit margins and interest rates might take the place of foreign loans. The essence of the argument is that American capitalists might as well be mulcted by domestic socialism as by foreign defaults. The argument, however, is unrealistic, like those of all other reformist programs. It assumes that individual conduct is governed by a collective rationality, an obviously absurd assumption, though one of the foundation stones of the ideology of democracy and liberalism. Individuals who bought foreign government bonds to yield from 6 per cent to 8 per cent or who bought domestic equities at forty times their current earnings were acting on the basis of optimism rather than rationality or average experience. If businessmen and investors were to begin weighing contemplated ventures in the scales of experience and logic, capitalism would forthwith cease. The average businessman or the average investor has to believe that he is wiser and abler than the average and that he will achieve better than an average result. The average man who goes into business fails. For the average man to believe that he is abler than the average and will outdo the average in business competition or investment selection is, collectively considered, most irrational. But it is a form of irrationality necessary for private capitalism.

An economy of abundance type of national policy which tried to maintain consumer purchasing power by a combination of government spending, taxation and artificially high wages, *with their corollaries of small profits and low interest rates, must, to the extent it is applied, paralyze capitalism.* This it must do by reducing hopes and incentives to private investment and enterprise. For purposes of capitalism it is better to mulct capitalists by losses on foreign loans and periodical domestic crashes than to attempt to mulct them by taxation and artificially maintained wage levels. Capitalism does not need the certainty of a small profit for every investor and businessman, but the possibility of a large profit for the lucky ones. Capitalism, to work, must have a basis for big delusions. Ninety per cent of those who go into business for themselves fail within ten years. Over three fourths of the small businessmen, especially storekeepers and service tradesmen, work for practically nothing. They would do better to invest their capital at two per cent in government bonds and go to work for a large corporation for wages as unskilled laborers. Only the capacity of human nature for limitless self-delusion could feed every year thousands of new business adventurers into the game to lose their savings and go broke while they work for nothing. Yet a *Fortune* poll survey indicates that slightly over half of the American people would like to be in business for themselves. Probably a higher percentage of them like to play games for money. Foreign loans and foreign trade facilitate self-delusion even better than domestic investments and trade ventures. Capitalists can delude themselves with false hopes about the profits of foreign investment and trade more easily than about domestic trade prospects, but they cannot well entertain illusions or false hopes about present taxes. Capitalism needs the incentives of wild hopes, not the certainties of statistics of business failures, science and logic. The frontier of human needs which could be satisfied by planned production is not one on which private profit seeking can possibly flourish. The profit system can flourish only on the illusive hopes of business adventurers. Such hopes, though still widespread and strong, are now inadequate due to the lack of expansion.

To utilize the present potential output of industry, it is necessary to increase mass consumption of luxuries or, of course, to resort to pyramid building or war. War has the advantage of being orthodox while pyramid building or an increase in the consumption of luxuries by labor would clash with the imperatives of the profit system in a highly competitive and nonexpansive phase. To increase mass consumption of luxuries requires a raise either of real wages or taxation on the rich or both. Either means fewer incentives to new investment and enterprise and more unemployment.

Capitalism faces a dilemma it never faced before: it cannot raise living standards without reducing profits and the incentives to new investment and enterprise; at the same time it cannot maintain the necessary market for full production and employment without raising living standards or real wages at the expense of profits.

This dilemma never existed for capitalism as long as it had a frontier, rapid growth, migration and a flourishing industrial revolution in progress. Nor has it arisen overnight. Slowly and imperceptibly it developed during the twenties. Then the saturation point in industrialization and marketing by means of forced expansion of consumer credit was reached. Then the peak of population increase was passed. In that gestative period of the economic crisis of the thirties and war crisis of the forties it became necessary for an ever increasing percentage of total industrial production to be devoted to luxury goods and an ever decreasing percentage to necessity goods. Thus, today, the only way to keep the steel industry busy without war would be to make more workers drive automobiles for pleasure. The only way to solve the farm problem would be to have the working classes consume more luxury foods like meat, fruits, green vegetables and dairy products and to have industry find more luxury uses for agricultural fibers and oils. Such increased consumption, however, could occur only as a result of higher wages and/or higher taxes which, in turn, would mean smaller profit margins, Yet economic experts and practical businessmen keep saying with virtual unanimity and entire correctness that the first essential for a revival of private investment would be a drastic cut in wages and taxes. The dilemma is inescapable.

During the frontier days there was no such dilemma: Business could expand on an ever growing demand for necessities resulting from new territory and new population. Such expansion of the business market did not require a narrowing of profit margins. Today business could expand only on a rise in consumer demand resulting from higher real wages or higher taxes. Expansion so effected could only narrow profit margins, eventually if not immediately, and reduce incentives to new investment and enterprise. Therefore, talk about the frontiers of human needs, science and technological change is largely bunk so far as the dynamic problem of capitalism is concerned.

The extent to which the virtually perpetual frontier land boom of the nineteenth century in this country maintained business prosperity and stability has received little attention from economic historians and writers on the American way. The chief functions of the continuous land boom of the frontier era were to provide a perpetual stimulus to new construction and a sort of never ending partial indemnification for losses on business operations. There were during the nineteenth century many localized booms and depressions and, also, prolonged periods of commodity price decline and what were then called hard times. So far as the comforts of life were concerned, the entire nineteenth century was a period of hard times if comparison is made between living standards then and now. From the end of the Napoleonic Wars in 1815 to the beginning of the Gold Rush in 1849 and from the end of the Civil War in 1865 to the resumption of gold payments in 1879, commodity prices had a downward trend. But during each of these long periods of falling commodity prices, both urban and farm land values generally rose in most sections of the United States, and for the country as a whole. In consequence, practically every small businessman and homeowner who was able to hold on to a piece of real estate through several decades, as many did, thereby accumulated a fortune or a considerable profit entirely on unearned increment in land. Literally thousands of inefficient enterprises were kept in operation for years and some were eventually enabled to recapitalize and reorganize under more efficient management solely with the aid of land-sale profits, which, in many cases, were realized repeatedly during the period. Tens of thousands of incompetent American businessmen died or retired well off in spite of all their mistakes and failures, entirely as a result of having acquired for a song large holdings of land in a fast growing community.

With rising land values, business and investment incentives were never lacking. If one were too poor to buy on Broadway or in Back Bay, one could buy cheap farm acreage only a few miles away, acreage which is now valuable business property. Or if one were then too poor to buy near the growing eastern cities, one could get land for nothing or next to nothing in the faster growing communities and agricultural areas, first of the Midwest and later of the Far West. For the rest, one had only to hang on to grow rich or well off. As late as the twenties, fortunes were quickly made by the lucky, often on a shoestring, in real estate in Florida, Detroit and Los Angeles, to name only three important and well-known real estate boom areas of that period.

The war and postwar boom in real estate, of course, was due to a combination of factors, all of which were necessarily temporary. The most important, perhaps, was war inflation; another was the big wave of immigration, held back for five years by the war, then, rushing in like a flood tide during the five years just after the war, only to be stopped by our restrictive immigration law and policy adopted in 1923. Another constant factor of urban land price inflation during the entire first thirty years of the twentieth century was the rapid rate of industrialization and urbanization which went on during all of that abnormal period.

Professor R. Burr Smith, in an article on "Replanning for Depopulation" appearing in the *National Municipal Review*, showed that urban population of the United States increased 108.5% or more than doubled between 1900 and 1930. Experts, however, now estimate that in the corresponding thirty-year period from 1950 to 1960 urban population will increase by only 8.4%. And it is by no means certain that the change will not be a net decrease in urban population over this period. During the twenties urban land values rose because there was an annual net drift of 750,000 from country to city. That movement, obviously, could not continue with the chronic unemployment of the thirties.

Actually the birth rate in the cities is so low that only three cities in the country with a population over one hundred thousand have enough births to offset deaths. For most cities, the deficiency is between twenty per cent and thirty per cent of what is required to keep the urban population stationary. This deficiency has to be met by migration from country to city. If the thousands of young couples bravely buying in the city suburbs new homes on the installment plan fully understood the import of current population trends for near-future land values, there would be even less new building than there is at present. It must not be overlooked that going land values, subject now to a growing number of exceptions, still represent a generous discounting of future appreciation. That is to say, the American way in real estate is to pay considerably more for land than it would be worth if population increase and land-price rise were expected to be about to stop. If current population trends were correctly discounted in current land sales in our cities and their suburbs, there would be a catastrophic overnight collapse in real estate values over the entire nation.

During the frontier era, railroad building and technological and industrial change tended everywhere to raise land values, while, in the thirties, the automobile, good highways and technological and industrial change were all tending everywhere either to put a low ceiling on *or, actually, to depress urban land values*. The explanation is simple, though little recognized as yet by optimistic traditionalists who blindly assume that all improvement in transportation and technology must produce the same blissful consequences these changes wrought during the nineteenth century: the new railway added to land values by the simple mechanics of population growth, while new industries and technique created work and subsistence for more people, thus encouraging further population growth. Today the automobile takes people away from the urban centers by making available for residence limitless adjacent areas. Today land values in any one improved suburban zone cannot rise much above the cost of duplicating its facilities—street paving, water mains, sewers and lights —in any nearby rural acreage. The automobile and good roads make virtually boundless territory available for residence. Industrial and technological change are also favoring decentralization in production and curtailment in the demand for new labor. These trends make for lower land values and thereby reduce one of the chief incentives to private enterprise.

The end of the major incentive to new construction, rising land values, might, in itself, be enough to spell the doom of private capitalism. During the nineteenth century the speculative builder usually counted on a secular upward trend in land values to protect him against loss on any houses he might not be able to sell as soon as built. The same land-boom factor guaranteed mortgage lenders and banks. It enabled mortgage guarantee companies to flourish on the profits of a guarantee which was good as long as it was not needed and worthless as soon as it was needed. All these companies folded up in the last depression. One had advertised truthfully that for fifty years not a cent had been lost by purchasers of its guaranteed mortgages. The same perpetual land boom that enabled hundreds of thousands of somber American bankers to keep straight faces as they talked about sound financial principles and practices enabled almost every buyer of a new house on mortgage to feel confident that a rise in land value over a period of years would more than offset wear, tear and obsolescence, thus netting the buyer a sound profit on his sound equity in sound American real estate. These well-founded expectations of sound profits on our perpetual land boom constituted a perpetual incentive to new building both as a long-term investment and a short-term speculation. In the America of 1938, by no means the bottom of a depression, most sales of improved urban real estate, except new houses, took place at prices below assessed value, where assessments are made on the basis of supposed present worth and below what any court would allow in a condemnation proceeding.

At present new construction has to be artificially stimulated by special government financing under the F.H.A. These arrangements operate in combination with the demand of newly married couples for smaller two-children-maximum homes with the newest equipment and insulation which permit low upkeep costs. The new financing terms of the F.H.A. allow possession on a ten per cent down payment. Installments are often less than rent for comparable housing space. If this type of building goes on and the present downward trend of land values continues, it must happen in a few years that most of the houses now being built and sold on this basis will be thrown back on the government by the thousands by mortgage debtors who will then find it advantageous to give up their equities which will amount to less than the accrued depreciation in value on these properties and to buy or rent similar old houses.

The present home-purchase finance plans of the F.H.A. are all based on the assumption of stable land values and an unduly low allowance for wear, tear and depreciation from obsolescence. A collapse of this mortgage credit structure will most likely be averted through monetary inflation for our next war. But it is significant to point out the following two considerations: First, the government has to induce building by means of financing which is not sound or feasible for private capital; Second, the government has to look to eventual monetary inflation to avert a catastrophic collapse of the real estate credit structure it is now erecting.

The government's depression agency for succoring distressed home-mortgage debtors, the H.O.L.C., now holds over a hundred thousand foreclosed properties. The banks, insurance companies and real estate credit institutions hold far more distressed real estate which they dare not attempt to liquidate in summary fashion, Notwithstanding the failure of creditors since 1932 to liquidate more than a small part of the foreclosed real estate of the depression, the government is coaxing with unsound loans persons of small means to buy or build new houses. The necessity for such financing to induce new construction and the necessity for eventual inflation to prevent its collapse give further proof of the end of the frontier dynamics.

Chapter VI
Rapid Population Growth
Cheap Labor and Expanding Markets for Necessities and Capital Goods

Population growth has been taken for granted in the democracies as a constant factor. It has not been given much thought for the simple reason that it has never been a problem. On the contrary, it has been the solution of most of the problems of capitalism. But it was a solution which no one had ever had to think out or work out. It was an apparently automatic solution which Mother Nature provided for capitalistic problems like depressions and public debts. It always made good the excesses of business optimism and public spending and borrowing for wars. It made capitalism and democracy virtually foolproof. It bred a lot of foolish political and economic theory and gave that theory a pragmatic sanction.

If investors and businessmen built too many residences, office buildings, railways or factories; if they expanded productive capacity far beyond current demand, rapid population growth quickly made demand catch up with potential supply. Thus the late Mr. J. P. Morgan was right in saying "Never sell America short" and the academic economists were right in talking about the harmonies of a system of economic freedom. Our present theory and practice in the matters of private investment and public credit are valid and workable only if population maintains a certain rate of increase. In the matter of paying off large public debts this is especially evident. The war debts of the American Revolution and the Civil War were easily reduced without the evils of extreme deflation. The reduction of the public debt is no longer possible because it cannot be offset by a corresponding expansion of private debt for new capital, and particularly because the per capita debt burden is no longer being reduced as before by a rapid growth of population. Three decades after the War of 1812 we had three times as many citizens to bear the debt burden as we had when the war ended. Thirty years after the Civil War, our population was twice as large and the public debt half as large as at the end of that war. That debt was easily paid off by the sale of public lands to a growing population and by the revenues from new tariffs for infant industries. Today, twenty years after the World War, the American population is only about thirty per cent larger than it was in 1919 and the public debt is not reduced but approximately twice as great.

If the assumption that population growth is a constant factor operating to make good excessive business optimism and government borrowing were true, the social philosophy and concrete recommendations of American conservatives and business leaders would be sound and the argument of this book would be false. As the assumption is false, the American conservatives are wrong and the thesis of this book seems correct. The issue is one of fact, not of opinion or preference.

Let us look at the record. In the matter of population this is comparatively simple. We cannot tell what the population of any country will be in any distant future, for we cannot foretell possible changes in current trends. But we can tell what the population will be any number of years hence on the basis of current, recent or assumed trends in the birth and death rates. We do not know the population of any given area in the distant past, or much before the opening of the nineteenth century. But we can be sure that the white population of the world rose more or less steadily from the discovery of the Americas to the opening of the nineteenth century, or from about 70,000,000 in 1500 to about 100,000,000 in 1700 and about 200,000,000 in 1800 and that during the nineteenth century it rose from about 200,000,000 to around 700,000,000 at present. We can be sure that the white population of the world will not double itself during the next hundred years and we can reasonably surmise that a hundred years from now it may not be much larger than it is at present. It may well be not as large then as it is now. Where the population of Europe only about doubled once during the nineteenth century, or increased by only about 150% between 1800 and 1930, that of the United States doubled no less than five times between the periods of our first census in 1790, when the total population was only 3,929,214, and our most recent national census in 1950 when it was 122,775,046. The rate of increase in our total population has steadily declined, the drop in this rate during the thirties being the sharpest of all. For the entire 140 year period, the rate of increase averages a doubling of the population about every thirty years. At the rate of increase during the twenties, the period in which we had our largest decennial addition, one of 17,064,426, it would take about 62 years for the population to double; at the rate of increase

Rapid Population Growth

during the thirties, now estimated at about 8,000,000, it would take the population of 1930 about 155 years to double.

In population, so far as dynamics are concerned, the vital factor is the trend. The most sensitive and the most revealing-for-the-future-index of the trend is the birth rate. The effects of a sharp drop in the birth rate are not seen in the immediate excess of deaths over births or in the net change in population. They are seen only twenty to thirty years later when the reduced number of babies becomes a reduced number of marriages and new families.

Professor Fairchild opened his recent book on population entitled *People* with the startling though true statement that "if the birth rate of the United States should continue to decline as it has during most of the present century, by about 1975 (just thirty-five years hence) there would be no babies born at all." Obviously no one expects this nadir in the birth rate to be reached in this or any other country. But if the current decline in the birth rate ceases and if the birth rate flattens out at any figure below that of the present rate, our total population must soon thereafter begin to decline. This is clear from another little noted fact about the present population trend, namely that the present birth rate is insufficient for replacement once the present birth rate is stabilized.

The full import of the population decline is not readily apparent in current census figures simply because the number of new marriages taking place today is determined by the number of births which took place twenty to thirty years ago when the total number of births was passing the peak in our history though the birthrate was then fast declining. In 1935 there were a million and a half fewer children under ten years of age than there were five years earlier. This means that twenty-five years later or between 1950 and 1960 there will be at least 75,000 fewer marriages and 75,000 fewer mothers each year than during 1930-1940. It must be borne in mind that if the present low birth were stabilized where it now is, the death rate would not be stabilized where it is at present. The reason is quite simple. The death rate is always determined in large part by the age composition of the population. In 1850 50% of the population was under twenty while only 8% was over fifty. At present about 40% only are under twenty while about 16% are over fifty. By 1950 it is estimated that only 32% will be under twenty and over 24% will be over fifty. Now the cut in the death rate since 1850 has been effected mainly among the young, especially among infants. This mortality reduction has now gone almost as far as it can go. During this time there has been no great reduction in the mortality of those over fifty. From now on there is likely to be little further reduction in the death rate, as medicine is doing little to prolong the life of the aged who are being exposed to more and more stresses and strains as a result of the increasing pace and insecurity of modern life. As a larger percentage of the population enters the old age group the death rate is certain to rise.

The National Resources Committee (in their report of May, 1938, on the "Problems of a Changing Population," page 24) estimate the total population of the United States for forty years on the bases of seven different assumed hypotheses of mortality and fertility, Of these hypotheses the one most favorable to further population growth allows for an increase of some 42,000,000 or a total population of 174,000,000 forty years from now; whereas the most pessimistic estimate, which assumes that the present decline in the birth rate will not continue indefinitely, gives a population ceiling twenty years hence around 1960 of 140,000,000, or only 10,000,000 higher than at present, and, thereafter a decline resulting in a population total some forty years hence or around 1980 no higher than that of today.

For our purposes it is relatively unimportant just when the curve of total population turns down or at what angle it turns down. It is enough that the population growth curve has already started flattening out. It is this flattening out which, more than any other single factor, is preventing full recovery. The important point here is that our system is not geared or gearable to a stable population. It can work only with a much faster rate of population growth than that we have enjoyed during the thirties.

This behavior of the population curve is in accordance with the mathematical theory developed by Raymond Pearl to the general effect that in any form of organic life a growth curve tends to conform to a logistic or S shaped curve on which the upper end or asymptote conforms to the lower end or asymptote. Such a curve starts slowly from the horizontal, then turns up almost vertical for a time and then flattens out at the top more or less as it moved at the beginning from the horizontal to the perpendicular. Whether this explanation is a valid theory or law or merely a coincidence observed in innumerable growth curves of colonies of bacteria or spores, is immaterial. Pure mathematics is certainly definite and indisputable in telling us exactly what any given rate of genetic growth in geometric progression will produce in the way of numbers over any specified period of time. And common sense, as well as physical measurement of available food supply, tells us that no such numbers of human beings, oysters, or bacteria spores can ever exist at the same time on this earth.

A preposterous result is always reached sooner or later by any geometric progression. Whether it is reached in a few hours, as in the case of certain spores, or in a few weeks as in the case of flies, or in a century or two as in the case of the growth of the white population of the world during the past hundred years, the principle is the same. If the total population of the world continued to increase as fast as it has during the past hundred years, it would outrun the limits of possible subsistence at the lowest possible level within a couple hundred years. If the dark races increase as fast as the white races have been increasing during the past fifty years, the dark races, now numbering a billion and a quarter, thus doubling every fifty odd years, would number ten billion within a hundred and fifty years.

Of course, there is no need to worry about population out-running subsistence as did Malthus, not that Malthus's premises and inferences were incorrect, but that checks to growth ignored by him always become effectively controlling factors long before the limits of subsistence are reached. The dilemma that Malthus saw is real only as a hypothesis. It will probably never even be approached. The dilemma Malthus and most of his defenders and critics did not and still do not see is of quite a different order. It is not, as Malthus feared, the dilemma of what to do *with* a steadily growing population but the dilemma of what to do *without* a steadily growing population. There would eventually arise a food deficiency if the population went on growing forever. But there arises immediately a dynamic deficiency if the population stops growing or slows down its rate of growth. Those who criticized Malthus for preaching population control, not by technical contraception but by means of premarital chastity, deferred marriage for the poor and moral restraint, based their criticism on religious or pious grounds. As the underlying religious beliefs have weakened, this criticism has lost most of its social force. The really scientific ground for attack on birth control or limitation of families is that a society to be healthy needs to be growing or that we have found no substitute for the dynamism of population growth. Scientifically it may be found possible and ethically it may be deemed desirable to find a substitute dynamism for population growth. But neither the Malthusians nor the anti-Malthusians have clearly seen or definitely attacked this particular problem.

The social problem of the world crisis today is one of finding sufficient dynamism, not of finding enough food. With wheat selling in Liverpool during the summer of 1939 just before the war started at the lowest price in sterling or in gold that it had ever touched since the time of Queen Elizabeth, and with the food and raw material surpluses everywhere, there cannot be said to exist a subsistence problem. On the contrary, the problem is one of what to do with food and raw material surpluses rather than one of how to feed an excessive population. The land-hungry great powers are seeking territorial expansion not because there is a shortage of food production for the needs of all mankind today but because, owing to high tariff and immigration barriers, the peoples of the overpopulated Have-not countries do not enjoy sufficient access to the unsalable surpluses of foodstuffs and raw materials being currently produced.

As the dynamic function of population growth has been neglected by the thinkers and theorists of democracy and capitalism, it would seem in order here to formulate briefly certain obviously dynamic functions which only a growing population or some yet undiscovered substitute therefor can perform.

First among the functions of population growth is that of creating a perpetual scarcity of bare necessities, so necessary for a healthy capitalism or socialism. This scarcity furnishes incentives for the leaders and compulsions for the led. This scarcity now affects only the Have-not countries; hence they alone are dynamic today. Capitalism in America was dynamic while world population increase assured food scarcity. Now that we have food abundance, capitalism is no longer dynamic. Hence the unemployed go hungry because we now lack scarcity. This explanation may sound paradoxical. Well, so is the situation in which farmers languish for buyers of their food and the jobless languish for food. A scarcity of bare necessities is a simple condition for the human mind to cope with. Such a problem admits of little disagreement and excludes the complications of taste and choice. Society is a complex and difficult business. Men need simple social problems and tasks. Abundance is much too complex a condition for the irrational mass mind to deal with. The existence of this problem of abundance moves our prophets of the irrational mass mind to preach more governmental economy and personal thrift. In this way the evil of abundance can be corrected by removing more workers and farm acres from production. The nineteenth century way of averting the evil of abundance was to have large families. The twentieth century way, now that we have small families, is to have large-scale unemployment and two world wars in one generation. Given the ideology of democracy and capitalism making thrift a virtue and given the shrinking size of families, it is hard to see any way of coping with abundance other than unemployment and war. And given our culture pattern, it is hard to see how we can operate society without the compulsions of a scarcity which a high birth rate, unemployment or war alone can maintain for us in a sufficient degree under our system.

The eighteenth century rationalists and the nineteenth century rationalizers never understood the dynamic function of scarcity. But we of the twentieth century, who have seen two world wars in one generation, should know better. The maintenance of order in a populous community is an extremely difficult business. A condition of having the necessary incentives and compulsions for the maintenance of public order is an abundance of unsatisfied needs, not an abundance of goods. Those naive neo-liberals who would solve the problems of the hour by stabilizing abundance have not learned that order is the first requisite of society, that order requires discipline, that discipline requires need and that need requires scarcity. For maintaining the necessary degree of scarcity a more humane way than unemployment or war would be perpetual pyramid building and peaceful squirrel-cage social activities imposed from above by a planning and coordinating will. In the absence of a dynamic scarcity, such activities are not self generating among the masses. A dynamic scarcity is one in which there is not enough food to allow the ruling classes to keep several millions unemployed on a relief dole. But unemployment and war, in lieu of large families, are obviously the course of least resistance. Besides, practically no one understands the disciplinary and dynamic function of scarcity. Broadly speaking, practically no one takes either an intelligently realistic or a purely humane view of any major social problem.

A second function of rapid population growth is to maintain a large percentage of youth in the age composition of the total population. The larger the percentage of youth in the age composition of a population, the greater the supply of initiative and dynamism; the larger the percentage of old people in the age composition of a population, the greater the tendency to stagnation and decline.

A third important function of rapid population growth is to assure great elasticity in social adjustments, especially in wages, and great pliability and fluidity of labor. An aging population tends to social rigidity especially in class relationships and social rigidity renders any dynamic readjustment difficult.

In a fast growing population there is a perpetual scarcity of producer's goods and a plethora of workers. In consequence, the leaders, who, under capitalism are the investors and enterprisers, and under socialism are the politicians, have the whip hand. Under capitalism, if wages can always be fixed at levels attractive to the investor and enterpriser, there is never a lack of new investment and enterprise and, consequently, never large-scale unemployment. There is always full employment because wages are sufficiently flexible always to be low enough to interest the profit seeker.

Under no system do workingmen create jobs for themselves. Jobs, or enterprises which employ labor, have to be created by the leaders who may be capitalists, politicians, priests or soldiers. There must be incentives for the leaders and compulsions for the led. These must inhere in a social situation and a social trend. The leaders must have vision and the led must have needs. The leaders cannot create the situation or the trend. They are rather created by the situation and the trend. Now that the conditions for the success of capitalist leadership are disappearing, the businessmen are headed for what for them will be the equivalent of the ghetto and a new brand of leaders appropriate to the new situation and trend will take charge. The necessary motivations for the leaders and the necessary discipline for the workers for the success of capitalism depended absolutely on certain trends, one of which was rapid population growth, a factor making for perpetual capital shortages. Once the population-growth curve begins to flatten out, capitalists cannot find enough incentives nor can they discipline labor. The correlation between capitalistic incentives and labor discipline on the one hand and population growth is too obvious to need much explanation. Some of the incentive part of it has been pointed out in the preceding chapter wherein was shown the connection between rapid population growth, rising land values and unearned business profits on such land appreciation, all tending to induce more building and industrial expansion. The discipline part of the correlation is equally obvious: During the days of heavy immigration, rapid population growth and a scarcity of food and shelter, labor could not have enforced its present real wage demands, which, to the extent they must be met at the expense of profits, are deterrents to new investment and enterprise.

It would be unfair to the classical or professional economists not to credit them with a belated recognition of the population factor. At the opening of the 51st annual meeting of the American Economic Association held in Detroit December 28, 1938, Professor Alvin H. Hansen in his presidential address to the association on the subject "Economic Progress and Declining Population Growth" said: "It is my growing conviction that the combined effect of the decline in population growth, together with the failure of any really important innovations of a magnitude sufficient to absorb large capital outlays weighs very heavily as an explanation for the failure of the recent recovery to reach full employment." At the same meeting Professors Glenn E. McLaughlin and Ralph J. Watkins read papers on "The Problem of Industrial Growth in a Mature Economy" in which they cautiously expressed more pessimism than hopefulness. The view of the vast majority of the economic profession, as well as of the conservative businessmen of the country as a whole, in regard to the population factor in recovery is doubtless expressed by Professor Wilford I. King in an article "Are We Suffering from Economic Maturity?" in which he confidently answered "No" and took Messrs. McLaughlin and Watkins to task for a mildly pessimistic view of the situation. The mental limitations of those who take Professor King's view were clearly revealed by him when he used an illustration which completely invalidated his whole argument. By way of refuting the present-day pessimists who find no adequate industrial expansion and building boom to end current unemployment, Professor King dragged out the old familiar argument of the frontier of limitless needs disposed of in the preceding chapter. In so doing, he asked whether George Washington would have been upset back in 1780 to have learned from one of his overseers that increased efficiency had enabled the plantation to get its work done by fewer slaves and that there was consequent idleness. The answer, obviously, is that George Washington would have been delighted to learn that he was getting more done with less labor and that most of the necessary clearing about the place had been finished, and he would have been most happy to order his overseer to put the idle slaves to work on elaborate projects of beautification of the estate and improvement of its facilities in every possible way.

The trouble with Professor King's illustration is that it completely gives away his whole case since the example chosen to show how increased efficiency and industrial maturity need never cause difficulties or unemployment was taken from slavery. Now anybody who does not recognize clearly the difference between present-day industrial capitalism and chattel slavery should not be teaching economics. Obviously, there can never be unemployment or depressions under socialism or slavery. Of course, a slave-owner who has to feed, clothe and house his slaves whether they work or loaf, will not leave them idle. He will either make work for them to do or sell them. If many slave-owners start selling slaves for lack of productive employment for them, the price of slaves will fall so low that owners will prefer to keep their slaves and employ them on works of beautification and creation of luxuries for the enjoyment of the masters, as occurred for centuries in many past civilizations.

The population factor has to be considered in the context of the system of private capitalism. Socialist dictators and owners of chattel slaves can obviously build pyramids or great mansions and hunting parks, thus forever keeping all the proletarian socialist workers or privately owned slaves employed all the time. This is exactly what happened in ancient Rome when it found itself flushed with slaves. Emperor Augustus, coming to power in such an era, said near the end of his rule: "I found Rome brick and I left it marble" But capitalists do not have individually to support their employees when the latter are thrown out of work. The incentive to industrial expansion under capitalism is not a desire for a higher standard of living for all the people but a simple desire for interest and profits. Professor King is correct in finding that industrial maturity would not matter if steps were continuously taken to make full use of all available labor and productive capital, thus ever raising living standards and lowering consumer costs of goods. But he is lacking in intellectual honesty when he adduces this argument without attempting to show why private capitalists and businessmen should take such steps or how they would profit more under present conditions by taking these steps than by hoarding their funds in tax-exempt government bonds as they are doing to an ever increasing extent. The chief dynamic factors which make capitalism work are those creating a sufficiency of motivations to private investment and enterprise and a sufficiency of disciplinary compulsions for mass acquiescence in the working of the system.

Raising living standards by building pyramids such as housing which the poor cannot afford out of their meager wages could insure full employment for any community in any phase of industrial maturity and with any conceivable supply of labor and abundance of food. But what is the motivation for a capitalist to raise living standards or build pyramids merely to eliminate unemployment and achieve full employment? This question Professor King, Mr. Herbert Hoover and all our conservatives advocating sound recovery conspicuously fail to answer. Rapid population growth was one of the five major factors which provided sufficient incentives for the capitalist, sufficient compulsions for labor and enough of the spirit as well as the material conditions required for the successful working of capitalism. The formation of new privately owned capital was continuously primed by the growth of population. Professor John Maynard Keynes in an article in the *Eugenics Review* of April, 1937, entitled "Some Consequences of a Declining Population," made the following estimates for England:

	1860	*1913*
Real Capital	100	270
Population	100	150
Standard of life	100	160

Most of this capital formation was made for supplying the necessities of a rapidly growing population and of the imperial state—a little for supplying the luxuries of the wealthy. And the creation of capital in Britain during this period was induced in large part by an increase in population in the British Colonies and America far more rapid than that taking place in England, where population growth was being greatly modified by heavy emigration all the while. Now an adequate rate of capital formation to end unemployment requires either a drastic raising of the standard of living of the masses by pyramid building or the destructive and consumptive processes of war.

Chapter VII
The End of Easy Wars

The function of war as one of the dynamics of democracy has been little recognized in the dominant social thinking of the past century and a half. The reasons are simple and obvious. One is that liberal thinkers have generally ignored the necessity and nature of social dynamisms as such. They have not recognized that, judging solely from history, stagnation in any culture is far more normal or usual than what we have been accustomed to think of as progress. Primitive or semi-savage peoples have perpetuated themselves for hundreds and thousands of years with slight cultural change or advancement and then, on the dynamic impulsations of large scale and organized warfare, swiftly developed a great civilization, like that of Athens or Rome. A second reason for prevailing ignorance about the dynamic function of war has been the historically unfounded dogma that war is abnormal, temporary and wholly destructive. The probabilities are that war will continue, as in the past, to be a normal and necessary human way. Certainly nothing has transpired under democracy or capitalism to render war less normal or less necessary as a social dynamism.

The fact is that democratic and capitalistic civilization has multiplied and intensified war motives and means. It has aggravated interest conflicts which produce war. This, capitalism has done by increasing disparities between the Haves and the Have-nots and by culminating in the economic stagnation which is now chronic under peacetime capitalism. This stagnation makes war a welcome way of escape to full activity. In addition to giving men more reasons to fight each other, our capitalistic civilization has given them better education, technique and tools with which to fight. Progress under our civilization has created more problems than solutions; more reasons for war than peace and more interest conflicts than interest harmonies. There is no need of offering proof. One has only to pronounce two words which the liberal optimists cannot argue away: the second world war and unemployment.

For the first time, two major world wars have occurred within one generation. So much for progress towards peace. For the first time in the history of the American nation, perpetual deficits to mitigate agricultural distress and unemployment are a necessity. These are facts, not opinions. So much for progress towards peace, order and abundance.

It is now the fashion for the believers in collective security to argue that, if war is not prevented, civilization will perish. They are doubtless right in calling war one of the mightiest factors in the destruction of a civilization—when a civilization is in decay. Where they err, however, is in not perceiving that if war destroys, it also creates civilizations, and that, also, a civilization can perish from stagnation quite as well as from war. Probably capitalism will perish in war rather than in stagnation for the simple reason that those in control will, before the system collapses in stagnation, turn to war. This indeed is already happening. But if, instead of slowly succumbing to stagnation, our capitalist civilization is destroyed in war, this will not prove that it could have been preserved by an avoidance of war. An old person may die of overexertion or any one of scores of preventable diseases or millions of preventable accidents. But it does not follow that any person can live forever by merely avoiding all preventable diseases and accidental causes of death. Old age is not preventable. The fact is that life is perpetuated by birth rather than the prevention of death. War creates as well as destroys civilizations. War is a process of birth as well as death.

The necessary dynamic forces of any society are effective motivations to social unity and social activity. Liberal capitalism has not developed an enduring sufficiency of such motivations as a dynamic substitute for war. War and religion since the dawn of history, and trade since the end of the eighteenth century, have been the great unifying and activity generating forces of human society. The pre-capitalist civilizations were unified and energized mainly by war or religion or some combination of both, with trade a wholly minor social force. Roman civilization, for instance, was a typical example of a war society and economy, while that of Egypt, for centuries, was pre-eminently religious. Rome, of course, was never without religion nor Egypt without armed might. The difference between martial Rome and priestly Egypt in the matters of war and religion was one of degree and emphasis. In neither civilization, any more than in other pre-capitalist cultures, was trade or the businessman ever a dynamic or dominant factor.

By the time of the discovery of the Americas some of the ruling classes in Europe, particularly in Italy and the Hanseatic cities of northern Europe, had become deeply interested in trade, as the Renaissance created tastes which could only be satisfied by considerable imports from the East. This era and these processes may be called the gestative period of modern capitalism. But, broadly speaking, in all civilizations prior to the nineteenth century, business, such as there was, had about the same function and importance as the quartermaster corps has for a fighting army: a useful but subservient service. The businessman, even under capitalism, was a camp follower rather than a leader in endless easy imperialist wars. He was a profiteer on the unearned increment of rising land and business property values, all resulting from growth of population and settled territories.

Below are given lists of the wars of the three major democracies during the century and a half preceding the twenties:

WARS OF ENGLAND

1776-83	North American (and with France).
1778-81	First Mahratta War.
1780-84	War with Netherlands.
1782-84	First Mysore War.
1790-92	Second Mysore War.
1793-1802	Revolutionary War (with France)
1801	War with Denmark.
1802-06	Second Mahratta War.
1803-14	War with France.
1806	Sepoy Revolt.
1807-12	War with Russia.
1810-12	War with Sweden.
1812-15	War with United States.
1814-17	Goorkha War.
1815	Hundred Days War (Waterloo).
1817-18	Third Mahratta War.
1824-25	First Burma War.
1824-25	Ashanti War.
1826	Burma War.
1826	Intervention in Portugal.
1827	War with Turkey.
1832	Intervention in Netherlands.
1838-42	War with Afghanistan.
1840-41	Egyptian Insurrection.
1840-42	War with China.
1843-49	Sikh Wars.

92   The Dynamics of War and Revolution

1845	Intervention in Uruguay.
1845-56	Intervention in Argentina.
1851-52	Kafir War.
1852-53	Second Burma War.
1854-56	War with Russia.
1856-57	War with Persia.
1855-60	War with China.
1857-58	Mutiny of the Sepoys in India.
1863-64	Ashanti War.
1863-69	Maori War.
1867-68	Wu with Abyssinia.
1874	Ashanti War.
1878-80	War with Afghanistan.
1879	Zulu War.
1880-81	War in Transvaal.
1881-85	War of the Sudan.
1882-84	Occupation of Egypt.
1885-89	Third Burma War.
1895-96	Ashanti War.
1896-99	War of the Sudan.
1897-98	Intervention in Crete.
1899-1902	Boer War.
1900	Boxer Insurrection.
1901-02	Somali War.
1903-05	Tibet Expedition.
1908	War on the Northwestern Boundary of India.
1914-18	World War.
1919	Afghan War.

(Total for 150 years: 54 wars, lasting 102 years, or 68 per cent of the time.)

WARS OF FRANCE

1779-83	War with England (North America).
1789-1800	Second Coalition War.
1791-1802	Insurrection in San Domingo.
1792-97	First Coalition War (against Dutch, Rhenish, Italians, Spanish).
1793-96	War in Vendee.
1793-1802	War with England.
1795-1802	Egyptian Expedition of Napoleon.
1803-14	War with England.
1805	Third Coalition War.
1806-07	War with Russia and Prussia.

The End of Easy Wars

1808-14	War with Spain.
1809	War with Austria.
1812	War with Russia.
1813-14	War against German States (Hundred Days War-Waterloo).
1823	Spanish Expedition.
1827	War with Turkey.
1829	War on Madagascar.
1832	War with Holland.
1834	War with Portugal.
1830-47	War in Algeria.
1838-39	War in Mexico.
1838-40	War in Argentina.
1843-44	War with Morocco.
1845	Expedition to Uruguay.
1845	War on Madagascar.
1847	War in Cochin China.
1849	Roman Expedition.
1854-56	Crimean War.
1857-62	War with Annam.
1859	Austro-Italian War.
1860	Syrian War.
1860-61	War for Papal State.
1861-62	Cochin-Chinese War.
1861-67	War in Mexico.
1862-64.	War with China.
1867	War in Rome (against Garibaldi).
1870-71	Franco-Prussian War.
1873-74	War in Tonkin.
1881-82	War on Tunis.
1883-85	War with Tonkin.
1883-85	War on Madagascar.
1884-85	War with China.
1890-92	War on Dahoney.
1890-94	War on Sudan.
1893-94	War on Morocco.
1893	War on Siam.
1894	War with Tonkin.
1895-97	War on Madagascar.
1900	Boxer Insurrection.
1907-12	War on Morocco.
1914-18	World War.
1925-26	Riffian War.

(Total: For 150 years, 53 wars lasting 99 years, or 66 per cent of the time.)

LIST OF PRINCIPAL WARS, MILITARY EXPEDITIONS, OCCUPATIONS, CAMPAIGNS AND OTHER DISTURBANCES, EXCEPT DOMESTIC TROUBLES, IN WHICH THE UNITED STATES HAS PARTICIPATED IN THE FIRST 158 YEARS OF ITS HISTORY

	Began	Ended	Time Consumed
War of the Revolution	Apr. 19, 1775	Jan. 14, 1784	8 yrs. 9 mos.
Wyoming Valley Disturbances and Shays's Rebellion	1782	Jan. 5, 1787	5 yrs.
Northwest Indian Wars and Whisky Insurrection	Jan. 1790	Aug. 1795	5 yrs. 8 mos.
War with France	July 9, 1789	Sept. 30, 1800	2 yrs. 3 mos.
War with Tripoli	July 10, 1801	June 4, 1805	3 yrs. 11 mos.
Northwest Indian Wars	Nov. 1811	Oct. 1813	2 yrs.
War with Great Britain	June 18, 1812	Feb. 17, 1815	2 yrs. 8 mos.
War with Algiers (Naval)	Mar. 1815	June 1815	4. mos.
Seminole Indian Wars	Nov. 20, 1817	Oct. 31, 1818	11 mos.
Yellowstone Expedition	July 4, 1819	Sept. 1819	3 mos.
Blackfeet Indian Wars	Apr. 1, 1823	Oct. 1, 1823	6 mos.
LaFevre Indian War	June 1817	Sept. 1827	3 mos.
Sac and Fox War	Apr. 1, 1831	Oct. 1, 1831	6 mos.
Black Hawk War	Apr. 26, 1832	Sept. 21, 1832	5 mos.
Nullification Troubles in So. Car.	Nov. 1832	Feb. 1833	3 mos.
Cherokee and Pawnee Disturbances	June 30, 1833	1839	6 yrs. 6 mos.
Seminole Indian War	Nov. 1, 1835	Aug. 13, 1842	6 yrs. 9 mos.
War with Mexico	Apr. 25, 1846	May 30, 1848	2 yrs. 1 mo.
Various Indian wars with Cayuse, Navaho, Comanche, Kickapoo, Snake, Sioux, Seminole, etc.	1848	1861	13 yrs.
Civil War	Apr. 15, 1861	Aug. 20, 1866	5 yrs. 4 mos.
Various Indian wars	1865	1890	25 yrs.
Sioux Indian War	Nov. 23, 1890	Jan. 19, 1891	2 mos.
Apache and Bannock Indian Troubles	June 30, 1892	June 30, 1896	4 yrs.
Spanish-American War	Apr. 21, 1898	Apr. 11, 1899	1 yr.
Philippine Insurrecrion	Apr. 11, 1899	July 15, 1903	4 yrs. 3 mos.

Boxer Expedition	June 20, 1900	May 12, 1901	11 mos.
Cuban Pacification	Sept. 29, 1906	Apr. 1, 1909	2 yrs. 6 mos.
First Nicaragua Expedition (Marines)	July 1912	Aug. 1925	13 yrs. 1 mo.*
Vera Cruz Expedition	Apr. 21, 1914	Nov. 26, 1914	7 mos.
First Haiti Expedition (Marines)	July 1915	Dec. 1915	5 mos.
Punitive Expedition into Mexico	Mar. 15, 1916	Feb. 5, 1917	11 mos.
Dominican Expedition (Marines)	May 1916	Dec. 1916	7 mos.
The World War	Apr. 6, 1917	July 2, 1921	4 yrs. 3 mos.
Second Haiti Expedition (Marines)	Apr. 1919	June 1920	1 yr. 2 mos.
Second Nicaragua Expedition	Aug. 24, 1926	Jan. 2, 1932	5 yrs. 5 mos.

In 158 years there was warfare practically all the time.

All great civilizations were brought forth in war. Ours is no exception. Only our creative wars were, on the whole, up to the end of the nineteenth century comparatively easy and usually most profitable for the victors, the now satisfied democracies. The main difference between the two great wars of this century and those of the

---

* The Nicaraguan Expeditions amounted to continuous occupations under the hollow pretexts of protecting American lives and property and assisting the Nicaraguan Government with the supervision of elections, the maintenance of order and economic rehabilitation. During one of the many bloody phases of these prolonged adventures in dollar diplomacy, the Sandino rebellion of 1927-1930, our marines lost 135 killed and 66 wounded in action while the Nicaraguan "bandits," the term applied by our Government to Nicaraguan patriots who opposed our intervention, lost over 3000. This was about one half of one per cent of the total population of Nicaragua. Had American casualties in the World War been in the same ratio to our population, our total killed would have been 550,000 instead of around 50,000 as they actually were. Our glorious little war against the Haitian Cacos in 1920 Cost 2500 Haitian lives. I am able to write advisedly as well as feelingly of these minor episodes of American imperialism because I happened to have served in the American diplomatic service in both Nicaragua and Haiti during brief periods of both adventures. I was the American charge d'affaires in Nicaragua in August 1926, who, at the direction of the State Department, sent the telegram asking for the marines to come back as being needed to "protect American lives and property." General Smedley Butler, who feels as I do about these chapters in American imperialist history, fought in the first marine intervention in Nicaragua in 1912 and also commanded the marines for a time in Haiti. He also wears two Congressional Medals of Honor.

seventeenth, eighteenth, and nineteenth centuries, is that the twentieth century wars of the liberal democracies have not been easy or profitable. This difference marks a turn for the worse in the history of democracy and capitalism. It is true that the first world war of the twentieth century was harder on Germany than on the victorious Allies and also that the latter gained nearly a million square miles of territory as a result of that war. Still it was a hard and unprofitable war for the winners. For the losers, it was merely a prelude to revolution and more war which will prove hard and may also be unprofitable for the Have-nots. Be that as it may, one thing is sure: the wars of this century between the Haves and the Have-nots will not prove either easy or profitable for the Haves. The dynamism of easy wars is over so far as democracy and capitalism are concerned.

Democracy needs easy wars, of conquest and exploitation. American democracy was founded by a feudal slavocracy and a mercantile plutocracy. The New England democrats caught in Africa, transported and sold the slaves whom the southern lovers of freedom subsequently exploited. Chattel slavery, a fundamental American institution of the founding fathers of our democracy, was based on the most naked possible use and violence. Greek democracy was also based on slavery and war, a fact often overlooked by those who idealize Hellenic culture. The Anglo-American devotees of what they consider to be Greek civilization have been for the greater part disciples of Plato, whose philosophic idealism was never exemplified by Greece in her prime. Plato was a product of Greek decadence who came well after the end of the great period of Athens. No great civilization in Athens or anywhere else has ever flourished on platonic idealism. Platonism has been an affectation of pre-Renaissance church scholars and Renaissance and Anglo-Saxon scholars living in retreat from the world. It has never governed post-Renaissance nationalism or Anglo-Saxon imperialism any more than it ruled the Athens of Pericles. It has made a major contribution to Western civilization in that it has furnished a philosophic basis for Utopianism which has been a potent cultural influence in the post-Renaissance culture of the West. Utopianism, alias escapism, however, important as it has been and still is as a cultural force, must be recognized for what it is, a part of the psychopathology of an advanced civilization. It attains its greatest historical importance as a factor of decadence. In terms of psychopathology, it represents the attempt of the mind to flee from reality into a world of ideals, i.e., dreams and wishful thinking, and to achieve by processes of rationalization what cannot be achieved through processes of realization. The psychopathology of idealism or escapism is not to be regarded as always or necessarily abnormal. On the contrary, it is normal for every one to seek escape from reality into a world of day-dreams some of the time. We are all part-time escapists or day-dreamers. Escapism becomes dangerous only when carried too far, as when an individual or a society indulges in it to the exclusion of an amount of realistic effort necessary for survival in the eternal struggle for existence. This psychopathology is the basis of much eighteenth-century rationalism and nineteenth-century liberal legalism. It is the psychological basis of the fictions and contrary to fact assumptions of our law, politics and economics. It represents the triumph of mind over matter—on paper and in dreams. The triumph of man is always the triumph of his will, served by the indispensable instrumentality of his mind or reason. The triumph of man, however, must always be the triumph of the entire man, of his emotions as much as his reason, of his viscera as much as his cranium. It is the triumph, not only of the whole man but of man really, not ideally, integrated with his society and environment. A bloodless triumph of an ideal presupposes a bloodless man. Heaven, not earth, is the abode of such men.

The territory of this republic was wrested from the Indians and developed by slavery. When chattel slavery proved less profitable than wage slavery, it was abolished by the dominant northern factory interests through a bloody victory over the weaker southern slavery interests. During the entire era of Anglo-Saxon democracy and capitalism, or from Queen Bess's piracy along the Spanish Main down to the Boer War (the last war to be won by British imperialism), force, violence and war were basic to the system. And this warfare was invariably easy and profitable for the Anglo-Saxons. It was gunpowder versus bows and arrows; the technology of the white man against the primitive or savage arts of the darker races. Anglo-Saxon democracy needed this unequal warfare and human exploitation just as Greek democracy needed slavery and perpetual war on inferior barbarians in order to flourish.

In the more equal wars between the British and the French or the British and the Dutch, or the British and the American colonists, there was always plenty left over for the losers, and there was never a necessity for the Anglo-Saxons to resort to conscription until 1916 or to capital levies until now. The loss of the American colonies left the

British still with the largest empire on earth. The British victories over the French and the Dutch still left the latter with vast colonial empires and allowed the French to build up a mighty colonial empire during the mid-nineteenth century after the French defeat at Waterloo. Even the wars between comparative equals, as between the British and the French, did not force Britain to adopt conscription or subsequently prevent winners and losers alike from acquiring further territories during the nineteenth century at the expense of the darker races. In those days the conquest of new territories, as in India, Asia and Africa or markets, as in China, was profitable as such conquest could not possibly prove today. In those days there was always plenty of demand at remunerative prices for all the raw materials and all the manufactures that could then be produced. To say that the nineteenth-century wars of the capitalistic democracies were comparatively easy and profitable is no disparagement of the courage of the soldiers and pioneers of that day. It is no reflection on the bravery or skill of the bullfighter to point out that the bull usually loses.

The ease or difficulty of war for any given people at any particular time is, of course, purely relative. It is practically always possible for a large nation to resort to war, however difficult war may be; and war, under the most favorable circumstances, is never without risks and difficulties. Granting that warfare or conflict is the dynamic principle both of capitalism and socialism, it is important that, by reason of the greater ease of war for the British in the nineteenth century than today, resort to this dynamism offered more attractions and fewer deterrents to the democracies during the nineteenth century than now. Formerly the Haves fought, usually with success, for more territory or markets. Such war objectives were always physically attainable and materially advantageous to the winners. Today the democracies are fighting for the security of their possessions, which is not attainable. It is hard for a realist to believe that forty million Frenchmen will ever win security by victory over eighty million Germans, or that the two hundred and forty million people of the satisfied democracies of America, Britain and France can ever enjoy security as against the four hundred million land hungry Russians, Germans, Japanese and Italians. The land rich Russians are as hungry for territory giving them outlets on the warmer seas as the land poor Germans and Italians are for more granaries. The Haves now want peace with plenty where formerly they wanted wars of aggression to get plenty. But the Have-nots do not now want peace with poverty. And it is the dissatisfied Have-nots who now call the tune the satisfied Haves must pipe to.

As already stated, the dynamic function of war has always been and still is today that of obviating stagnation and anarchy by creating the necessary drives to social activity and unity. Without these products of war, a high civilization has hitherto been impossible. It remains to be demonstrated that a requisite quantity and quality of social unity and activity for a high civilization can be achieved otherwise than through war. Welfare and civilization have flourished only where and when people have been collectively united and motivated, as in war, by common aims and a common danger. Europe emerged from the barbarism of the Dark Ages when and because the discovery of new continents, the birth of new religious cults and the growth of nationalism gave rise to wars which created the necessary drives and disciplines for social unity and activity. Luther gave Europeans new religious passions and Columbus gave them new territories to fight over. It proved better for welfare and the advancement of culture to have national than private warfare. By reducing warfare to that occurring only between nations and by reducing the number of states through the formation of large empires, welfare is served and civilization advanced. In these ways, larger areas within which social cooperation may be successfully practiced are created and preserved.

The substitution, of large-scale public for small-scale private warfare since the rise of nationalism, following the Renaissance and the Protestant Reformation has been mistakenly acclaimed by many as good ground for the hope that public warfare would eventually go the way of private warfare into limbo. The taking of this view shows again a failure to grasp the central point of the present chapter. The great gift to welfare and civilization of nationalism was a pattern of warfare which imposed social unity where the preceding pattern of private warfare had failed to create such unity, but had rather promoted disunity. Public warfare was not only a substitute dynamism for private warfare but a vast improvement, socially considered. And the great civilizations of the past, like that of Rome, exemplified the superiority of a regime practicing public warfare over contemporary and more backward regimes tolerating private warfare because they were insufficiently civilized and unified to practice public warfare. An essential difference between a tribe of cannibals and a civilized people is to be found in their respective ways of warfare.

In the trend of the past four centuries from private to public warfare, from small political units to larger ones, there has never for one moment been a trend towards peace or away from warfare. Least of all since the Wilsonian collective security myth was made the rationalization of the most foolish declaration of war in history, the one we made on Germany in April 1917. Most significant of all, there has not even been a serious quest after a substitute dynamism for public war. The peace movements, schemes and machinery of the past forty years have not aimed at the development of a substitute dynamism for war but merely at the prevention of war, not for the benefit of all mankind but for the benefit of the satisfied who wanted their plenty with peace while the dissatisfied majority endured their poverty in impotency. The peace crowd, of course, have sought to formulate and put into operation substitutes for war as an adjuster of international differences. But they have simply not grasped the more important function of war as a necessary social dynamism. If one told the leaders of the different peace movements as late as 1932, the depth of the depression, that unemployment was the most serious war danger, as I did in my *Is Capitalism Doomed?* published in March 1932 and written in the autumn of 1931, one was met, as I was, with incredulous and pitying glances from liberal thinkers who could then see no connection whatever between unemployment and war.

This incomprehension of the economics and social dynamics of war is mainly due to the almost complete failure of the thinkers and writers in all fields of the social sciences during the rise of modern capitalism ever to take a realistic view of social facts like war and the necessary function of dynamism. This failure was due partly to humanitarianism and partly to hypocrisy, During an era in which the American, British and French empires were being built by almost continuous warfare, it may have been commendably humanitarian to wish for a social order free of war but it was downright intellectual dishonesty not to recognize that continuous warfare was one of the major dynamisms of the democracies in that era and, it was sheer hypocrisy then to argue as did the liberals, that war was exceptional, abnormal and avoidable. A commendably honest exception to the general rule may be found in Professor Carr's history of the two decades from 1919 to 1939 in which he frankly recognizes that international peace has become really "a special vested interest of the predominant powers" rather than a general interest. This must remain true as long as present inequalities of economic opportunity prevail both among nations and among individuals within nations.

Religion, it would seem, is the only probable substitute for war as a social dynamic. It has, of course, served most often as an auxiliary of, rather than as a substitute for, war. Interestingly enough, Christianity, on its face a cult of universal brotherhood and peace, has, as yet, never produced a civilization or been identified with one which was not continuously characterized by war. In all the great Christian civilizations the main function of Christianity, so far as war has been concerned, has been to sanctify, multiply and intensify wars.

Volumes can be filled with documentary evidence of the foregoing statement. Professor Ray Hamilton Abrams, a University of Pennsylvania sociologist, published seven years ago a book entitled *Preachers Present Arms* which he was easily able to fill with facts showing how American churchmen helped put America into the first world war of the twentieth century. In 1916 Rabbi Stephen S. Wise asked "Are we to enter the armament gamble in which every nation loses?" A year later he was calling for "slaughter of the Boche." In 1914 Bishop William T. Manning was praying for peace. In 1918 he was calling peace talk "thinly disguised treason." Cardinal Gibbons was blessing the boys with the injunction, "Go forth to battle and victory, and God will be with you." Alfred C. Dieffenbach, editor of the *Unitarian Church Register,* wrote: "Christ . . . would take bayonet and grenade and bomb and rifle and do the work of deadliness." Henry B. Wright, a Y. M. C. A. leader, said, "I would not enter this work till I could see Jesus himself sighting down a gun barrel and running a bayonet through an enemy's body." Newell Dwight Hillis, one of the nation's leading Congregationalist ministers, went up and down the land making speeches to sell Liberty bonds in which he worked his audiences up to a frenzy of passion and hate by a dramatic recounting of tales, largely false, of French and Belgian victims of German rapists. The men of the gospel and peace retailed atrocity stories and the religious publications ran Liberty Loan ads such as this: "KILL THE HUN—KILL HIS HOPE. Bayonet and bomb—both kill! One kills the Hun, the other kills his hope. Buy U. S. Government bonds." Christian ministers and preachers of moral idealism have to wait for a war to go to town. Only then are they really potent moral forces. Only then are their hearers in considerable numbers and to any significant extent swayed by their oratory. War makes the Christian ministry and church temporarily dynamic and influential. That, doubtless, is why they invariably are so enthusiastic for war. It enables them to sell religion, temporarily, and to make it, for the duration of the war, important. It gives the Christian minister a brief spell of social importance and compensation for his chronic inferiority complex. As this book went to the publishers a front-page headline of a New York daily screamed in bold type, "Churchmen say Christians can't remain neutral. Thirty-three leading Protestants aver ethical issues in war force 'responsible' stand." It is inconceivable that a headline should have carried the news, "Bankers say the rich can't remain neutral." It would be easy to find thirty-three leading bankers who think that, but they would not have the effrontery to formulate such a view in the didactic tones of these thirty-three men of God and lay brethren. It takes the ministers of the gospel to whoop up a modern war. The plutocracy are mere camp followers of modern wars. The preachers furnish the moral leadership for war. Only they can mobilize the folk deity and the public conscience for the big killing.

Christianity, of course, has not been the dominant creative force in any Christian civilization since the Renaissance. Christianity has been distinctly inferior to war and trade as a dynamism. It has made the following not unimportant contributions, however, to the prevailing culture: (1) It has provided moral sanction for the legal safety and enforcement of property rights; (2) it has encouraged attitudes necessary for capitalism such as those favoring abstinence, thrift, saving, investment, interest, profits and private enterprise; (3) it has helped to keep the poor, poor in spirit and the meek acquiescent in their earthly lot. In short, Christianity has not developed a dynamic substitute for war. It is merely on tap when needed as an emotional auxiliary to war and property rights.

The economic mechanics of religion are similar to those of war and are obvious and simple. To demonstrate the role of religion as an employment creator in the past, it should not be necessary to rehash ancient or medieval history or to spin much economic theory. It should suffice merely to gaze upon the colossal religious ruins of the past all over the world and upon the churches and temples built hundreds of years ago which are still in service. The construction of the religious public works of the past fully and continuously absorbed the surplus labor and production of entire communities for centuries. Given enough religion or enough war, there will never be unemployment. The reasons are simple and obvious: First, there is no limit to the expenditure a community can make on war or religion except its capacity to produce minus its minimum requirements for subsistence. Second, religious or war motives have always proved sufficient to call forth maximum expenditure and sacrifices. The big point is that the activity or inactivity of any community is determined by the adequacy or inadequacy of the motivations to activity it can develop. No machine will move without sufficient motive power. Our economic machine has not been slowed down by reason of technical defects, inadequate resources or the satiation of human desires. It has been slowed down because it is dependent on profit motivations which, in the changed circumstances of current trends, are no longer adequate. Therefore, the civilized world turns to war as the only escape from stagnation.

War and religion are two creators of economic demand which do not have to depend on profits. Expenditures on war or religion obviously afford satisfactions deemed by the people who make them to be worth the sacrifices and costs involved. Otherwise, they would not be made. War and religion generate their own motivations for centuries on end. The pursuit of individual profits does not. For centuries the Romans found plenty of motives to carry on wars and the Egyptians to build pyramids. But capitalists have run out of motives for building railroads and Empire State buildings in less than a hundred years. The saturation point in capitalistic investment is soon reached. In war and religion it never is, and that is why capitalism is a temporary way while war and religion, like the poor, are with us always.

The essence of our economic difficulty today is an insufficiency of new private investment which, in turn, is due solely to an insufficiency of profit motivations. This failure of private investment, as we are told ad nauseam, is due to changed conditions reducing profit incentives and opportunities. The solution, we are told by professional economists, businessmen and conservative investors is to end these changed conditions diminishing the number of opportunities to make profits. They do not for a moment entertain the question whether this be possible. I am sure that it is not, otherwise, I reason, it would take place since there is such unanimity of desire to have it happen. If people fail to remain young, I am forced to infer that it is impossible not to grow old. It is as simple as that. I do not any longer waste my time trying to prove to doubting optimists that it is impossible to restore the necessary conditions for the successful functioning of private capitalism. Those who take my view do not have to prove their case. They need only challenge the optimists to prove their theses by achievement. After all, the tax collector presents my case much more convincingly than I can possibly do. The democracies are proving it by turning to war because they cannot otherwise escape from stagnation.

In terms of the concrete or specific, it may be said that, as between the building of a million dollar movie house and a million dollar church or armory there is no difference so far as current employment and production are concerned. There is, however, this important difference: the movie house can be built under capitalism only as long as it appears likely that the masses will have enough purchasing power to pay the necessary admissions to make the building a profitable venture. But in the religiously and militarily dominated society, the wealthy or the ruling class, along with the masses, always contribute enough to the cult or to the state to insure full employment. If there is a limit to what can be invested for profit, there is no limit to what can be spent for the glory of God or for war. An economic historian has calculated that during the thirteenth century France built over a billion dollars' worth of churches and cathedrals. In precapitalist days the building of pyramids, the Inca temple at Macchu Pichu, which I once spent a day climbing a mountain in the Andes to visit, a Roman wall or a medieval fortress was much more of a job provider than similar projects would be today with the use of modern technique and labor-saving machinery. All of which merely proves that, with our present labor supply and productive efficiency, we shall need to build several times as many pyramids and temples or to fight several times as costly wars as did our ancestors centuries ago. And the probabilities are that we shall.

The theoretical case for capitalism and democracy rests upon a denial that unemployment is ever anything more than temporary and local. This denial rests on the further refusal to admit that the rich will ever hoard their savings. These ostrich-like reactions to now current facts are obviously absurd.

The spiritual aspect of war and religion as social dynamisms is even more important than the purely economic aspect just discussed. The central fact of the spiritual aspect of the break-down of capitalism and democracy is a loss of faith in the values of the system. This, of course, is receiving widespread attention by disturbed liberals. The more naive and intellectual of them are earnestly crying out for a revival of faith in the values which are often verbalized in such terms as liberty, individual initiative, private property rights and free competition. The more *terre á terre* businessmen merely ask for a revival of confidence. The trouble is that the chief values of capitalism and democracy are no longer either credible or practicable. But the values of religion and war are always both credible and practicable.

The cardinal value of capitalism is prosperity. Other values are competition and laissez-faire. But you cannot revive confidence in prosperity when it is not just around the corner. And you cannot believe in competition when you cannot successfully practice it. Materialistic values can be believed in only as long as they can be materialized. The values of war and religion, on the contrary, can always be realized. One can always suffer and die for one's faith or one's country. One cannot always get six per cent with safety, buy land or stocks on a rising market or have two cars in every garage. And there's the rub for capitalism. The rich and the poor can always follow a St. Francis into a life of asceticism and suffering or a Hitler into a war to build a greater Germany. But one cannot always get rich quick.

The spiritual values of war and religion are collective heroism, suffering, self-sacrifice and discipline—the will to suffer as well as the will to power or mastery. Religion and war can always realize and rationalize these values. War and religion give men something to suffer and die for. They give suffering a purpose and meaning as well as a satisfying and exalting quality. The failure of capitalism makes men suffer without giving to their suffering either a decent purpose or a rational meaning. If a man suffers in war, he is a hero; if he suffers for his faith, he is a saint; if he suffers under capitalism, he is a sucker. There is dignity as well as fulfillment in being a hero or a saint but not in being a jobless failure under capitalism. There is a vast difference between suffering for something and suffering from something. People will suffer in war for their country or under persecution for their faith. They will suffer in war for their country until the failure of their government makes their suffering seem futile. They may then revolt as the Russian people did in 1917.

Today capitalism or business is not fighting or leading a fight for the people. It is merely stagnating, in the absence of war, and thereby imposing untold hardship on innumerable victims. Those who imagine that people will not readily turn from stagnation to war or some crusading new political faith merely because the change may increase the people's suffering do not know human nature. People are not instinctively averse to suffering and hardship, only suffering and hardship must have a meaning and purpose. Even death on the battlefield or martyrdom for one's faith has been for millions of people in the past life's grandest and most exalting experience. But how can anyone feel exaltation over suffering due to the failure of business to provide employment and a decent living? How can one feel that he is heroically upholding the glorious values of liberty when he is merely a passive victim of business impotence or incompetence? The appeal to heroic devotion to the liberties of capitalism is naive. If these liberties are worthy of devotion, of practicing rather than preaching, they must inspire it.

The values of economic freedom and competition fail to inspire faith when they cease to be practicable or when their practice leads to anarchy and chaos, as at present. One can, of course, make a philosophic value of anarchy. But capitalism and democracy have not given the people that type of philosophy. On the contrary, they have made values of order, efficiency and ease. Businessmen and workers have no taste for the joys of philosophic anarchy. Nor is the anarchy resulting nowadays from extreme competition and economic freedom the sort of thing a philosophical anarchist might long for in a life comparatively free from moral, legal and conventional restraints. The worker in the bread line has as much regimentation as the soldier, but the latter has regimentation with dignity. The businessman being put through bankruptcy is subject to coercion equal to that of any authoritarian government, but it is uncompensated by security. Neither the worker nor the businessman enjoys the type of anarchy which results from the breakdown of prosperity or excessive competition. A taste of such anarchy breeds a deep and abiding sense of frustration and futility, not of freedom.

In any brief review of the dynamic function of easy wars in the successful rise of capitalism and democracy it would be a serious omission not to call attention to the fact that nationalistic wars tempered the anarchy and contradictions of private competition. Both war and religion necessarily impose collective unity. Their practice unites large numbers of people in interests and feeling. Private competition, on the contrary, must always tend to destroy social unity. During the nineteenth century, two conditions permitted at the same time the preservation of the private competitive system and a satisfactory degree of national unity: The first was the already discussed factor of continuous warfare of a sort that was generally easy and lucrative for the peoples of the three great democracies of the present day, whether such warfare was ostensibly imperialistic as that of Britain and France or whether it was, as in the case of the American colonies, frontier settlement warfare against the aborigines. The second condition was the political immaturity of a vast majority of the electorate of that period, wherefore, in general, they competed under and not over the rules, leaving the making of rules largely to the landed slavocracy of the South and the mercantile plutocracy of the North in the case of the United States, and, in the case of Britain, to a single and fairly compactly knit together ruling class.

An entire community can practice competition in an orderly way only in war or in competition with an outside community. Thus, in war-time, each warring community operates internally on the basis of cooperation and externally on the basis of competition. In this way there is order within and anarchy without. It is obviously an inevitable condition of any society of sovereign nations that it be characterized by anarchy. Multiple sovereignties are merely a synonym for anarchy. International anarchy is a corollary of national sovereignty. That numerous company of idealists and theorists who profess to wish to substitute in the international sphere the rule of law for the rule of anarchy while at the same time preserving national sovereignty is composed of persons who are either singularly obtuse or intellectually dishonest. Anyone who does not understand that, under the rule of law, there can be but one sovereign, not several, does not understand the meaning either of law or sovereignty.

But, although war has been throughout history a force for anarchy as among nations, it has been a force for social cohesion and order as within nations. Between chronic international anarchy and national order there is no necessary contradiction. The fact is that capitalistic democracies have needed the centripetal force of foreign warfare to offset the centrifugal force of private competition. It may be that socialism within the nation can develop enough forces of unification to obviate the necessity for the internally unifying forces of foreign war, though this may now well be considered doubtful. Certainly, ever since the Renaissance and Protestant Reformation, Western civilization has needed the unifying forces of national and imperial wars. Individualism, or the disuniting force of private competition, has made this need of foreign war all the greater. The free play of individual or minority group self-interest tends to make any community go to pieces. The counter forces of unification necessary for social order under capitalism have had to be largely generated by the continuous waging of easy and successful foreign wars. Now the democracies no longer have easy foreign wars to offset the disuniting forces of capitalism, which, in its maturity, is nothing but unmitigated class war.

CHAPTER VIII
The Masses Go To School and the Polls

During the nineteenth century the cure for nearly every social evil was supposed to be more democracy. Broadly speaking, this meant more votes and more education. Faith in more democracy and more education, with its accompanying trend of an ever growing electorate and an ever improving system of public instruction, helped avert for the time being many of our present difficulties. As long as it was possible to make reforms, such as curbing the absolute powers of the Stuarts, ending taxation without representation in the American colonies, cleaning out the rotten boroughs in England or removing property requirements to vote, and as long as it was possible to show a steadily decreasing percentage of illiterates in the population as a result of a steadily expanding and improving system of public instruction, democracy could point with pride, justify large hopes and dissipate agitation.

Now we have about reached the limit or saturation point in reform, civil liberties, extension of the suffrage and elimination of illiteracy. We, therefore, can no longer say with plausibility that more democracy is the cure for any major social evil. It rather appears that democracy has created more problems than solutions. Specifically, we cannot now offer the jobless the vote, free schooling or new civil liberties in lieu of a job or a dole. They have the vote, free schooling and civil liberties—to starve—and they have not jobs. It is obvious what they need and want. And nothing else can take its place, the place of a job. The vote is now enabling the underprivileged to form minority pressure groups to extract a handout from the government at the expense of other classes. The role of education in our present crisis is to make the masses susceptible as they never were before to propaganda and demagogic manipulation. The greater the number of people who can vote and read, the greater the irrationality, the greater the conflict of minority interests and the greater the anarchy in the political and economic processes under a system of parliamentary democracy. The people can rule with rationality and success only through a single leader, party and governing agency. Public order and welfare require administration not conflict; the imposition and performance of duties, not the playing of a competitive game.

Democracy and education have not brought peace or social justice. On the contrary, they have intensified and implemented class warfare with new techniques. This was to be expected. It is not democracy gone wrong. It is democracy grown old. It is not an imperfect but a mature democracy. The age of reform ended with Lloyd George's passage of the Parliament Act in 1911, emasculating the House of Lords of its final veto power, with Woodrow Wilson's new freedom and with Theodore Roosevelt's Bull Moose party in 1913, phenomena of similar futility. The direct election of senators, woman's suffrage and in some states the referendum and recall came along in this twilight of democracy.

The chief error of democracy or laissez-faire as a social doctrine lay in the assumption that there are certain natural laws under which and not over which the people will compete. The assumption is obviously false both as to history and human psychology. Life is not a game to be played under immutable rules. It is, among other things, a grand free-for-all fight over what the rules shall be. The eighteenth and nineteenth century champions of laissez-faire, democracy and capitalism assumed that the masses would accept the rules, as well as the rule, of money. It is only fair to most of the early exponents of democracy, even in America, to say that never for a moment did they believe in universal suffrage, labor unions or organized political pressure groups except by the well-to-do.

The simplest example of how the democratic game breaks down once everybody starts playing it, may be found in government subsidies. As long as the manufacturers were the chief subsidy receivers, in the form of a highly protective tariff, American democracy could work fairly well. But once every large economic group like the farmers, the unemployed, organized labor and the aged is in a position to enforce a demand for a similar subsidy, the parliamentary or democratic jig is up. Subsidies do not make sense or work when everybody gets one. The essence of successful democracy is subsidies for the few and taxes and votes for all. What had to doom the system was the obvious impossibility of having votes for everybody without attempts to get subsidies for everybody. The fact that the game could be played so long was due simply to the natural lag of the masses in catching on to it. It is, however, too simple a game, that of grab as grab can, for even morons not eventually to catch on to it.

It is amusing to hear present-day exponents of the American Way in the pay of the National Association of Manufacturers, the nation's most important aggregation of government subsidy seekers and receivers, wax indignant over the selfishness and nerve of the new pressure groups like those of the C. I. O. Ugly charges of class warfare and class legislation are leveled at these newly organized minorities. The making of these charges is obviously a case of the pot calling the kettle black. It is like-wise nonsense for the social scientist or idealist living in the ivory tower of some endowed institution to pontificate about the ways of sound democracy and unctuously call for an end to subsidies, monopolies and pressure groups. Every meal he eats is subsidized and the very institution which shelters him enjoys usually the unjustifiable subsidy of complete tax exemption. It is nonsense for this subsidized pensioner to denounce subsidies for others because there has never been a moment in the history of the British or American democracy and capitalism when special subsidies and monopolies have not been basic to the system.

There never has been and probably never will be a society without subsidies, monopolies and favored classes. The trouble with democracy today is not that it is characterized by these features but that the battle over them results in stagnation and chaos. It is the playing of the game that has to be stopped now and, fundamentally, for no other reason than that too many people have learned to play it and to play it too well.

The rise of capitalism and democracy marked an era in which emphasis was on rights and the assertion of these rights which was the playing of the game. It was assumed that the playing of this game yielded the greatest good to the greatest number. The role of the state was that of umpire or policeman, to protect and enforce the rights of the players. It never seemed to be recognized by the theorists of the game that a necessary feature of any game is the loser. Naturally, those having most rights and getting most state aid were the players owning most property. There was a right against a trespass on one's property but not against being thrown out of work. There was a right to just compensation for one's property taken by the state in war but not for one's life thus taken. One was supposed to deem it an honor to give one's life to one's country but to get paid for one's property given to it. Briefly, there was security for property and, in a limited way, for the person but not for personal employment and personal survival. One of the major concerns of the founding fathers in drawing up a more perfect union was to get the then nearly worthless paper of the revolutionary government (which they had bought up in large amounts for next to nothing) redeemed subsequently in gold. The fact that it was done by 1835 was one of the great triumphs of American democracy. The battle for democratic rights and liberties began against Charles I in the early seventeenth century as the fight of the economically privileged merchants for the safeguarding of their property rights against an old-fashioned monarch who naively and undemocratically thought that private property was no more sacred than human life. The American and French revolutions about settled all arguments everywhere over civil liberties. Subsequent progress has been mainly a matter of extending the application of the principles established in these revolutions. Today no significant number of the underdogs are anywhere interested in their civil liberties. They are interested in jobs, doles for farmers, relief for the unemployed, pensions for the aged—in general, ham and eggs. None of the things they are now interested in is a matter of right under democracy.

Civil liberties are a means, not an end. The English city merchants of the early seventeenth century and the American city merchants of the late eighteenth century wanted certain rights in order to be able to take advantage of certain opportunities. Where there is no opportunity, there is no right. One does not hear these days American farmers clamoring for freedom to do what they please with their land and labor or to enter the free market of capitalism. What they want is subsidies, production curtailment and government interference with the freedom of the market. Why are the farmers not satisfied with their liberties under the bill of rights? The answer is that they cannot eat freedom and they cannot, in many cases, get enough to eat by the exercise of freedom. A freedom to starve is meaningless as freedom.

The cry for civil liberties today is not heard from the under-dogs but from the top dogs. As present trends are moving, the cry of the rich for their constitutional rights and liberties becomes essentially a plea for the capitalists right to hoard, to throttle down industrial production, to peg prices and to make the best of stagnation for the interests of property and management. This is the right of the investor to do as he pleases with his money, the right of the businessman to run his own business and the right not to be put out of business by government competition or government regulation. When capitalists demanded rights to enable them to take advantage of opportunities for expansion they stood on firmer moral, psychological and political ground than when they now demand rights, the exercise of which only enables them to maintain business stagnation.

We are now hearing less about the old and more about the new rights, the new right to a job, the new right to a living from the production of farm products and the new right to old age pensions. The emphasis is also shifting from the winning and assertion of rights to the imposing and fulfillment of duties. These changes have come, not as matters of public taste or opinion but of public need. Democracy in America will finally perish when our government, for the first time, in a war, will have to impose on industry a totalitarian social discipline in the coming war, such as formerly democracy imposed only on its conscript soldiers. When business for the first time has to be regimented the same as the conscript, democracy is over.

Before concluding this chapter on the end of the age of reform, it will not be amiss to include a brief comment on the connection between propaganda and democracy and universal public instruction. No one will deny that political discussion on the level of the Federalist papers could not secure wide publication in our papers or magazines today. The reason is obvious: such discussion would be above the level of the lowest common denominator of readers in practically every publication. It would, therefore, be commercially unprofitable as material for publication. Is the general level of public education, literacy or intelligence lower now than in the days of the American Revolution? No, quite the contrary. The difference is that in those days the elite set the tone of political discussion whereas today the "people" set it, having come into their own in the maturity of democracy.

To say that democracy has now brought it about that political and other questions must be discussed in terms understood by the masses is false, since the principal effort and achievement in most political discussions are to create and exploit misunderstanding for the obtaining of desired practical results. The purpose of political discussion as of good advertising copy is not to stimulate critical thought but to create a desired state of mind or emotions, desired attitudes, habits, choices, decisions and actions. This purpose, of course, is democratic. It evidences respect for the people's votes or commercial patronage. It is both the triumph and the finish of democracy.

Once good advertising technique becomes good political technique, a country is ready for a Dr. Goebbels. Such efficient means of manipulating the public mind as are in use by our advertising men, publishers and political experts cannot be left indefinitely to the ends of any selfish individual or minority interest. The inevitable anarchy resulting from the unbridled use by private interests of the new techniques of misleading the public and manipulating public opinion makes the monopoly of these techniques by the state as necessary as was in an earlier day the monopolization by the state of armed force within its borders. Propaganda technique and a monopoly of the large newspapers used for private interests are as dangerous as would be today the carrying of firearms by special groups for the furtherance of minority group interests. For a great corporation or a group of rich men to subsidize propaganda for their ends is as much of a social menace as it would be for them to use private armies to intimidate voters at the polls or buyers in the market place.

The Jews in Germany were the victims of too much democracy. Hitler realized at the outset of his war on international capitalism that it would be good political strategy to blame everything on the Jews, since the moronic public mind is not capable of assimilating abstract ideas or developing indignation against a multiplicity and complexity of evils. It is the same political strategy which today makes the good American demagogue blame everything that is wrong with America on Hitler. Although Hitler is a little more remote from America than the German Jews were from Germany, the idea that Hitler is the cause of all the world's troubles finds easy credence with the American masses. It is no strange thing that the nation which, before the war, was the leader in education, whither our youth going into the teaching profession trekked by the hundreds to get Ph.D.s, should now be the most efficient exponent of the technique of the American advertising men and of Dr. Goebbels, who is the last word in that technique. The fact is that democracy worked only while an aristocracy ruled. The world is getting back to aristocratic rule by new elites because one of the necessary accompaniments of maturity in a democracy is an increasingly unintelligent and incompetent direction of public affairs, as proved by the present state of the world despite the resources and the military and economic supremacy of the democracies since Versailles.

Part III. The New Revolution. Mars, the Midwife

Chapter IX. Necessities and Frustrations

Chapter X. We Fight Because of Democracy's Failure

Chapter XI. From Capitalist to Socialist Imperialism

Chapter XII. The Return of Discipline. The Old Freedom and the New Discipline

Chapter XIII. Power Politics

Chapter XIV. Realism Ends in Foreign Affairs When the People Rule

Chapter XV. The Bloody Futility of Frustrating the Strong

Chapter XVI. After War, Pyramid Building

Chapter XVII. We Stagnate Because There is No Common Will to Action

Chapter XVIII. Out of War a New Revolutionary Folk Unity

Chapter IX
Necessities and Frustrations

The new revolution is the product of necessities and frustrations rather than of opportunities and aspirations, as was so largely the revolution of capitalism. The Germans who put Hitler in power had no opportunities, as formerly—the Germans of the revolution of '48 for instance—to migrate. Nor were they able to achieve prosperity through foreign trade. American, British and French tariff and immigration barriers doomed Germans to seek expansion through war in Europe.

Also the new revolution was started by the first world war of this century and is by way of crystallizing into a fairly recognizable pattern in the second world war of this century. The period from 1919 to 1939 was one of transition from the capitalist revolution of the past two or four centuries, as one cares to date the beginning, to the new socialist revolution. The capitalist revolution may be dated from the Renaissance or from the rise of the factory system about the time of the American Revolution.

In any case, there is a definite unity to the pattern from the Renaissance down to the World War. And there is rapidly emerging a fairly definite unity to the new revolution. The capitalist collapse enters its third decade with the beginning of the forties. The twenties marked the era of spurious prosperity and unworkable arrangements. In October 1929 the lid blew off when the American stock market collapsed. The thirties were the decade of depression, social upheaval and preparation for war. The lid blew off again in September 1939 when the peace of Europe collapsed. The entire period from Versailles to Poland was one of the progressive deterioration of the old order.

To discuss, as is done in this book, a new revolution in terms of its causative necessities and frustrations rather than of its inspirational opportunities and aspirations is, in itself, revolutionary. Ever since the Renaissance, social change has been geared to opportunities and aspirations rather than to necessities and frustrations. Throughout this period dominant social thought has fairly consistently shown the influence of an irrepressible optimism which has been more often justified than disappointed. Of course, during all these centuries since the Renaissance men have had to bow to certain necessities of their situation. But, generalizing broadly, it may be said that the big difference between then and now is that opportunity and aspiration were then in the saddle, whereas necessity and frustration now rule mankind. And this is as true of rich Britain and France facing the Westwall or of rich America facing irreducible armies of the unemployed and federal deficits, as it is of Germany facing the blockade or Russia everywhere facing closed outlets to the warmer waters, or of Italy and Spain facing everywhere immigration barriers and shrinking foreign markets.

There was never an actual necessity to end feudalism but there is a necessity for the democracies to end unemployment. There was no real need to inaugurate democracy, capitalism and industrialism. There were just attractive opportunities for certain people to do so with profit to themselves. So these things were done with effects which, on the whole, were beneficial for all mankind. There is today a need to inaugurate socialism or some form of collectivism, call it what you will. Feudalism did not break down. It was overthrown by the emergent trading classes. Capitalism is actually breaking down. Contrary to Marxism, it is not being overthrown by enemies on the outside. If it is not to be allowed to die a natural death but has to be destroyed, it will be killed, not by its critics but by its warmest friends waging a war for its defense.

A book written in terms of twentieth-century necessities and frustrations cannot possibly prove as inspiring or appealing as one written in terms of nineteenth-century opportunities and aspirations. People do not like to have explained to them unpleasant and imperious necessities of their situation; nor do they care to be reminded of their individual and collective failures. Practically every present-day purveyor of a social message who desires or obtains a large audience still talks in terms of opportunities and aspirations. This is why most current talk about the problems of the hour is so largely meaningless. The aspirations may be there but the opportunities are lacking. The simplest proofs are unemployment figures, current trading volume on the New York Stock Exchange, money and interest rates, new capital issues, new construction and so on. Businessmen may laugh at this book but they cannot laugh off their present and future taxes.

It may be said that there are abundant opportunities to reorganize society for the more abundant life, or along lines of democratic socialism. But that is not what the American people now want done.

They want to have brought back the prosperity of a young and growing capitalism; some want the security of the Haves, all want the damnation of the Have-nots other than themselves. Just now the German Have-nots are supposed to be the cause of all the trouble. Individuals want jobs for themselves, but do not give a hang about jobs for others. Farmers want twice the market price of their products and the unemployed to be left to starve so as to reduce taxes, and so on.

In a democracy, if the people want to be deluded, those who believe in and successfully practice democracy must try to delude them. American entry into the present war is probably necessary to shatter deep-seated illusions of the peoples of the democracies. A realistic approach to current problems on the eve of America's going to war can be inspired by no hope of changing the minds of the masses, since the minds of the masses are wholly inaccessible to any realistic examination of the situation. The main purpose of a realistic approach to current problems must be to prepare the minds of the elite minority capable of leadership when the time comes for such leadership. The time is not yet ripe for leadership. The people now want crooners, not leaders; promises, not discipline.

It is understandable that the people in the democracies still demand each day their daily delusion. The people in the capitalist democracies are used to a steadily rising standard of living and improving social order. Ten years of depression are not enough to shake a faith in progress acquired over prior decades if not centuries. As a matter of fact, the promises of capitalism and democracy were fulfilled to a much greater extent during the nineteenth century than have been those of Marxist communism in Russia or the Roosevelt New Deal in America. Capitalism promised prosperity and made good. Marxism promised a classless society, the democratic rule of industry by the workers and greater abundance for the workers than they had ever known before or could ever know under capitalism. These promises, obviously, have not been kept and do not seem likely ever to be kept, which is no reason why the Russian regime will collapse. There is no reason to suppose that any other regime would have done much better for the Russian people during the same period and under the same circumstances. The New Deal promised prosperity, full employment, the more abundant life and a balanced budget. These promises have been no better kept than those of Marxism, which, again, is not a reason for the early liquidation of the New Deal. As long as Sovietism and New Dealism can rely on war they are secure in power unless and until they lose a war. The Fascists and Nazis made fewer promises of Utopia and told their followers more truthfully that they were in for war and hardship, on which the Fascists and Nazis have made good. But it was not promises of Utopia which put the Bolsheviks or the New Dealers in power any more than the Fascists or Nazis. It was the breakdown of the preceding order or the necessities and frustrations of the situation.

The big point to remember about the new revolution is that it does not have to be sold in advance to the people. They will get it whether they like it or not. Their attempts to avert it will only hasten it. The quickest and surest route to an American Fascism or Nazism is a war to end Nazism in Europe; the next best route, perhaps, is vigilantism and witch-hunts against subversive movements at home. Only there are not enough and not important enough witches of this variety to make it possible for this route to lead very far. The so-called subversive movements in the United States are a joke. Their only social significance will be to furnish homespun demagogues easy targets for rabble-rousing and legalized or public opinion sanctioned violence and intolerance, all of which make excellent revolutionary preliminaries, if there is a revolution really in the making. These movements will make no ideological contribution to our revolution since most of their leaders and followers are well below the idea level. It would obviously be absurd to pretend that Americans will not take any ideas for a new revolution from Europe, whence we got most of our ideas for the revolution of 1776, but Americans will not take their ideas from Europe via German bus boys or New York East Side cloak and garment workers. In the sphere of action, no movement in America can be important, the majority of whose following do not have English names and are not of Protestant ancestry.

The new revolution the American people are going to have will not be sold to them. They will, instead, be sold a war to stop revolution in Europe, and in this way they will get a stiff dose of the same revolution in America. The American people are not in the market for a revolution. They are in the market for international righteousness, a war, prosperity with a balanced budget, lower taxes and sundry other crackpot schemes of the funny money or ham and eggs varieties. In the pursuit of various will-o'-the-wisps, the American people will get experience, disillusionment and a revolution they are now not bargaining for. The real leaders of the new American revolution will at some stage of the collapse have to sell themselves personally to a considerable number of the people. But this will be possible only after the necessities of the situation and the frustrations of the people have taken command.

Just for the moment it may be said that the more truthfully the facts of the present and the possibilities of the future are presented in discussion, the better it will be all around, except for democratic politicians who want to get on the public payroll immediately or to remain on it. An interesting difference between the patriot of today and his counterpart in the rise of the capitalist revolution of yesterday is that today's patriot will really try to avert developments like American entry into the European war and to mitigate the anarchic practices of domestic politics which will produce the mature phase for the full inauguration of the new revolution, whereas the decent believer in the liberal revolution fifty to a couple hundred years ago, tried to hasten its coming or progress as much as he could. The patriot in 1776 did not mind burning British tea in Boston harbor, but the American patriot of 1940 is not eager to pour American oil on the European conflagration. It is the friends of democracy and capitalism who can be relied upon to land this country in war and thus to hasten the new revolution. Patriots who believe in the new revolution would retard its coming by preventing its coming through war. Those who do not believe in the new revolution would hasten its coming by going to war against it. The enlightened patriot in 1940 is an isolationist of the variety branded by President Roosevelt as an ostrich. If he is intelligent, he knows that the war party is bound to win the first round. Democracy and a commercial press and radio make America a push-over for Mr. Roosevelt and the British to take into war whenever it suits their interests.

So the enlightened and realistic patriots of today are for a time condemned to playing a passive and inglorious role. They cannot share the illusions of the masses and those who will lead them into the most futile and disastrous war in our history. But they will not be able to oppose effectively that war and, once it is declared, they will have no choice but to fight for their country right or wrong. As long as they can legally express an opinion about it, they will point out the futility of our fighting twice in one generation for the selfish interests and phony idealism of Great Britain and international capitalism. After war is declared, they will have but one thought, the coming of the day when those opposed to our entry into the war will have their innings.

American patriots of 1940 cannot check the follies of democracy on its last legs. Beyond the point at which war is declared they must help to exaggerate these follies. They must leave it to war to deliver the new revolution. The second world war will destroy democracy and capitalism to the pious prayers of its friends and the frenzied plaudits of the rabble in this country, where these plaudits will be wilder than they were in any of the European belligerent countries at the beginning of the conflict.

Chapter X
We Fight Because of Democracy's Failure

The immediate causes of the present world war and the new revolution are the failures of the victorious nations and of the Versailles system, and, in addition, of course, the fundamental reasons for such failures. These reasons were extensively discussed in the five chapters of Part II. The post-Versailles failures have been economic, diplomatic and political. They occurred mainly during the twenties while democracy and capitalism rode high, wide and handsome. They were not due to Hitler. He was due to them.

The essence of these failures was an inability to preserve the old or to create the new. Now war has come both to destroy the old and bring forth the new. That war has to do this, is an indictment of democracy and a refutation of the enlightenment. The American patriot of today deeply deplores the tragedy but marks it down as the final proof that democracy has failed. War has come to give us the new revolution simply because we, in the democracies, were unable to achieve it bloodlessly during twenty years of peace and world supremacy. No victorious alliance was ever more powerful than that headed at Paris by the two greatest liberals and ablest politicians of twentieth-century democracy, Woodrow Wilson and David Lloyd George. Over twenty million lives were sacrificed in order to give these liberal messiahs power to make the world safe for democracy and capitalism.

For the many reasons developed in Part II it would doubtless have proved impossible for any quality or type of democratic statesmanship to have averted either October 1929 or September 1939. Be that as it may, it has to be admitted that allied statesmanship did not even try intelligently to do so. This was clearly pointed out by John Maynard Keynes in a book published just after Versailles and entitled *The Economic Consequences of the Peace.* The performance of democracy triumphant and capitalism rampant during the twenties cannot be dismissed now with an airy, "They'll do better next time." The first blunder of the democracies at Versailles, of course, was an indecent refusal to show prudent moderation as was displayed by the victors at the conference of Vienna in similar circumstances a century earlier.

They wanted a peace of blood and iron enforced by words and paper. The same mass irrationality in America at the beginning of 1940 wants the destruction of Nazism but not the necessary American contribution to this end. Of course, an irrational mass mind, torn between conflicting emotions, will unquestionably, in the final analysis, be carried away by its passion rather than held back by its pusillanimity. Nothing could be more pusillanimous than the prevailing combination of American opinions that Europeans should be encouraged to fight to the bitter end for the right and the freedom of the world and that Americans should keep out of the fight. Obviously, if a nation takes the moral view of the war affected by the American mass mind under the incitation of long sustained and cleverly directed propaganda, then the only self-respecting thing that nation can do is to back up with its arms its convictions, its moral principles and what it believes to be the defense of its own freedom. Either our beliefs about the war are wrong or our staying out of the war is shortsighted and pusillanimous.

Another important inconsistency or irrationality of the victorious democracies at Versailles was that they sought on one hand to perpetuate the institutional status quo of capitalism and democracy and on the other hand to introduce the most radical innovations, such, for instance, as the creation of the successor states. In other words, they upheld at the same time the internationalist ideal of a world capitalism and the nationalist ideals of numerous petty ethnic minorities in Europe. Their hope, of course, was that the power of the international money system would prove mightier than the forces for economic disintegration generated by the myriad national systems being set up or inflated at Versailles. They regarded different nationalisms more or less as the American rich have long regarded Tammany politics or, for that matter, all American politics, something the muckers can be allowed to play with, enrich themselves with and keep the populace amused with as long as the plutocracy is able to have the really important things done or upheld by government as the plutocracy desires.

The Wilsonian idealists were politically and psychologically too naive to perceive that if militant nationalism were to be raised to a factor of the first magnitude in the postwar world, it could only transpire that the two largest racial groups in Europe, the Russians and the Germans, the former dominated by the crusading Bolshevist faith and the latter animated by a fierce defeat and humiliation-engendered hate, must sooner or later come to supreme power over most of Europe, as has since happened. The reasons were as obvious in 1919 as in 1939: The Germans were twice as numerous as the Italians or the French and three times as numerous as the next largest ethnic minority, that of the Poles, while the Russians were three and a half times as numerous as either the French or Italians. The German annual total of births greatly exceeds that of Britain and France while twice as many Russians are born every year as Americans and three times as many as Britishers and Frenchmen combined. In quality for industrial or war purposes, the Germans were and are second to no people. The Allies, of course, hoped by self-determination to place a swarm of ethnic Lilliputs over the great Germanic and Slavic Gullivers. And Mr. Wilson's legalist mind doubtless took it for granted that factors as real as German population-and-industrial-production superiority in quantity and quality could be held in check by a few lines of contractual lawyerese set down in treaties and League covenants.

It is not merely hindsight to say that if the Allies were interested in preserving the institutional status quo of democracy and capitalism, they should never have unleashed on Europe a wave of self-determination. Doubtless that institutional status quo could not be preserved. Be that as it may, the victorious Allies made no rational attempt to preserve it. They should, instead, have used their victory and resulting power to force upon a greater rather than a smaller Germany—say the greater Germany after the treaty of Brest Litovsk—and on a reconstituted central European federal state, now supposed to be the supreme war objective—with its capital at Vienna, a free-trade regime. The Allies should then have used their monopoly of power and food supplies to force upon all the Balkan states membership in a Pan-European customs union upon which they would also have imposed extensive free trade with themselves. The chief reasons the Allies did nothing so intelligent for the attempted preservation of international capitalism and democracy as to use their power in a rational effort to create European economic unity were: First, their leaders, including Messrs. Wilson and Lloyd George, had not the slightest idea of the economics of capitalism or the mechanics of political power. They knew, of course, how to win elections and lawsuits under the democratic regime, but they did not know that these rather specialized forms of contest for power are not all there is to the struggle for political power. Second, the stage had been reached in American as well as French industrialization at which protectionist monopoly had become vitally essential to stability and profits. American and French industries were not geared to world free-trade competition and knew it. The British also were not and did not then know it. They recognized it in 1932 when they went protectionist.

In financial and monetary matters the British at and just after Versailles expected to outstrip their competitors. This expectation has been rewarded with as fine a basket of dead sea fruit as any crew of international bankers ever harvested. Following the advice of the Cunliife Committee drawn up just before the armistice, the British attempted to do all the sound things for recovery such as deflating the currency and bank credit, balancing the budget, retiring the public debt and returning to the gold standard. American bankers rushed in to take part in and profit from the supposedly world-wide return to normalcy. The movement profited mainly the American bankers. The American investors who bought the now worthless foreign bonds gave the party for their bankers. British bankers could not sell so many bonds but they did reap large profits on the high money rates caused by wild German short-term borrowing and by the Wall Street speculative boom. So, while the two crazy booms lasted, a good time was had by both Wall and Threadneedle streets. But the profits of high money rates have since been largely wiped out by the losses suffered by all international lenders on the German and central European standstill agreements by which over a billion dollars of short-term loans have been liquidated on a basis of a fifty per cent and sometimes a higher discount.

Briefly, the whole attempt of the twenties to restore the pre-war money system operated from London and for London ended in complete failure, American investors being among the biggest victims. The failure was first officially acknowledged when the British struck their financial colors in September 1931 by going off gold. Our corresponding devaluation of the dollar in 1933-1934 made the abandonment of the world money system unanimous, since what Britain and America do in monetary and exchange matters has sooner or later to be done by every other nation. At the outbreak of the world war in 1914 the pound temporarily went to a premium, being quoted in some transactions as high as $5.70 as against a parity of $4.86. It was pegged until March 1919 around $4.75. Since the outbreak of the World War in 1939 the pound has been allowed to break from $4.60 to $3.60-$4.

The moral of the failure of international finance or the British system during the past two decades is simply this: If this system could not right the world after the victory of Versailles, why suppose that it can right the world after another Versailles victory to be won, as before, with American aid? In other words, what allied propaganda now seeks is again to enlist America to fight for the lost cause of capitalism. This time the war is more clearly than before for the preservation of international capitalism since this time the enemy is consciously and avowedly anti-capitalist. In 1914 Germany was really fighting international capitalism but did not know it until near the end of the war, and even then probably most of the German ruling classes did not understand who their real enemy was. This time the Have-nots know what the war is all about. It is easy to say that the Allies are fighting not for capitalism but for justice, righteousness, honor, truth, freedom and self-protection. Granting all this, it remains none the less true that, if they should win, the problem of organizing peace would still be one of making capitalism work as it was not found possible to do during the twenties. The Allies enthroned righteousness, truth, honor, justice, freedom, etc., etc., at Versailles and we cannot question that the military and economic supremacy of the triumphant democracies during the twenties was the rule of the high principles and ideals for which they stand. Still and all, this rule of the saints, did not work economically. Is there any reason to suppose that, with the system unchanged, it would work any better after the angels had once more triumphed over the devils?

This point also has relevancy to what may be expected of the German people if the warfare against them is intensified, in the name of righteousness, of course. Can they, in the light of the post-Versailles failures of capitalism, expect any economic improvement if they surrender on the terms of the Allies? They can see the ten million unemployed in America. They can recall the six million unemployed in Germany in 1932 before Hitler came to power under an Allies-imposed democracy from which Wall Street had shut off its lifeblood of loans from gullible American investors. They can reflect that Germany defeated or victorious would not have the wealth of the United States to mitigate with colossal relief deficits chronic unemployment such as democracy and capitalism cannot now avert. The proof that democracy cannot solve unemployment, of course, is the American record of the past ten years. War may be terrible, but stagnation as a result of defeat or surrender would be no less so. If Hitler's war regime is a harsh dictatorship would the occupation of

Germany by a French African army be any less harsh or distasteful?

Taking a realistic view of the facts of the past ten years and the continued failure of democracy to solve unemployment and balance the budget in America, it may be said that the peoples of the Have-not nations have no incentive either to keep the peace as imposed by the Haves or to accept an Allied peace which could hardly offer the German Have-nots more than it offers the underprivileged third of the American population now living at a sub-decency level.

The most insane kind of a war is one for a lost cause, the very fighting of which must help doom that cause. If the new revolution comes about through war, its coming in that way will be the fault of the Haves who were in peaceful enjoyment of a large measure of world economic power for over a decade after Versailles for not having recognized the breakdown of their system and inaugurated under peaceful circumstances, before it was too late, the inevitable new revolution.

If the new revolution has to come about through war, it will be the fault of the Haves or the defenders of capitalism and democracy for having made war the only practicable way to world reorganization. The war cry at once raised by the British in September 1939 that they were fighting only to end Hitlerism and the Nazis makes sense only if it means that the revolution begun and carried on up to date by the Nazis has to be stopped if the Allies win. Obviously, it would not make sense for the British and French to fight a modern war against Germany simply to effect a change in the leadership of a German revolution. If the new revolution goes on, it can make little practical difference to the Allies, to ourselves or the people of Germany what changes take place in the personalities of the leaders.

CHAPTER XI
From Capitalist to Socialist Imperialism

One of the hardest facts about the new revolution for Americans as well as the British to understand is that it means the end of the British Empire. The new revolution, obviously, does not mean the end of imperialism, of political and economic concentration of power, of the rule of the weak by the strong, of the absorption of the small by the large or of the rule of naked power. But the new revolution, in its very essence, is the erection of socialist imperialism on the ruins of capitalist imperialism. This must mean, among other things, the liquidation of the British Empire, the keystone of which is money or money lending and money manipulation. The United States over the Western Hemisphere, Germany over a considerable part of Europe, Italy over a considerable part of the Mediterranean and North Africa, France over her self-sufficient territory in Europe and some of North Africa, Russia over eastern Europe and central Asia and Japan with/or China over the Far East can survive by going national socialist. In so doing each of the great powers just named can practice imperialism as indicated by the exigencies of special situations, needs and relationships. The smaller Scandinavian countries, Spain, Portugal, Switzerland and the low countries, to the extent and in the manner approved and prescribed by the great powers immediately concerned can also survive independently on a national socialist basis, each being largely self-sufficient and not dependent on parasitic forms of foreign income.

But the British Empire can never go national socialist since the essence of the present relationship of the home country as money lender, investor and banker to the colonies is a parasitism which no conceivable variety of workable socialism and economic autarchy can long tolerate. That is the supreme tragedy of the British people in this fateful hour of their destiny. Majority public opinion in the British colonies at the present time, of course, would indignantly, sentimentally and loyally repudiate this pronouncement. That, however, is of no long run importance any more than the gold clauses on American government gold bonds and currency gold certificates were in the face of the imperious pressure of revolutionary economic change to force repudiation.

The British have foreign investments totaling some £3,292,000,000 or some $16 billion at the old parity of dollar-pound exchange. Most of these investments are in the British Empire. In 1937 they yielded Britain an income of £210,000,000, or roughly a billion dollars, which was about 4% of the total national income of Great Britain. This is not a large percentage. But it is a highly important financial quantity as it means a source of supply of foreign exchange. In 1937 Britain's net import of commodities, that is of commodities retained for British use and not re-exported, was £952,000,000. They were paid for with exports valued at £521,000,000 (F.O.B.) by foreign investment income valued at £210,000,000; shipping services rendered to other countries amounting to £130,000,000; by commissions earned by banks, insurance companies and other institutions amounting to £40,000,000; by £5,000,000 of miscellaneous receipts; and by some £45,000,000 from the liquidation of foreign assets. All in all, over £400,000,000 or some $2,000,000,000 in foreign cash from foreign investment income and liquidation and for services sold to foreigners was needed in that recent year of comparative prosperity to balance the British accounts with the world.

If the world went national socialist or autarchist, most of this cash income from abroad would be permanently lost to Britain. Her imports would have to be cut correspondingly, if not in excess of this figure, since her commodity exports would be sure to decline in a world of nations all pursuing policies of increased self-sufficiency and all industrializing; the less industrialized nations, of course, industrializing most.

If Britain had to cut her commodity imports forty per cent to match her diminished foreign money income, she would have to lower real wages, thus inviting revolt by labor, and she would also have to raise taxes and curtail the capital or unearned income of the wealthy, thus inducing a large-scale flight of British enterprisers and stagnation among those who remained. Economic retrenchment in Britain would entail a whole series of disasters for the British polity and economy. Wiping out foreign cash income on investments and services, which amounts to only some eight per cent of the total national income, will be a far more serious business than this percentage would indicate. It will not mean merely an eight per cent lower standard of living. It will mean the difference between the bearable economic stagnation of the recent past and an unbearable economic stagnation of the near future.

To get a proper basis of comparison by which to appraise the new British economic situation after the world has gone national socialist, it is necessary to bear in mind the following: When British economy was in a healthy state before the war, its commodity exports were so large in relation to its imports that its combined income from sales of goods and services (shipping and financial) and from foreign investments was large enough not only to pay for all imports but, also, to allow a yearly increase of some seven hundred million dollars to twelve hundred million dollars in British portfolio foreign investments. Recently the British have been reducing the total of their foreign assets by two or three hundred million dollars a year. During the war they will reduce the total as much as the day-to-day possibilities of liquidation will allow. After the war, socialism will practically wipe out such investments. Then the British economy, which is geared to a velocity of operation and to types of production of exports and shipping services which allowed a net yearly increase of around a billion dollars in foreign investments, will have to operate almost without income from foreign investments or shipping. In other words, the British economic metabolism flourished for a long time putting on foreign fat; then, for a short time, it lived on that fat; and, finally, as a sequel of a serious illness, it has to lose all its foreign fat and thereafter to live, an emaciated, anemic shell of its former self, wholly without foreign fat.

There is an almost universal tendency among American economists to assume that the British Empire can go national socialist as easily as an economically self-contained and geographically integrated Germany, Russia or United States, once Britain exchanges the rule of the old school tie for that of the new breed of socialist Caesars. The assumption will not bear analysis. Canada, Australia, New Zealand, South Africa and India, to mention only the major economic units of the British Empire, would never, as national socialist states, pay toll or tribute to the English investor, the English banker, the English manufacturer, the English merchant or the English crown. Why should they? They can print their own money, manufacture their own bank credit, manufacture all the goods the British manufacture, sail their own ships and defend themselves.

The notion that the British defend their colonies is largely erroneous. The colonies defend England—just why, they are bound sooner or later to ask themselves. We defend Canada. If the Australians or the Indians needed defense from Japan, the English could not supply it. The British Empire today simply is not a unit for defense purposes as is Russia or the United States. The English need all their fleet to defend their home islands and insure supplies. They, therefore, are of no practical use for the defense of their major colonies.

It may be argued that if the British fleet were not able to hold off Germany and to blockade other potential aggressors, none of the colonies would be safe from them. The problem has to be considered from another angle. Of course, England's fighting Germany and holding a naval threat over the heads of the Japanese and Italians adds to the defense factors of the British colonies. But that is not the question. The question is whether in the present or rather the future state of world economic organization the British can afford to maintain their fleet and fight a major war with the Have-nots every twenty-five years. If the British cannot afford to contribute heavily to this brand of protection for the colonies out of the profits of their foreign trade and out of their foreign financial income, there is nothing to hold the empire together.

In brief, the financial and defense sides of the British Empire are mutually complementary and dependent on each other. If British finance capitalism has to succumb to socialism in and after the war, and no socialism can tolerate absentee finance capitalism, Britain cannot thereafter afford empire defense and a world war with Germany every generation for the safety of the British colonies. The British colonies, therefore, willy-nilly must then look to other arrangements and policies for their defense as well as be their own bankers and manufacturers.

If British capitalism will not pay, British imperialism will not work. This does not mean that imperialism will pass with capitalism. It merely means that, without capitalism, without the power of money and without world-wide respect for the money system, its ways, myths and contracts, without all these, a little island of nervy adventurers cannot rule a third of the earth. Money knows no geographic limits that is why the British people did not laugh when they guaranteed Poland), but socialism does, and so does military strategy. In the mysticism of money, credit and British ideology, the British Empire is a unit. But in the realism of geography, military strategy and socialistic policy, the British Empire is not and never can be a unit for political administration, economic planning or military defense.

America from the North Pole to the Cape of Good Hope is already, geographically, a unit for defense by a preeminent United States. This hemispheric area could possibly be made a unit for economic planning and barter under our hegemony. For our complete political domination, the area from the North Pole to the Rio Grande is a natural unit, and possibly also from the North Pole to the Panama Canal. The Russian empire is clearly a unit for political and economic administrative and military defense purposes. A French empire in North Africa, an Italian empire in another part of the Mediterranean and a German empire from the Baltic and North Seas to the Black, Aegean and the Adriatic Seas, could all become workable political and economic units and defensible military units. But the British Empire, in the breakdown of finance capitalism and the world-wide dominance of socialism, is an utterly impossible unit, politically, economically and militarily. Hence the utter folly of our lighting for it.

The British have overpopulated the British islands on the assumption that foreign tribute to British money and other monopolies would always take care of a population in excess of the islands' means of subsistence. For more than twenty years now the British have not been able to market the output of three of their oldest and best monopolies, coal, shipbuilding and textiles. The evidence and consequences may be observed in the "special areas" of Wales, the Tyneside, the Clydeside and parts of the midlands in which men have grown to middle age on the dole without ever once in their entire lives having held a steady job. What has happened during the past twenty years to British coal, shipbuilding and textiles will happen in the next twenty years to British finance. As it does, the curtain will fall on the greatest imperial pageant of history. And, as the world goes national socialist, the British isles will turn into a settlement house, or world charity case No. 1. It is not strange, then, that, in fighting for the perpetuation of their doomed economic power and system, the British make their war objectives synonymous with every moral absolute men are known to cherish. For the British, the new revolution and their war effort to stop it are life-and-death matters. For us they ought to be only a great historical spectacle and lesson. But education, apparently, comes only through experience; and experience comes high. So we shall probably have to sacrifice hundreds of thousands of American lives and billions of dollars worth of American resources to learn that when an empire or a system has to go, it has to go.

ENTER SOCIALIST IMPERIALISM

The failures of the democracies since Versailles in diplomacy as well as in economics augur ill for their success both in and after the present world war and both presage and suggest the outline of the new revolution. The outbreak of war in 1939, of course, was, in itself, the most shattering single proof of democracy's post-Versailles failure. The fact that a nation as badly beaten and as completely overpowered as Germany was in 1919 should be able twenty years later to defy her victors of two decades earlier is a fair measure of the failure of diplomacy and statesmanship among the democracies. Having made in 1919 a peace harsh enough to create Hitler, the Allies, as late as 1935, or four years before the outbreak of the world war, had not the intelligence or the unity to prevent the re-militarization by Hitler of the Rhineland. Players holding poor cards usually play them badly.

It is easy to explain as typically British muddling the blunders of imposing a harsh peace on the world's most warlike and efficient people and Europe's most numerous breed, and taking no subsequent steps for its enforcement. It is plausible to account for the non-application of effective sanctions against Japan in 1931, against Italy in 1935-1936 and against Hitler in 1937 on the same general ground. But these facile and popular explanations will not hold water. For one thing, the British are not a stupid race nor, in foreign affairs, are they inexperienced or naive. Still less are they congenitally incapable of long-run calculation or quick action. They did not get their empire by being ninnies or in a fit of absent-mindedness. If their statesmanship has failed to avert a second world war in one generation, the explanation is to be found in a changed situation and a bankrupt system rather than in the deterioration of British statesmanship.

From Versailles to Warsaw, the statesmanship of the democracies played a role of weakness and impotency because money had lost its power. The British and their American and French disciples never believed up to September 2, 1939, that a bankrupt Germany could, if it would, challenge the armed might of the richest nations in the world. Even after the British had declared war on Germany, they continued for a considerable time to cherish the fond illusion that, by virtue of their money superiority, they could win the war almost without fighting. Gold, God and the fleet were supposed to do most of the fighting necessary for the defense of Britain. The fact that British and American statesmanship never, until the last, believed money could be successfully defied by bankruptcy, God by Bolshevism and sea power by land power, is not so much a reflection on the intelligence of the responsible statesmen as an indictment of the scholarship and social thought dominant in the democracies during the twenties. The so-called social scientists of the democracies have not prepared their peoples for the events of the forties for the simple reason that, by and large, the social scientists of capitalism are commercialized, intellectual prostitutes who pander to the tastes of their patrons. The simplest way to prove this is to try to get a realistic discussion of a current social problem published in an American publication or aired over an American radio network.

After Versailles the British could have acceded to the French demand for an ironclad Anglo-French military alliance to keep Germany down and to uphold in a realistic fashion the Versailles system. French military men, with the contempt for capitalism apt to be characteristic of their profession, argued that such an alliance, implemented by a perpetual military occupation of the Rhineland and complete and effective military control of Germany was the only formula for continued peace and security along Versailles lines. They were entirely right. British statesmanship had faith in the power and hopes in the future of money. With such faith and hopes, the British shrank from the costs and implications of a purely military policy on the Continent. Of course, if the power of money made a military enforcement of Versailles superfluous, then, from the British point of view, it was doubly undesirable, since the military repression of Germany in perpetuity was obviously uneconomic in capitalistic terms. The simple logic of it all was that if such measures were necessary and were, as in the nature of things they had to be, extremely bad business, then Britain and capitalism were doomed anyway and Versailles had been won in vain. Obviously, the British were reluctant to make any such admission.

The truth is that if the power of money is finished, so are the power and prosperity of Britain. She has far too many mouths to feed to operate on any basis of pay-as-you-go, produce-what-you-consume and international-barter, national socialism. The tragedy of all this for Americans is that we shall have to be dragged down with the collapse of money and Britain, because British propaganda and the ideology of capitalism have made us the ultimate support of the system.

As Voigt points out so clearly in *Unto Caesar*, other nations may lose wars and recover, but Britain can lose only one war, her last war.

Since the Reformation, Britain has never lost a war, except, after a manner of speaking, that of the American Revolution. Subsequent developments, however, have so subordinated the United States to British interests that the American Revolution can no longer be considered a loss for the British Empire. We are still, now more than ever, a British colony, and by reason of our technical separation from Britain we have been able to develop into an infinitely more powerful and useful ally of the empire than any of the other colonies. If Britain loses a war, she loses her empire and her financial primacy. If socialism triumphs, she has to lose them anyway. With these lost, Britain is through, not only as a great power, but also as a self-sufficient nation.

No other nation in Europe is so dependent on capitalism as Great Britain. No other nation faces as great difficulties in the course of a transition to socialism. If the British have to go under as a great power with the passing of capitalism, it is in keeping with their tradition that they as a people should go down with their ship, fighting to the last. But it is rather silly of us Americans who are the most favorably situated of any people in the world to get on noncapitalistically, to stand with the British on the burning deck of their sinking ship until it goes under. The more Englishmen who are killed and the more their fertility is diminished by prolonged war, the easier will be their ultimate task of living on reduced territorial resources. But no matter how many Englishmen die fighting for capitalism they cannot save it in war this time any better than they could in peace during the twenties and thirties when they, in common with all the triumphant Allies, were flushed with the fruits of the Versailles victory.

From a purely humanitarian and British-loving point of view, it would be vastly more sensible for America to bid England and France stop the war, which they might do, if we told them that they could under no circumstances count on our assistance in the event of its continuance, and if we then assumed full responsibility for the rehabilitation of Britain and the defense of such parts of the empire, under our flag, as we might decide, on strategic grounds, we could reasonably carry out. The real question for us, so far as the British are concerned, is whether we take them over before they are ruined or afterward. There would appear to be a strong case in logic for doing it before instead of afterwards. But logic, like the flowers that bloom in the spring, has nothing to do with the case, and, as habit and passion have everything to do with it, the British will probably have to be ruined with our assistance before their rehabilitation along permanently workable lines can ever receive serious consideration. After we have assisted them through war to the lowest depths of collapse, they may be harder to rehabilitate than at present.

Rehabilitation of Britain by the United States to adjust it to the requirements of the new revolution would, of course, be possible only after we had undergone revolutionary changes ourselves. We should have to revamp our economy so as to permit of the absorption into the United States and Canada of some twenty million British immigrants. That we obviously could not do with ten million Americans already unemployed in this country. We should have to take over Canada and Australia and write off all the British possessions in Africa, Asia and the Mediterranean as well as absorb the excess population of the United Kingdom. Australia could be made invulnerable to invasion by means of appropriate coast defenses, industrial diversification and economic organization. The defense of the entire American hemisphere by ourselves would present no insuperable difficulty. We should abandon Britain's African, Asiatic and Mediterranean possessions and stations to those best able to grab and hold them.

A gigantic reorganization of the parts of the British Empire which we could defend under an American receivership and reorganization could create a new Anglo-Saxon world which would be not only invincible in a military way but workable in an economic way. The United Kingdom would become another Sweden. The royal family might be kept as a tourist attraction like the quintuplets in Canada. The English would be humbler but happier. It is a revolutionary project, but this is pre-eminently a moment in which new revolutionary projects are necessary for survival. The trouble with our squandering billions of dollars and millions of lives trying to save the British by exterminating bad Germans, bad Japanese and bad Russians is that such expenditure, no matter how successful in destroying British foes, will not—cannot, create for the British a post-war bread-and-butter solution.

Of course, my suggestion for an American receivership for the British before instead of after their total bankruptcy and collapse will not receive serious attention in any responsible allied quarter, either here or abroad. I do not make it with any such expectation. It is my fixed conviction that the British have to commit imperial suicide as a *beau geste* in keeping with their glorious past and that we Americans have to accompany them quite far in their Götterdämmerung in keeping with the sentimentalism and irrationality of a democracy untempered by enough recent suffering to make realism comprehensible to the masses of the people.

I am, however, deeply sincere in expressing a wish to help the British people. This interest in the British as people and not in their system has its basis in race and not in money. I respect and cherish the values of British blood but not the values of capitalism or any other form of a now doomed internationalism. I would do anything feasible to perpetuate the British as a people and to amalgamate as many as possible of them with ourselves. I am opposed to our taking station on and going down with their sinking ship, international capitalism, as I feel sure we shall do. I value people more highly than systems. The new revolution will go on. The British people can survive by adjusting themselves to the new after centuries of adjustment to the old or they may suffer incalculably by a hopeless defense of the old order and futile opposition to the new order.

There are many thinkers in the democracies today who recognize the inevitability of revolutionary change, but would have it carried out everywhere by their crowd, which, of course, is the great democracies. Thus Clarence Streit's much discussed *Union Now* and innumerable other similar proposals emanating from allied sources as propaganda these days, all favor a rather drastic reorganization of the world by the right people, meaning the British, assisted by ourselves, the French, the small neutrals and generally the international satellites of the British. Actually, these proposals, if carried out, would constitute a more revolutionary change than anything so far envisaged by the Fascists, Nazis or communists.

From the point of view of this book, which is anything but pacifistic, the main trouble with these proposals is that they call for the imposition on all mankind of an Anglo-American revolution, something which seems preposterously unattainable to any realist. Revolution, every nation and people must have, but it has to be carried out by each nation. In the name of democracy and freedom, the British and the French are in 1940 fighting to end in Germany a German revolution appropriate to the 20th Century and there to impose the 17th and 18th Century revolutions of Britain and France which are over everywhere. Revolution must come from within, not from without. I should oppose a proposal for an Anglo-American-French conquest of the world for the same reason I oppose the Streit or any other similar plan for a world order conceived and enforced by the aforesaid three power combination. Reasons: It can't be done and the attempt to do it will be an unmitigated disaster. We can extend our moral or legal control only as far as our guns can shoot and only as long as they can shoot that far. Any sort of hegemony envisioned in terms of other assumptions or hypotheses is a pure chimera as all past experience shows.

It is easy to formulate a hegemony of the democracies on purely moral or legal bases. But the creation and maintenance of such a hegemony, to the realist, presents only the following questions: Whom do we have to fight to impose it? When? Where? How? And with what chances of success? We can answer summarily that any such hegemony is, ipso facto, a scheme of the Haves which will have to be imposed by arms on the militant Have-nots who now greatly outnumber and outwork the Haves, even if they are inferior in economic resources to the Haves. A realist cannot take seriously any proposal, however piously or idealistically it may be dressed up, which is tantamount to an attempt to force upon four hundred million Germans, Russians, Japanese and Italians a world order which is unacceptable to them and would be essentially discriminatory in favor of the two hundred and forty million white British, American and French Haves. This view is by no means taken out of sympathy with the four hundred million dissatisfied. Anything the British and French can put over on the Germans, Russians or Japanese or any other people outside the Americas is all right as far as I am concerned, provided they can do it without our aid. Conversely anything the Germans, Russians or Japanese can put over on the British and French or any other people outside the Americas is equally not my concern. To take a different view is logically to commit one's country to a permanent military alliance with the countries one assumes one must protect and preserve in their present boundaries. And to make this commitment of the United States to a perpetual defense of any foreign empires and boundaries, would entitle us to a large measure of control over the policies of the countries we guarantee. Otherwise we should be in the position of a person who guaranteed all the liabilities of a partnership, shared title to none of its assets or income, and had no voice in its management. Such a person would not be a partner but a sucker. If the money system cannot support British hegemony without necessity for a world war in which we must take part against the wicked challengers every twenty-five years, there is something wrong with the money system and something impractical about the British hegemony.

Chapter XII
The Return to Discipline
The Old Freedom and the New Discipline

The old revolution of capitalism was a revolt for economic freedom. The new revolution of socialism is a revolt against economic freedom. The old revolution was a revolt for power for money. The new revolution is a revolt against the power of money. Great Britain as the world's oldest and still its premier banker is obviously indicated to be the first victim of this revolt. This new revolt, of course, is due mainly to the failure of the money power either to avert or end the depression unaided by government spending and to the failure of the money power also to prevent a second world war in one generation.

To understand the revolt against free trade and economic freedom, one must understand the past raison d'être and the present failure of free trade and economic freedom. One of the many anomalies of the topsy-turvy world since 1914 has been the support given by free traders, internationalists, idealists, bankers and college professors to the multiplication and defense by allied statesmanship of small nations whose economic nationalism has been in complete variance with the imperatives of liberal economic freedom. The same internationalists have been loudest in denouncing the efforts of Japan, Italy, Germany and Russia to enlarge certain areas under their respective controls within which free trade can actually be practiced. The explanation of this inconsistency, of course, is that the internationalists do not want regionalized but universalized free trade; they do not want greater power for great powers but greater power for big money.

The logic of economic freedom and free trade is simply more power for money. The objective is most power for those having most money. Free trade is the self-interest of money. The free market was the interest of a submerged and emerging trading class in the days of feudalism and the ensuing commercial and industrial revolutions. The free market is not today the interest of a submerged and steadily sinking class of farmers and unemployed in the declining days of democracy and industrialism. The proofs are simple: the farmers cannot obtain a remunerative price and the unemployed cannot find jobs today in the free market. Yet they number nearly half of the working force of the nation. Free trade calls for a world economically and politically so organized and administered that money can move from one country to another as freely as migratory birds. Thus money can dictate to governments everywhere its own taxes and regulations and to labor its own wage scales, without the appearance of applying physical force. It is truly a marvelous system when it works according to the liberal storybooks. If the terms of capital are not met satisfactorily in one place, it can make its coercive power felt by the altogether lawful and thoroughly non-violent procedure of flight or passive resistance. Thus it puts pressure on the gold reserves and security markets, on banks and their debtors, and on labor employed in industry and trade in the area not meeting money's demands, which is euphemistically called failing to act in a way to inspire business confidence. This is the freedom for money for which hundreds of thousands of Americans must die on European battlefields though they, themselves, never had enough money from one pay day to another to get clear of debt.

The money power, if free trade and economic freedom are upheld generally, can be exercised with total anonymity and irresponsibility so far as persons and corporations are concerned. Mr. Roosevelt is to blame for every failure of the New Deal, as, for instance, that of not balancing the budget or maintaining recovery. But, thanks to economic freedom, American business cannot be blamed for the failure of American finance to keep the banks open in 1933 or of American industry to keep men at work. The money power can make millions jobless and destitute without once firing a single shot or emitting an audible sound or explanation of what it is doing. It is, of course, nonsense to try to personify or identify the money power as a given group, clique or individual in Wall Street, Lombard Street or anywhere else. The rare charm of economic freedom is that nobody is ever responsible for anything that happens. No conspiracy can be proved if international capitalists start taking their money out of one country, as our Committee of the Nation did in early 1933. Why has no government investigation ever exposed the names of the bankers, gentlemen and patriots who sold dollars for foreign currencies and shipped gold abroad during the first two months of 1933? No one is to blame if the action of capitalists forces banks to call loans and curtail lines of credit, thus inducing a panic of depositor withdrawals and liquidation on the security markets. The responsible capitalists are simply private citizens legitimately and properly exercising their constitutional right as free individuals to do what they please with what is their own. In committing the acts which add up to a national disaster, these myriad rugged individualists have no intention of producing such disaster. In fact, they neither know nor care what the result will be to which their individual acts contribute. They have the word of Adam Smith and all the pious humbugs rationalizing liberalism, democracy and capitalism ever since that the result can be only for the common good. An invisible hand guides all this. If you do not believe it, you lack faith in democracy and freedom. If it is not true, democracy does not work. No conspiracy or illegal acts can be proved if a number of companies shut down factories in New England and transfer production to the South because wages and taxes are lower there. Given free trade, if a number of companies shut down factories in a country where wages and living standards are high to transfer production to countries where wages and living standards are low, they are guilty of no wrongdoing but rather of the exercise of sound business judgment.

It is not strange that Wall Street and the holders of great fortunes in America and throughout the world generally believe in free trade and economic freedom, or that the rich in this country are the main contributors to the Liberty League or that the husband of the richest woman in the world, the Social Register and the colleges and foundations they endow are for Britain, liberty, democracy and war. In 1940 America the rich want liberty and the poor want ham and eggs and there is no connection between the two. Millions of simple souls have imbibed the indoctrination of the classroom about liberty and now believe it as gospel truth. The doctrine of free trade, economic freedom and laissez faire was developed in England in connection with a shift in policy from the monopoly of the eighteenth century to that of the nineteenth century. The British in the eighteenth century pursued monopoly by means of mercantilism; in the nineteenth century they pursued it by other means—free trade. In *The Wealth of Nations*, published in 1776, Adam Smith showed the unsuitability of mercantilist policies and the suitability of free trade to British ends under the new conditions created by the rise of the factory system. The transition from mercantilism to free trade went on up to the middle of the nineteenth century when the last of the English corn laws were repealed. This change enabled England to achieve and exploit for over a century the biggest and juiciest series of monopolies ever enjoyed by any nation, to wit, monopolies in banking, shipping, coal, textiles, and the heavy industries. The irony of it was that free trade, the essence of which our sophomoric economists still believe to be the opposite of monopoly, was conceived, developed and propagandized by the British for over a century with great success precisely because, during that period, it was the very best possible system for making the British monopolists and yielding them monopolist profits.

But if American and Continental professors fell for Adam Smith, David Ricardo and John Stuart Mill, it did not take American and continental statesmen and businessmen long to see that free trade was nothing more or less than a British racket. So they quietly began, here after the Civil War, and in Germany after the Franco-Prussian War, to fight the British free-trade monopoly with specially protected and subsidized monopolies of their own. The essence of the British monopoly under free trade was the ability to buy cheap and sell dear. To break this up, it was necessary mainly for foreigners, by the adoption of tariff protection and subsidies, to curtail the ability of the British to sell dear. Under free trade England stood in relation to the rest of the world exactly as the American manufacturer now stands in relation to the American farmer. American industrial prices and profits are stabilized by means of price and production control, such as only monopoly can achieve, while American farm prices fall below a remunerative level. In consequence, American farm profits disappear and American farmers go on the dole, Meanwhile successful American industrial monopolies and semi-monopolies maintain prices and profits.

According to the college professors, economic competition, like cricket, is a game to be played under rules; according to experience, it is the war of all against all under which monopolies and the abuse of the weak by the strong are as inevitable as it is for big fish to eat little fish, in another sphere of competition. Fair competition is simply competition under rules and conditions which suit the interests of the person using the phrase. The most essential fact about competition of any sort is that everybody does not win. In a phase of economic expansion, the winners are abnormally numerous because of expansion and in spite of competition. Then competition proves tolerable, as it did in the nineteenth century.

Long before the World War of 1914-1918, British free trade had begun to lose out due to the rise of tariff-protected industries all over the world. But it was not until 1932 that they were forced to haul down the flag of free trade and get in step with the protectionist, state capitalist times. The main reason was that free trade had ceased to be a useful means of monopoly for the British. The British enjoyed over a century of free prosperity while they were getting away from eighteenth century mercantilism. Then they enjoyed about half a century of holding their own while the rest of the world was getting back to mercantilism. From 1914 to 1932 they suffered two decades of trade decline after the world had got back to mercantilism. From 1932 to 1957 the British had a mild prosperity under a return to state-subsidized industry or a new streamlined mercantilism, with a strongly socialist accent. The new revolution of today and tomorrow may really be said to have begun back in the seventies and eighties when America and Germany led the challenge of British free-trade monopolies by fostering tariff-subsidized domestic monopolies. The state socialism of Adolf Hitler is simply the final phase of the protectionism begun by Bismarck and McKinley, long before Hitler had cut his second teeth.

Free trade, with the money system often called the gold standard, though, in reality, never anything but the Bank of England managed currency of world trade, elaborated theoretically in the British Bullion Report of 1844 and hundreds of dull tomes by academic economists, constituted a world formula of monopoly by the British and for the British but later generously placed at the disposition of the moneylenders and money-changers of the world. This is why, for generations past, "the best people" everywhere have been fanatically pro-British. Britain made the world safe and easy for money. The best people, therefore, now feel that they should make the world safe and easy for Britain. If this costs millions of American lives, so much the worse for America.

Britain created for moneylenders and money-changers a system by means of which they could wield power and reap profits with a minimum of social responsibility. Property owners under feudalism had to accept responsibility and power, and they had to perform functions exposing them to danger. They were not free to do what they pleased with their property or to carry it around the world on a piece of paper. They had not the advantage of the British banking system, gold standard and continuous market for paper securities. The British gave money a new freedom and power. This was the birth of democracy. The system now gives millions chronic unemployment and insecurity. It, therefore, has to go and is going. Millions may die for freedom or the power of money, but they will die in vain.

It is neither hyperbole nor literary license to say that the British developed the money system or that they made of it an instrument of power and profitable monopoly first for the British and later for the moneylenders and money-changers of the world. It was the London goldsmiths of the seventeenth century who discovered in keeping gold for clients who did not trust the Stuarts that it was not necessary for the custodian of gold ever to have physical possession of as much gold as he had given out receipts for, the reason being, quite simply, that all the depositors (then bailors), of the gold never at the same time demanded their gold. The bankers later shaved down the bailee responsibility at law to that of a simple contractual relationship under which the depositor merely has a right of action or a right to sue the banker for breach of contract if he fails to honor the depositor's drafts up to the limit of the depositor's credit balance with the banker. Banking grew out of the discovery that a deposit receiver could lend out more money than he had or operate on a fractional reserve against his deposit liabilities.

The essence of the banker's monopoly under modern banking, a British discovery, is the banker's power to create money, and the essence of his racket is the ability, as long as the system works, to earn a return on more money than he actually has in his own capital plus the deposit of cash. For this monopoly to work, the banker must be able at all times to meet all demands for cash. Practically, this means that confidence in the banks must always be such that there are no serious runs on them for cash. It also requires that bankers cooperate with each other whenever one or more of them needs more cash than he has on hand. These conditions of the successful operation of the banking monopoly or racket can be met only if a worldwide system of central banks, the mother of which is the Bank of England, and of large modern banks, operates smoothly to lend each other money or gold when needed on reasonable terms.

Another feature of the British financial system was their bill of exchange by means of which imports and exports between countries all over the world were financed, i.e., payment made by the importer after ninety days and payment made promptly on shipment to the exporter, all through the medium of a sterling bill, usually a ninety day I.O.U. of the importer, guaranteed by a British bank. Through this ingenious device, British bankers and bill brokers collected a parasitic interest on lending to foreigners money kept on deposit in English banks by foreigners, and a parasitic commission for changing one foreign money into sterling to realize payment by the importer and then from sterling back into another foreign money to effectuate payment of the importer's money to the exporter. Thus, if a German bought wheat from Rumania, he had to pay in Rumanian lei via London and sterling, while another German, if he sold steel rails to Rumania, had to collect his German marks via London and sterling. Now, by means of rational barter and clearing arrangements, all this financing through London of trade which never touches England is completely short-circuited to the loss of London and to the gain of other countries, who today find ways of balancing their accounts with each other without paying toll to British moneylenders and moneychangers.

For reasons too numerous and complex for brief and easy explanation, this world-wide system whereby bankers created money and credit on which to collect interest and commissions could work only during the boom phase of world capitalism. Only such a phase could engender the necessary public confidence in such phony fabrications of credit by private monopolists of the money function. Once this phase was over, the maintenance of the system during recurring crises of ever growing severity imposed strains which society could not stand. These strains involved measures of deflation of bank credit, collection of loans, liquidation of securities, denials of new bank loans and other financial processes of a deflationary character too onerous for the community to bear. In short, the state had to suspend and reverse these processes. This meant the beginning of the end of private banking and capitalism.

Government had to suspend or, rather, end the right of private holders of currency to redeem it in gold. Government had to assume directly or indirectly, in one way or another, responsibility for all bank deposits. To assume such responsibility, the government had to exercise, without the banker-imposed limitations of the gold standard, the function of creating money. This the government achieved in various ways, all amounting to an indefinite expansion of the quantity of money and bank deposits with the result of cheapening money or lowering money rates to the vanishing point to the loss of the banks which live largely on lending money they are able to create in the form of deposits and keep outstanding. The whole function or purpose of the gold standard was to keep money scarce and dear for the benefit of the bankers whose interest it is to lend money for as high interest rates as the traffic will bear. One of the ways in which government increased the supply of money was to mark up the value of gold, thus, in our case, printing $35 instead of $20.67 against an ounce of the precious metal. In this way Washington made $4,000,000,000 of gold it had in January, 1934, worth, overnight, about $7,000,000,000. And in this way it has attracted to this country over $11,000,000,000 of gold against which paper money has been created to be held by the Federal Reserve Banks. The countries from which all this gold has come have increased the quantity of money in circulation and bank deposits while losing gold with the benefit of devaluation and without the benefit of gold or the leave of the private bankers, thus showing how superfluous both gold and private bankers are to a government printing press. Gold as a monetary instrument is doomed along with capitalism.

The big difference between bank and government created money is that bank money has to rest on confidence whereas government money rests on coercion. For banker money to be good, conditions must be such as to inspire confidence in the banks and in business. Government, on the other hand, does not have to inspire confidence in its paper or other money. Government makes its money legal tender, refuses to convert it into gold or foreign currency, and bars the use of other money. Government cannot control the purchasing power of its money except by controlling all economic production. But government can force the use of its money to the exclusion of any other money.

Government control cannot make a given quantity of money worth more than the current speed of spending and the current rate of production of goods and services will allow. Fluctuations or a slow decline in the value of money are of no great importance in a socialized economy. The only important monetary desiderata under socialism are (1) to have an unlimited supply of money always available for spending and (2) to spend enough of it or to spend it fast enough to have no unemployment. Under capitalism stable money is a vested interest of the rich or those whose fortune on net balance is in obligations. Under socialism, there is no public interest in preserving the fixed integrity or purchasing power value of fortunes in bonds or mortgages—rather just the contrary. The simplest and easiest way to tax and discourage oversaving is a slow and continuous depreciation of the currency. When the monetary unit gets too low in purchasing power, a new unit equaling so many of the old units can be adopted and the creeping inflationary process repeated ad lib. In this way the burden of the public and private debt is continuously alleviated thus making it possible continuously to create new debt for new investment.

Perpetual monetary depreciation is the only alternative to perpetual population growth, since under any money-using system, perpetual monetary inflation is an empirical necessity. This is exemplified in Stalin's and Hitler's socialism or Coolidge's and Hoover's capitalism. The only significant difference in this respect between Russian or German inflation and our inflation of the twenties is that our inflation had to collapse in a terrific deflation and could not be started up again under capitalism. It has had to be resumed since 1930 in the form of relief deficits. Socialism is a formula for perpetual inflation without periodic deflations. Depression has cut our private debt $12 billion and raised our public debt $20 billion.

The rise of government-managed money or the increasing assumption by government of the money function, the world over, has come since 1931, not as a reform demanded by the people but as a necessity demanded by the breakdown of banking in 1931-1933. These changes, which need not be explained here in detail, have involved, among other things, a great loss of freedom and a great increase in government coercion. The loss of freedom has not greatly affected individuals who can now buy more for a paper dollar than they could in 1929 when we had a kosher dollar. But this loss of freedom has meant less profit, prestige and power for bankers and the financial district.

The big point to retain about it all is that these changes were not initiated by revolutionary leaders, either in America or England. Our stock market collapsed, our commodity prices crashed, and all our banks closed under Hoover, not Hitler. For private finance now to call for a fight for economic freedom is like a man in a hospital, who has been picked up unconscious in the gutter in a fit of apoplexy, protesting against an invasion of his personal liberty and demanding its restoration, while he lies on a bed of anguish half paralyzed waiting for the next stroke of paralysis which will probably be his finish. Private banking, such as it is today, is lucky still to be in the government's hospital and in the governments iron lung waiting for the next and last stroke which the war should administer.

President Roosevelt has driven more nails into the coffin of economic freedom in America than Hitler and Stalin. He has laid the institutional and bureaucratic foundations of the new revolution in America. Yet he may lead America into war against the new revolution in Europe which has gone a little further than he has yet had time or need to go in this country. The essential reasons why the money power or economic freedom has been curbed here and virtually ended in other countries are the same. They do not derive from *Das Kapital* or *Mein Kampf* but from the necessities of specific situations and the frustrations of people in these situations. Money, or ownership and enterprise, cannot be allowed to hold monopolies and exercise power for gain while, at the same time, failing to inspire enough confidence to prevent bank closures and to provide enough jobs to obviate necessity for government relief and pump priming.

In considering the future reorganization of economics along the lines already being traced by the new revolution, one can only try to understand the larger objectives. One cannot foresee needs or uses of ways and means. The first thing, perhaps, to understand, is that, freedom, facility, economy and advantage for private initiative are no longer paramount values or objectives of public policy. Under capitalism it was axiomatic that goods should be produced and bought where they could be produced or bought cheapest. Under the new revolution it will be found necessary to produce, buy and order economic affairs generally according to the indications of public interest, rather than private advantage. It may be advantageous or necessary for America to produce synthetic rubber in this country or to have it grown in nearby Mexico or Central America at a cost far in excess of that at which rubber is momentarily obtainable from Malasia. The norms of economic freedom are no longer valid.

A nation can no longer be run according to the calculations of business which need take no account of social costs such as depressions, unemployment and war. Preparation for war and prevention of violent industrial fluctuations will impose costs which must be met. There is no economy for the community in allowing individuals to make decisions with a view to securing maximum economy and efficiency and minimum cost when many important social costs are passed on to be taken up in other accounts. There is no sense to our buying Argentine wheat, corn or meat because it is cheaper in dollars at present prices and exchange rates than the domestic product and because to do so will enable some of our manufacturers to export more if, in consequence, we have to increase relief to American farmers, and if the resulting increase in relief cost cannot be taken out of the manufacturer's increased exports profit.

Free-trade theory errs in assuming a stability of prices and supply as well as an easy fluidity of investment capital and productive labor, all of which are now wholly out of the question. Wheat may be obtainable one year in any needed quantity from abroad at forty cents a bushel, a year or so later in smaller quantity at one dollar a bushel, another year or so later at two dollars or more a bushel in insufficient quantity for our needs if domestic production has been curtailed meantime. Foreign prices and supplies are not stable or dependable. Domestic factors of production such as industrial labor, factories, farmers and farm equipment cannot be shifted about from one line of production to another as fast as Price differentials and supplies change or as easily as a farm hand can be shifted from doing one chore to doing another.

If we increase automobile exports or cotton exports by buying more wheat, shoes or textiles from abroad and less from our own producers, the consequently disemployed American labor and machinery cannot be promptly shifted to producing articles of which we may, as a result, be able to export more. Nor can labor disemployed in one industry be promptly absorbed into some new and fast expanding industry. That was possible in the days of expansion, but is no longer possible. Then too, in the past when living standards were lower, industrial and farm workers were more fluid than now. They could carry all their belongings from one place to another on their backs. And they left behind them no unpaid installment or mortgage obligations. Today the disemployment of several thousands of industrial workers in a New England town must create a severe local crisis which is not compensated for by gains from tariff reductions to other industries and regions. Peter suffers more by being robbed than Paul gains by being paid.

In the present economic situation, tariff reductions can never be justified by gains offsetting losses. Contrary to the classical economists, it is cheaper to subsidize through tariff protection industrial employment already efficiently organized than it is to terminate such employment through tariff reduction and then turn around and subsidize the resulting industrial disemployment through relief, which is costly to administer and demoralizing far beyond the measure of money. The whole case for free trade assumes that unemployment is not a chronic factor. For a country with ten million workers chronically unemployed, it is nonsense to talk about the saving on labor to be achieved by buying some commodity from abroad. Our problem is not how to save labor but how to create work. Any notion that the disemployment of labor can be an economy for a country in our situation is basically fallacious.

It is an economy for an individual or corporate employer to reduce labor costs. But for the country to reduce employment can never be an economy. It may be a real economy and advantage for a great corporation like the United States Steel Corporation to buy control of and shut down the principal industry of Newcastle, Pennsylvania, thus ruining that entire community. The social costs of a ruined Newcastle are not borne by the United States Steel Corporation. It may result more economically or profitably for a great automobile industry to produce seasonally and leave the city of Detroit to take care of its seasonally unemployed. Those who say that the interests of an employer or capitalist always coincide with those of the communities within which they operate or that the interests of all national industries are complementary simply do not observe accurately and fully or else they do not report the facts honestly. Low farm prices during 1930-1933 were disastrous for American agriculture and beneficial for British industrial and building recovery. Just as American industrial protection in another period was beneficial for American corporate profits and disastrous for British industry. Economic interests under freedom and competition are rarely complementary except during an abnormally expansive phase.

The argument for greater individual freedom is but a plea for greater individual power for money, not for labor. The argument for freer foreign trade is a plea likewise for more power for money. If individuals have recently been losing economic power on some levels, it is a result of the breakdown of the system. Individuals cannot expect the state to restore to them powers they could not maintain under competition. If the opportunities which give content to certain economic liberties are reduced or gone forever, the government cannot bring them back. Mr. Hoover did not enact a curtailment of economic liberties. Economic liberty and power must be held once it has been won by the individual. Let those who want these boons restored, try to win them back if they can. Those who want power and are most likely to get it in the future will ask it in the public interest and not for private enrichment.

Economic freedom and free love are alike in theory and in practice, in principle and in results, except as modified by the exceptional circumstances of 19th century frontier expansion. Only, under democracy, the one is glorified as well as legally practiced while the other is both conventionally execrated and legally repressed. The believer in freedom for private enterprise says, "Hire 'em when you need 'em and fire 'em when you don't." The believer in free love says, "Love 'em where you find 'em and leave 'em where you love 'em." The democracies have always practiced collectivist discipline in sex and family relations while, in respect to greed and enterprise, they have practiced individualism, freedom and irresponsibility. The expansive processes, possible only for a brief century or two, no longer render economic anarchy socially tolerable. Therefore, it now becomes, like sex anarchy, immoral, unethical and impracticable according to any defensible social standard. Even Bertrand Russell's extremely mild attempt to carry over into the realm of sex the norms of democracy and individualism, duly qualified by an exception for all cases where children might be involved, recently made his appointment to a teaching position in New York city the occasion of a storm of protest. Many were found to defend his right to teach philosophy in spite of these particular views, but no one publicly said a kind word for such views.

The inconsistent defenders of freedom in economics and regimentation in sex—in the holy bonds of matrimony—will, of course, say that the same standards do not apply to business and the family. I deny it. So far as society is concerned, I see absolutely no ethical or practical differences worth mentioning in this connection between a deserted wife, an abandoned child, a disemployed industrial worker or a distressed farmer. All are, equally, social problems. All involve grave social maladjustments and disorders. All call for public relief. The interest of society in sex and economics is the same: public order and public welfare. Both are incompatible with the hire-'em-and-fire-'em ways of American industrialists and the love-'em-and-leave-'em ways of free lovers. Today, the ways of American economic freedom, specifically of our big industries like steel and automobiles and of our free market price system, are creating at least one hundred farmers and unemployed for the community to support or assist with relief to every one bastard being created by rugged individualists and liberty lovers in sex matters to constitute a similar charge on the community. Individualism and liberty, whether in sex or business, must be judged by the fruit it bears. The industrialists of America declare their dividends and spout their ethics while the community has to take care of their employees part of the time.

In view of the foregoing ethical considerations and the relief facts of the hour, I have no hesitation or reservations whatsoever in declaring categorically that I personally find the ethics of economic freedom and individualism, as applied in today's America, as despicable and intolerable as the ethics of free love. I make this statement forceful because I am aware that my views and the ways of totalitarian collective discipline are now being denounced generally in this land on supposedly high moral grounds. Well, I am meeting that denunciation, not with an apology for my views, but with a counter-denunciation of those of my critics, which I am sure no one will have any trouble understanding.

There are just two things to do about the unemployed: Give them work or give them relief. The totalitarian way is to give them work. The democratic way is to give them relief. I do not have to defend the former. I denounce the latter. I challenge my critics to prove with deeds—not words—that I am wrong and that American democracy, i.e., capitalism, can give the unemployed work or the farmers a remunerative price today without going to war. As long as they cannot meet this challenge with performance instead of appeal to morals, sentiment and tradition, I shall continue to feel flattered by their reproaches.

The special pleader for freer international trade can always cloud the issue by showing our need of certain commodities like coffee, rubber or other articles not obtainable at home; or, point out how home industry may be disrupted or even bankrupted by the loss of foreign markets. He can score heavily by painting a fantastic picture of what conditions might be like were all foreign trade to be completely stopped. Such arguments cannot be answered as categorically as they are formulated. The reasons are that the factors are relative while thesE arguments are in terms of absolutes.

No so-called isolationist or believer in government-controlled foreign trade and maximum regional self-sufficiency, be he national socialist or a Republican, capitalist or New England high tariff manufacturer, ever favors putting a Chinese wall of foreign trade exclusion around his or any other country. The best proof of this is the fact that the autarchic regimes of Russia, Italy, Germany and Japan have recently been making every effort, and with considerable success, to increase their foreign trade. The head of autarchy No. 1, Adolf Hitler, said, "Germany must export or die," yet free traders go on charging that the autarchies aim at the suppression of foreign trade. The etymology of the word autarchy, meaning self-rule, should suffice to refute the charge that autarchy means the elimination of foreign intercourse. Actually, the amount or percentage of foreign trade a collectivist autarchy will have in a given period will be determined, not by the application of any general principles, but mainly by needs and opportunities for advantageous foreign exchanges; advantageous to the total economy, not merely profitable to a special class or certain regional interests. The liberal doctrine of the harmony of interests under law, liberty and competition is obviously bunk as the American Indians, the negroes, the losers in business competition, the farmers and the unemployed, now living on the dole, should be able to attest. The statement that, under competition, the interests of the losers and winners are the same is arrant nonsense. It is also the keystone of the law, doctrine, morals and institutional practice of capitalism and liberal democracy.

The special pleaders for freer trade simply do not state the issues with adequacy or honesty. These are not, as the free traders try to make it appear: foreign trade versus no foreign trade. They are not more versus less foreign trade. By some the issues may be called more versus less freedom, more versus less government control of foreign trade; or, more versus less dependence on the uncontrollable fluctuations of foreign prices, supply and demand. The autarchist, or believer in the new revolution, would merely say that the issue was one of order versus anarchy in foreign trade. In simple fact the autarchist or the new revolution does not stand either for more or less foreign trade, more or less freedom, more or less state control, as ends in themselves or, even, as infallible means in themselves to given ends.

The new revolution or the autarchist of today simply wants more or better order. The new revolution finds that better order calls for better control. In most cases this will mean less individual freedom and less dependence on foreign economic factors beyond the control of any one nation trying to stabilize its production and employment. The liberal revolution said, as a matter of faith and doctrine, "Lower international trade barriers. Maximize individual freedom in production and exchange and everything will go better." The new revolution denies this, not as a matter of faith and doctrine but as a result of observation and experience. It might have worked out satisfactorily the free-trade way for England during the high noon of modern capitalism or, roughly, from the beginning of the industrial revolution down to the Second World War. But it no longer works that way, and that's that. The issue in respect to foreign trade and economic freedom today is wholly one of fact established by continuous experiment. Every autarchist wants all the possible advantages of a maximum amount of foreign trade. But he sees no advantage in a momentary gain in cheapness or efficiency at the price of a permanent sacrifice of order and economic stability.

The free traders preach. The autarchists practice. The free traders, like Mr. Hull, lay down principles nobody is willing to observe. The autarchists carry out administrative control. The autarchists are in power. The free traders are not, though some of them are in office. The autarchists have to get results. The free traders like Mr. Hull get applause while the farm and unemployed relief administrators pass out the dole to the victims of economic instability. Freedom and foreign trade are means, not ends. No one anywhere proposes to suppress all individual freedom of choice in economic matters or all foreign trade. It is merely proposed to control economic choices and action and, also, to regulate foreign trade as a necessary means to better social order. There simply is no free trade or freer foreign trade issue anywhere in the realm of the practical. The issues raised by Mr. Hull and his staff of pedantic yes men are wholly academic and irrelevant. American business and labor will never allow these starry-eyed doctrinaires to try out their theories on an already economically stagnant America.

Chapter XIII
Power Politics

A recent reviewer correctly remarked that the phrase "power politics" is as tautological as would be the phrase "sexual fornication." Perhaps a little qualification is necessary. In the realm of action there can be no politics without power. In the realm of speculation there can be any kind of politics. Anglo-Saxon law and political theory are largely a mass of fictions. During the hundred odd years from Waterloo to Sarajevo, the might of Britain and money were wielded so smoothly that the underlying facts of power came to be almost completely lost to sight. The obscuring of the power factors was not accidental but studied.

Property rights, of course, have always rested and must always rest on naked power, else why would a destitute man see his family starve while observing the rich flaunt abundance in comparative security? But, under feudal and other earlier regimes, the power factor behind property was not deliberately obscured. On the contrary, it was ostentatiously displayed. The lord of the manor carried a sword conspicuously and was a swordsman of distinction; so were his knights. And the poor villains were denied the right to bear arms. Property then went to great pains to exhibit its power. Ownership and naked power were honestly identified with each other. Today a far mightier but much less visible power protects the barons of the bags than that which formerly guarded the barons of the crags. But, thanks to the institutions, folkways and ideas inaugurated by the English revolutions of the seventeenth century and the French and American Revolutions of the eighteenth century, modern property rights have been made to appear to the average man to rest on contract and consent interpreted by unarmed judges and enforced through the peaceful processes of law, the coercive aspects of which are obscured by reason of the virtual impossibility of effective opposition. In logic or fact the chief fallacy of this popular ideology is that it supposes that majority consent equals freedom for all and the absence of coercion. There need be no antithesis between consent of the governed and coercion of the governed. Much legally happens to people to which they never consent. The governed may consent to be coerced by their government. Do our governed consent to unemployment? Is destitution not coercion? Consent often demands and imposes coercion. The coercion of an overwhelming majority can be much harsher and more effective than that exercised by an individual or a class. The coercion of economic necessity is real though not a subject of consent or refusal of consent.

Democracy and capitalism developed a new technique of coercion in the interests of property. During the rise of capitalism there was within capitalistic nations general assent to its peculiar coercions largely because opportunities to share in property rights to power over and coercion of others were sufficiently numerous; while within the society of nations those dissatisfied with the coercion of the mighty imperialists like Britain were, as a whole, the darker races for instance, utterly powerless to oppose it. The later comers into the imperialist game, like Germany, Austria-Hungary, Japan and Italy, found enough opportunities during the nineteenth century to expand at the expense of the weak not to think seriously of then challenging the really mighty Britain. The idea that the nineteenth century Pax Britannica, such as it was, consisted of an era of more or less unbroken peace is, of course, utter nonsense, as was shown on pages 91-92 in a list of British imperialist wars of that period.

What is now meant by power politics is, in reality, just a new frankness in discussing the use of power in politics. When the British subjugated native races in the imperialist processes of the nineteenth century, such measures were not considered either in the popular or learned thinking of that period as having anything to do with politics or power. What American founding father or signer of the Constitution ever thought of African slavery or killing American Indians for their lands as having any remote connection with the philosophy of either politics or power? American intellectuals like Jefferson could write and talk endlessly about our governments being founded on consent and law rather than force and violence, having all the while a plantation full of slaves, with armed overseers and manacles, and while fighting the Indians and the French more or less all the time. Thus was born Jeffersonian or Jacksonian democracy. Both Jefferson and Jackson, like the Athenian democrats, were slaveowners. Even our having a four year Civil War which gave birth to the Republican party does not shake the popular American illusion that, so far as we were concerned, the nineteenth century was a period of law and order and peace. One just does not consider such facts as our Civil War, the Mexican War or incessant warfare on the Indians, up to the fourth quarter of the nineteenth century, when one moralizes about the new political cults being essentially phenomena of force and violence.

One of the great secrets of Anglo-Saxon success is the imposition on others of their canons of definition, taste and ethics. According to these canons, anything the Anglo-Saxons do in the furtherance of their interests is, by definition, not a use of force or violence. If they have slaves, theirs is still a government based on consent. When they worked nine year old children in textile mills, it was with the consent of the children whose right to freedom of contract Anglo-Saxon justice respected. Anything we do is merely the upholding of law, order, justice or human freedom, etc., etc. The imposition of these concepts, definitions and theories has been one of the greatest of British imperial conquests: the intellectual subjugation of the world to the exigencies of British and capitalistic interests.

The new revolutionary ideologies and leaders have challenged these canons. That challenge, an essential feature of the new revolution, has brought into use the relatively new phrase "power politics." The leader of a new revolution must talk frankly to his followers about power. After a revolution has triumphed, its leaders and regime grow more and more reticent and equivocal about power, if the regime be democratic. It is during an important shift of power that one hears a lot about power politics. The reason is not that power in politics is then coming back into use, for politics is always essentially a conspiracy of power. The reason is merely that new hands are being laid on power and old hands are losing it. Those who lose power denounce the power-hungry barbarians who oust them; those who come to power denounce the abuse of power by their predecessors. Both are right, though their respective charges are as unimportant as they are true. One now hears more about power, not because it is more important or more active as a social agent, but simply because the shift in power calls attention to the existence of a recently concealed factor.

The masses may be affected somewhat by a shift in power, though rarely as much as is commonly believed. Thus, in Russia the coming of socialism has meant a shift in power from the hereditary and largely incompetent elite of Czardom to an elite which was suppressed under the Czar. The shift has meant a lot to the outs who came in and the ins who went out, but to the masses who are always out (of power), swapping masters has meant little real difference. They still have to rise early, toil late and undergo hardships as before.

The essence of the beginning of a new revolution is a shift in power, hence the current emphasis on power politics. The chief reasons a shift in power has to occur are (1) incompetence or failure, for whatever the reasons, on the part of the holders of power; and (2) an organized attempt to exclude too many from power who are as competent as those holding power. Shifts in power are not really caused by mass preferences, though the masses and their perennial discontents are always exploited by an out-elite in a bid for power. The most frequent cause of the downfall of one regime is that it fails to provide for a sufficient circulation of the elite.

The real cause of the American Revolution against George III or the later Latin-American revolutions against Spain was that the colonial elite resented the favors, jobs and revenues going to the elite of the mother country. Czarist Russia was a dictatorship of a bureaucracy, exactly like communist Russia, Nazi Germany or Fascist Italy. Only Czarist Russia attempted to perpetuate the dictatorship of a hereditary bureaucracy, which must always prove impossible. A dictatorship of a bureaucracy, to survive, must provide for the easy access to power of most of the elite. Capitalism is a dictatorship of money, impersonal, anonymous and hard to put your finger on because of the ways of money under such a system. To work, it must provide opportunities for a large percentage of the elite to make money and must not perpetuate inherited fortunes too long. It must maintain a three generations from-shirt-sleeves-to-shirt-sleeves tradition. The overthrow of any regime can be averted mainly by buying off enough of the elite of each generation through advancement to power. So far, war has proved the surest, if not the only, workable, system of selection to keep the powerful in power by a continuous process of selection and elimination.

What, more than anything else, doomed the Weimar Republic in Germany or the Czarist regime in Russia was the frustration of too many of the elite. In Germany, from the Kaiser to Hitler, roughly half of the young graduating from the institutions of higher learning found no jobs suitable to their intellectual and social rank. In many cases, their middle-class parents and relatives had been ruined by the postwar inflation. It was not the proletariat who made the revolution in Germany, though in its rise to power the Nazi revolution did attract large numbers of the unskilled or semi-skilled workers. Similarly, in the Russian Revolution it was not the proletariat but the frustrated elite who created the revolution. A non-hereditary bureaucracy is probably the most stable regime possible for human society to achieve. In the present state of enlightenment, a stable rule by an hereditary aristocracy is unthinkable. The restoration of monarchy, therefore, is about as likely as the restoration of chattel slavery or polygamy. A new Caesarism cannot survive on the hereditary principle. Rome's Caesars were not a hereditary caste.

Whatever the chances may be for a restoration of an hereditary ruling class, a revolution is essentially a shift in power from an in-elite to an out-elite, most of the dynamism for the change coming from the out-elite. The growth of a dissatisfied elite is more an incident of the working of the system and changed conditions than the result of deliberate suppression of the outs by the ins. In this country and both Britain and France, it is probable that revolutionary change will occur without civil war or insurrectionary violence of any magnitude. The present ins in the democracies are neither organized nor class conscious. The changed mechanics, after we go to war, will at once work for a clarification of thinking about power by the outs or marginal ins among the elite.

Changed mechanics will create a new bureaucratic corps of the elite, strategically well situated, who will be too numerous and powerful after a long war to turn, when it is over, to selling pencils on the sidewalks, while the present gentry of trade take back the running of the nation's industries. For the bureaucratic new elite to take over, it should be enough for them to see clearly that, in any attempt to return to private capitalism, they cannot be taken care of as they have become accustomed. The new bureaucratic elite will feel their oats before the end of a long war. As the war goes on, investors, or those merely owning wealth, will grow poorer and poorer as a result of heavy taxation to avert inflation, while businessmen will grow weaker and weaker by reason of increased regulation and regimentation brought about by the military exigencies. As capitalists and businessmen grow poorer and weaker, the bureaucratic elite of government and organized labor will grow stronger and more cocky. Add to this the popular disillusionment and bitterness over the failure of the war to produce anything but bereavements and sacrifices, and you have enough dynamism for a drastic phase of revolutionary change. The essence of this dynamism, of course, will be hate for the persons, ideas and institutions responsible for our entry into war. The point to emphasize in this connection is that revolution does not follow any fixed pattern.

Here it will almost certainly not in any way conform to the pattern of the French Revolution or the earlier English Revolution of Oliver Cromwell. Still less will it follow the Russian or German precedents.

Revolution in America should not be thought of as a wave of reform or unrest. The American people voted against the Hoover Depression rather than for the Roosevelt New Deal. In 1940 America, on the verge of war, there is some unrest but far from enough to warrant any serious talk about revolution. The revolution which has been going on for seven years under the New Deal has not been at all the result of a desire for revolutionary social change. In so far as it has been a revolution, it has been the result of the necessities of the situation rather than the preferences of the people. The people do not want revolution and have not wanted it at any time since 1929. They have wanted only business or, rather, prosperity, as usual. In default of this, they have wanted only handouts from the government. In receipt of these, they have wanted mainly from their leaders bedtime stories told with a soothing radio voice.

At the opening of 1940 the American people are not politics or power conscious in respect to their domestic economic problems. At the opening of 1940 they felt more violently over the poor Finns, the poor Poles, the poor Czechs and even the poor Chinese than over poor Americans out of work. The American people are more worried over democracy for Europeans than jobs for Americans. This being their mood, it is obvious that they are going to do something about Europe or China before they do anything about America. They will revolutionize America in their attempt and failure to stop revolution in Europe. This they will do, not in a humane, constructive or patriotic impulse to save America, but in an irrational and destructive impulse to damn Hitler and Stalin. Possibly conditions could eventually become bad enough in America to precipitate a violently revolutionary phase in this country without our going to war. But there is no point to speculating about that possible eventuality when it appears so much more likely that our situation will become explosive and our revolution dynamic through our entry into war to stop Japan, Germany, Russia, world revolution and sin abroad.

It may even be better for us to get our revolution through a foreign war than through an indefinitely prolonged deterioration of our domestic economic situation. For one thing, if we go to war, the power conflict between our Haves and Have-nots, incipient in 1940, will take the subtler form of the progressive ruin of the American Haves to the strains of the "Star Spangled Banner" (taxation and regulation will do it) and the accompanying expansion of power and inflammation of feeling of the American Have-nots through war measures and experiences. If it happens this way, the cruder forms of class struggle may be entirely avoided in this country. Our bemused rich and economically powerful will be crushed amid the incense of patriotism and in a great *élan* of enthusiasm to save the British and French Haves. This would be following the tradition of the Czar and his nobles. A ruling class about to perish usually facilitates and hastens its own destruction. It will be ironic, but most of our rich will not have the wit to see the humor of it until it has been spelled out for them in history books written a decade hence. What simpler or more painless way of wiping out private fortunes than that of having them voluntarily put by their owners into government bonds, the value of which will be wiped out by slow inflation in a long-drawn-out war?

In international affairs the same fundamental conflicts of interest and power prevail as in domestic politics. The Haves are pitted against the Have-nots, with everything to be settled in terms of power, armed, economic or ideological. In the long run the patterns of distribution, both internationally and intranationally must conform to the changing patterns of force or power factors. Since 1917 the chief trouble in Europe has been the incompatibility of the distribution pattern with the force or power pattern. For that incompatibility the United States is mainly to blame. By taking the side of the Allies in 1917, we enabled them in 1919 to dictate a peace and a redistribution of territory which the play of the force factors in that war, without our interference, would never have permitted. Then, having enabled the Allies to impose a peace which would have been impossible without the aid of our might, we withdrew our might from the equation. And so, twenty years later, the war resumes. If the European power factors had been allowed to make the peace without our interference in 1917 or 1918, they probably would not have changed enough in twenty years to upset that peace. As it happened, the withdrawal of our support from the Allies after the peace of Versailles was enough to create the necessary unbalance for another war.

The theory underlying our entry into the war, of course, was that the world's troubles were due to one personal devil, then called the Kaiser, whose removal, with our aid, would permit the establishment of a permanent rule of righteousness. This theory erred in one basic assumption, namely, that the international order can rest on anything except a balance of power. As a matter of fact, though we refused after the World War to enter the League of Nations, we did lend considerable support to the impossible world order created at Versailles by keeping up until 1929 a stream of loan funds to Germany and other European countries. When we withdrew that support from the Versailles system, we made its collapse only a matter of a short time.

Almost exactly the same issue confronts us in 1940 as in 1917, only this time it is more clearly drawn. There is now a more unanimous moral indignation against Hitler than in 1917 against the Kaiser. But the power problem is substantially the same in that the Allies have not the slightest chance of winning without our assistance, the situation now being much worse for the angels than in 1917. In 1917 Japan and Italy were on the side of the angels and Russia had just gone under after putting up a hard fight which was at the outset invaluable to the Allies. Today Russia and Japan are against the angels and Italy cannot be counted on their side.

The issue again confronting us is that of whether we shall add our might to that of Britain and France to dictate a peace which they alone have not the power either to impose now or enforce once it is dictated. The American people have recently indicated, both in innumerable polls of public opinion and in diverse other ways, that they feel that we cannot stand for political regimes like those of Hitler and Stalin. But there is no sense to our making periodical crusades to overthrow regimes like those of the Kaiser and Hitler if we are not willing to enter a perpetual alliance with Britain and France forever to prevent the subsequent rise of similar regimes in Germany, Russia, Italy, etc., etc.

There was just one way in 1917 and there is just one way in 1940 to keep America out of war. That way is to make our people see the issues in terms of power rather than morals or sentimentalism. But almost no American isolationist or opponent of our going to war is willing so to state the issues. Consequently isolationist opposition to our going to war is futile and doomed to failure the moment our President decides that the time has come for us to move in that direction. The moral case for our going to war cannot be answered except by challenging its major premise, stated in President Roosevelt's message to the opening Congress on January 3, 1940, that it is our business how European governments behave in Europe. The case for intervention in Europe on moral grounds can only be assailed effectively by discussing alternative courses of action in terms of power. The moral argument for our partnership in a European crusade for righteousness is best refuted by pointing out that it calls for a continuing exercise of power over European destinies which we are neither able to make nor willing to undertake.

CHAPTER XIV
Realism Ends in Foreign Affairs When the People Rule

Up to 1919 the great capitalist powers, in their foreign policies, were fairly realistic about power. They sought security along balance of power lines. That is to say: 1. They accepted the balance of power between nations as an inevitable fact in a society of sovereign states, which are most unequal in economic and military power. 2. They sought at times to change the balance of power through war and diplomacy, but never to substitute for it a monopoly of world power of one nation or one league of nations. With the late world war, came the British need of Woodrow Wilson's United States, which was to be had only at Wilson's price of acceptance of the ideal of the League of Nations. This British need imposed on them acceptance of the ideal of collective security and some subsequent pretense at the pursuit of an unattainable monopoly of power for the League. The British and French met Wilson's price in form but never in substance. The first welshers from the League, of course, were the American people. They were entirely right in repudiating the League and entirely wrong in having fought for something they were unwilling to uphold. It was never more than a sham, put forward by Wilson in all sincerity to the American people as the high moral objective of our entry into war, subscribed to in all duplicity by the Allies as Mr. Wilson's price for our coming to their rescue and fought for in all futility by the American soldier.

The League had served its purpose when, as an iridescent dream, it had helped get us into the war and when the war had been won by the Allies. Thereafter, it was only a hollow mockery because no great power was willing to surrender any part of its sovereignty towards the constitution of a League of Nations monopoly of power for the enforcement of international law, justice and collective security.

Now that the British and French are again at war with Germany, the ideal of collective security is once more being dusted off for use in bamboozling the American people and in rounding up the United

States and other neutrals for another Armageddon. The Allies are not really for collective security any more than Senators Lodge and Borah were twenty years ago, because the Allies are not willing to pay their part of the price of its attainment, which is the relinquishment of national sovereignty to an international agency to be vested with a monopoly of power. It would make little difference, of course, if the Allies were sincere in their professions of loyalty to collective security, since, if they were, there are at least four, not including the United States, of the seven great powers which would never ratify any counterpart of Article 10 of the League covenant, and which are inalterably opposed to collective security; and since three out of seven do not constitute a majority, even if the three are for righteousness and collective security or anything else.

So much for the collective security record of the democracies. It is one of bad faith from start to finish, including our asking American soldiers one year to die for the ideals of the League and then two years later promptly repudiating these ideals once the war had been won. As for the new revolution, it may be said that it is definitely not moving towards collective security but back to the balance of power theory and practice. The Marxist Communist International envisaged a collective security Utopia based on a monopoly of power by a proletarian world-wide socialism, whatever that might be. Just how such an international authority could be constituted and made to function, assuming the world-wide adoption of Marxist communism, has never been satisfactorily explained, even in theory. It would seem probable that there would be as many interest conflicts and power clashes between nations in a socialist as in a capitalist world. There is not much point in speculating about the possibility of a socialist world monopoly of power, however, as socialism in action, in Russia, Germany and, to a slightly less extent, in Italy, has its back turned on collective security and its face turned towards the traditional balance of power theory and practice. The democracies preach, but do not practice, collective security; the socialist dictatorships are neither preaching nor trying to practice it.

In theory, or rather in propaganda, the democracies are seeking to revolutionize the world by establishing the rule of one brand of righteousness under one monopoly of power, something which has never yet been realized. That is to say, the counterrevolutionary Haves are seeking peace on the basis of a revolutionary and visionary monopoly of power in lieu of the present or any other balance of power. The present balance of power is unsatisfactory to the Haves because in it the German, Japanese, Russian and Italian Have-nots are too powerful; it is equally unsatisfactory to these Have-nots because in it they are too poor. What the Haves really want, of course, is to change the post-Munich balance of power into one in which the Haves will be more powerful and the Have-nots less powerful, but what they say they want is to create a power situation in which justice and law will be all-powerful, which is just so much hokum, as no two great nations can ever permanently agree about justice or law. The revolutionary Have-nots, on the other hand, with greater intellectual honesty, are proclaiming, more or less truthfully, what they are actually seeking, namely, a change in the balance of power, or a new balance of power in which the Have-nots will be more powerful and the Haves, notably Britain, will be less powerful. This objective is a traditional pattern of change which is honestly avowed by the Have-nots. The Have-nots explicitly disavow any desire or intention to set up a monopoly of power through any form of international organization.

The facts that the capitalist democracies say that they are fighting for collective security, or a monopoly of power, and that the socialist Have-nots say they are not fighting for any such thing are most significant. These facts, presenting such a sharp contrast, suggest many important inferences about the democracies, the new revolution and the choice confronting America on the issues of the war.

In the first place, the off and on or insincere quest of the Allies after collective security on the basis of an unattainable monopoly of power is strongly indicative of the decadence of the democracies. Dynamic civilizations in the ascendant do not think in terms of Utopia, universal security, impossible guarantees of their early loot and world peace on the basis of its retention. Britain on the rise did not rely on America or any other country to come to her rescue. She relied rather on her own realistic diplomacy and mighty navy. These were adequate largely because her diplomacy always frankly recognized the balance of power and sought to divide and rule rather than to unite the wicked and then mow 'em down like Charlie McCarthy or Popeye the Sailor.

In the second place, this decadence of the democracies, notably of Britain, is symptomatic of a hardening of the democratic arteries. Why does British statesmanship chase the will-o'-the-wisp of collective security, knowing full well that the necessary monopoly of power for its achievement is impossible? Why does Britain get into wars she has no chance of winning without American help? The answer in one word is "democracy." Actually, neither Mr. Chamberlain nor any other intelligent Englishman really could believe in the war aim of collective security with its preposterous corollary of a monopoly of power. But British realists know that the British masses, in their mental and moral feebleness, need such illusions, and also that in their electoral might they will not permit the pursuit by any British government of a strong realistic foreign policy appropriate to present world realities. Formerly the hard heads and harder hearts of the British ruling classes shaped British foreign policy. Now the soft heads of the British masses determine British foreign-policy decisions. British statesmen now know further that, being inhibited by British democracy from pursuing a realistic foreign policy, they need America and that America can be had only by means of the lure of an unrealistic idealism such as collective security.

In the third place, the new revolution, being a revolt against the shams, illusions, frustrations and failures of democracy, naturally tends to complete realism and intellectual honesty about power.

In the fourth place, the real war choice of America lies between going to war for an unattainable monopoly of power, and allowing the new revolution of realism to continue its course without our opposition while we work out an American policy to keep our present place in the sun in the new balance of power.

The moral case for a second American crusade in twenty-three years on the side of the angels is valid only on the assumption that the angels can win and thereafter maintain permanently the monopoly of power necessary for the stability of their heavenly world order. Few people realize this. Hence the overwhelming majority of Americans are on the side of the angels, merely because the angels are the best people. The moral case for our entering war goes unchallenged principally because no one cares to attack the idea of heaven or the person of an angel. And it is considered bad form to raise practical questions in connection with heaven, angels or moral imperatives. In present-day America it is thought to be a mark of decent instincts to, ignore power in politics just as, in Mid-Victorian England, it was deemed bad taste to mention sex in polite conversation. To make clear the issues of the present war, it is necessary to plunge into some rather abstract political theory. To make the abstract concrete in every particular, which it would be easy to do, would unduly expand the thesis.

The first thing to understand about Utopian schemes of world peace and order and about the exigencies of practical politics is this: To enforce any kind of public order it is necessary for the enforcing agent to command within the area of enforcement a virtual monopoly of power. The nation, if it is a sovereign state, has a monopoly of power within its boundaries. No League of Nations and no alliance, past or present, holy or unholy, has ever had a monopoly of power throughout the entire world. This difference between the power of a nation within its borders and the power of an international alliance within the limits of the entire earth is fundamental. A war for territorial conquest may make sense because it may succeed for one nation. A war for the establishment of a world monopoly of power cannot make sense because it cannot succeed. According to allied propaganda, the war of 1914-1918 was, and the present war is, just that sort of war. Of course, allied propaganda has never had the intellectual honesty, either in the preceding or the present world war, to state frankly that the objective of the world rule of international law can be achieved only on the basis of a single world monopoly of power. This obviously is no reflection on allied propaganda since, to be good, it has to be deceptive.

The Allies at Versailles had what came as close to being an international monopoly of power as anything a victorious coalition ever had in world history. There is no point to going back further than the Congress of Vienna for examples, since in no earlier period of history could any single victorious power or any combination of states ever have had the slightest pretension to a world monopoly of power if only for one reason: Before the nineteenth century no single nation or coalition of nations ever had physical access, either with its ships or its armies, to all parts of the world. Japan, for instance, was closed to foreign ships until past the middle of the nineteenth century. The mighty Roman Empire, for example, was unknown to the Far East or to the great American Indian civilizations of Mexico, Central America and Peru of that period. The Allies at Paris in 1919 counted among their number Japan and China as well as the United States. Russia was the only major world power not participating.

But the unity of command and purpose which carried the Allies to the pinnacle of their power in November 1918 had dissolved even before the plenipotentiaries met in the famous Hall of Mirrors. It had been disintegrating still further all the way down to Munich. By that time Japan and Italy had abandoned the angels, while Russia was definitely with the Teutonic devils. All during the twenties and down through the thirties to Munich, the victorious Allies of 1919 had been working at cross purposes. Their failure, once the peace treaties were signed, to maintain unity of purpose to say nothing of perfecting a permanent monopoly of power on the continent of Europe, is not strange. The interests and ideals of the Allies coalesced only for a brief moment in the temporary war effort to defeat Germany. They wanted Germany beaten for different reasons. Once Germany was beaten, they had no further common interests as a basis for unity or cooperation. Their conduct proves this. And their behavior, whether during the French occupation of the Ruhr or Hitler's re-militarization of the Rhineland, completely refutes the entire case of the international idealists who promise a better world order if only the foes of Hitlerism triumph in war. The British and French can never triumph in peace because they can never agree in peace. They never did.

In the postwar period Britain wanted a weak German navy and a strong Germany on land to checkmate militarist France, while France was indifferent to the German navy and concerned only to have a militarily weak Germany. Because of this conflict of interests and policies, Hitler was allowed in 1936 to rearm the Rhineland when it would have been the easiest thing in the world for the French and British to prevent it.

The basic fallacy of internationalism is a refusal to recognize that the nations of the world are united by no common set of values, standards or interests. Russia, the largest great power in the world, is anti-Christian. Japan, another great power is non-Christian. Yet Mr. Roosevelt wants us to fight for Christianity or, at least, God. At least two great powers, Germany and Russia, are definitely anti-capitalist. Four of them, Russia, Germany, Japan and Italy are expansionist. Three of them, Great Britain, America and France are anti-expansionist. Ideologically, institutionally, economically, and militarily, world trends are now more than ever before away from international unity in peace. The only formulas of international unity today worth considering are Roman Catholicism and international capitalism. Why should Protestant or poor Americans die for either? There is no international agreement about either religion or property. The most vocal exponents of world unity are the subsidized spokesmen for the Anglo-Saxon plutocracy. They want war to save capitalism. Another vocal exponent of world unity, the Vatican, wants peace to save Christianity. But Mr. Chamberlain and the Pope, presumably both good Christians, do not agree on what to do to save

Realism Ends in Foreign Affairs When the People Rule 175

Christianity. Yet Mr. Roosevelt sends a personal emissary with a view to a Papal-American effort to save the world. Well there may have been some sense to the idea of uniting the world under the Cross or under the crescent. But the idea of uniting it under the dollar and pound sterling signs is too silly for words. That, of course, is the central idea of the social scientists and thinkers of liberal capitalism, the idea endowed by great wealth in nearly every American college. It is especially the idea of all international money and credit idealists. At least four hundred million Germans, Russians, Japanese and Italians are unwilling to bow to the rule of the dollar and the pound, a fact which makes the internationalism of Woodrow Wilson, Franklin D. Roosevelt, Cordell Hull and Neville Chamberlain merely the side of the Haves versus that of the Have-nots, with the Have-nots in the numerical majority. A monopoly of power by the Haves, for the rule of righteousness is simply unthinkable under such conditions.

It is interesting in discussing the monopoly of power idea to recall that the British in their long history up to 1917 always spurned this particular dream. After the Napoleonic Wars, they were most emphatic in their rejection of overtures to join the Holy Alliance for the realization of just this chimera.

The chief reason no nation can, or ever will, live up to the obligations of collective security is that to do so would mean a surrender of sovereignty to an agency attempting to exercise a world monopoly of power. No nation, least of all Britain or America, is yet prepared to consider such a surrender. For a nation to surrender its sovereignty to another international power, after all, is neither more nor less than for it to cease to be a nation.

The traditional British policy has been wisely to rely on the balance of power for their security. This policy rests mainly on the historically and logically well-founded assumption that no coalition can ever achieve a monopoly of power. Therefore, it aims to divide and rule. An essential of this policy, of course, is the playing of one powerful nation against another, not the defying of four of the seven most powerful nations in the name of righteousness, international law, collective security or what have you. For the first time in their long history as a great power, the British in 1939 deviated from this traditional policy, first by inviting war with Germany through the guarantee of Poland and, second, six months later, by going to war with Germany to make good that guarantee.

Munich, the only instance of important international change by peaceful agreement between 1919 and 1939, was in entire harmony with the balance of power policy. The guarantee to Poland a half year later was a reversal of that policy for one of collective security, an infallible formula for world war. The theory of Munich was that if the small succession states of central and eastern Europe were left to their fate or to such bargains as they could drive with Germany and if Germany were allowed a completely free hand in that part of Europe, she would sooner or later clash with Russia. Thus two great powers, who have long been traditional enemies of Britain, would check and weaken each other to the enhancement of Britain's strategic position in the world. No calculation could have been better founded in experience and logic. The only rational alternative to this policy would have been a collective-security policy followed consistently from the end of the World War. Collective security is obviously a policy which, to be followed rationally, must be followed consistently and almost invariably over a considerable period of time. Even so followed, the policy *may* fail; but, followed spasmodically and inconsistently, a collective-security policy *must* fail.

It was madness for Britain to scuttle collective security at Munich for the balance of power policy and, incidentally, to hand Hitler the keys to central and eastern Europe, if the British intended to fight a year later for collective security. It is sheer nonsense to say that Britain and France had to do Munich in September 1938 because they were then unprepared to fight Germany and that, one year hence, they would have raised the Anglo-French war potential enough to more than make up for the liquidation of Czechoslovakia's army of a million and a half men, the loss of the Czech Maginot line, the sacrifice of her strategic position penetrating the heart of Germany and her valuable arms industries. It will take the British at least three years to create as much military power as they gave to Hitler at Munich. It is even more absurd to say that Mr. Chamberlain handed Hitler the Czech key to Poland and southeastern Europe in the faith that Hitler would keep his promise not to use this key. What is a key for if not to be used? Hitler's only reason for desiring the Czech key to Poland was to use it, and Britain's only logical reason for giving him that key was that he might use it exactly as he did. The British, like other rational beings, must be assumed to know the logical consequences of their acts.

The explanation of the absurdity of giving Hitler the key to Poland one September and going to war against him for using it the next September is simple. It is the working of democracy. A politician needing votes and observing democratic procedure in England dared not tell the truth about Munich in its defense, either before or after. A democratic statesman cannot act rationally without telling the people the truth and he cannot get elected if he does tell them the truth. He must, therefore, act as irrationally and lie as much as the exigencies of getting elected require. Munich was a piece of rational British balance-of-power politics. Chamberlain hoped to be able to get away with it by concealing and misrepresenting his real, underlying calculations and motives, which he could not frankly avow in a truthful statement of the whole problem. He was unsuccessful, thanks to the workings of democracy. He ran into the difficulties which usually beset the untruthful. He was found out. Being a good politician in the democratic way, he, therefore, jumped out of the Munich frying pan into the Polish guarantee-world-war fire. By so doing he saved his political skin. This was a political triumph in a democracy. The fact that Britain is now at war with Germany as a result does not mar that triumph. Chamberlain was neither a weakling nor a fool. He was a clever and successful politician who knew how to get and keep power in a democracy.

When, under the pressure of democratic politics, Chamberlain scuttled the balance-of-power policy, or playing Germany against Russia, for a sure road to war, he did so under the worst imaginable conditions for British success. That, however, was not his fault. By scuttling a policy of traditional British realism for one of an impossible collective security in the guarantee of Poland in the Spring of 1939, Chamberlain killed three birds with one stone: 1. He made himself solid with democratic public opinion at home and abroad. 2. He united Germany and Russia, normally enemies of each other as well as of Britain. 3. He committed Britain to war against the two greatest land powers in Europe, having together roughly seven times the man power of France, about the most disastrous blunder possible for British foreign policy to make. It was a democratic triumph for Chamberlain to be a war premier and a disaster for Britain to be committed to fighting Germany and Russia over spilled Polish milk. It was a democratic triumph because Chamberlain stayed on top and because the rabble was continuously pleased, first at the Munich surrender to Hitler because it meant "peace in our time," and second at the Polish guarantee slap at Hitler, because it meant righteousness, i.e., war in our time. It must be a British disaster because it will be a long and costly war from which Britain cannot possibly reap any advantage commensurate with her losses. In a democracy propaganda governs policy. In a totalitarian state policy governs propaganda.

Some readers will perhaps say that if the balance-of-power policy and Munich, one of its necessary corollaries in the situation of September 1939, were so unpopular, and if collective security was so popular with the peoples of the democracies, including particularly the British people, Stanley Baldwin and Neville Chamberlain, each in his turn, erred in not espousing the democratically popular policy of collective security from the beginning of the Japanese aggression in China in 1931 and in not upholding it all the way through—Manchukuo, Abyssinia, Austria, Czechoslovakia and Albania.

It is in answering this particular observation that the general argument of this book is especially apposite. The facts generally stressed here are that while the peoples of the democracies are overwhelmingly in favor of collective security as an abstract ideal and opposed to realism as a policy, they are equally opposed to assuming in time of peace the responsibilities implicit in collective security. Briefly, the people in the democracies do not understand the implications of their desires and will not elect candidates who tell them the truth. Liberals have never understood that truth has prevailed in the past not by reason of the preference of the masses but by reason of the pluck and pertinacity of an elite minority. The only way to get the peoples of the democracies behind collective security is to bring on a war situation and get them mad enough to go to war. Appropriate action for collective security is only possible in the democracies when it is war action. This means that collective security works only when it calls for war, which is to say when it has failed to work. To swing the people into a collective security mood, it is necessary to cook up a war situation. Until that is achieved it is necessary to follow a more or less realistic policy which ordinarily means, for England and every other great power, a balance-of-power policy.

The people, of course, are not to blame that collective security will not work. They are to blame only for not being willing to face the fact that it won't work, and for electing statesmen who delude them as they like to be deluded. When democracy was less mature, the British masses had less influence on the course of foreign policy. Then statesmen had to lie and delude the public less simply because they had to explain less. And, because they had to lie less, they had to blunder less. The public knew less and cared less about the conduct of foreign affairs. In the days of Pitt, Palmerston or Disraeli, if a British

Minister had done a Munich with a view to pitting Germany against Russia, he would not have had to undo it all by guaranteeing Poland seven months later. In those days billions of dollars had not been invested in publishing and radio enterprises in the democracies requiring a continuous exploitation of human imbecility, ignorance and emotionalism for a return on the investment.

Of the power situation in September 1939 it may be said that Britain and France only about equaled Germany and Russia for balance-of-power calculations. Therefore, Britain and France, following a balance-of-power policy, would never have dreamed of challenging Germany and Russia, since to have done so would have given control of the balance of power to other and hostile powers like Japan or Italy. Even assuming the strongest probable combination, that of Britain, France and the United States, against the combination of Germany, Russia and Japan, it would be a pretty evenly matched contest. Balance-of-power policy does not risk evenly matched contests. It would never put Britain and France into what might easily be a war against Germany, Russia and Japan. Britain and France may well be able, unaided by America, to defeat Germany and Russia or even Germany, Russia and Japan. A balance-of-power policy ventures no predictions as to the outcome of given contests. It merely forbids a great power to start a war unless, in so doing, it begins with the odds clearly in its favor. Britain and France definitely have not the odds in their favor in the present war unless they can secure as allies America, Japan and Italy, as before. There was plausibility in 1914 to the calculation that, with France, Russia and Japan against Germany, Austria-Hungary and Turkey, the war declaration of Britain on the side of France and Russia would prove decisive in favor of the latter. Actually it did not so turn out, as in 1917 it proved necessary for the Allies to bring the United States in on their side in order to win. In 1939-1940 there was not even plausibility to the supposition that Britain and France alone had the odds in their favor in a war against Germany and Russia, with Japan and Italy ready to jump on the British when their exhaustion after prolonged war might make them seem an easy mark. It is not necessary for any unity or community of interests or purposes to exist between Japan or Italy and Germany and Russia for either of the first two named countries to attack Britain for territory when Britain is weakened by war.

The question may be raised, "Can any great power always follow a balance-of-power policy?" The answer would seem to be "Practically always." Obviously, small nations cannot always profit from the fact that large nations follow it. For a great power, following a balance-of-power policy will mean, broadly speaking, that it will not start a war with another great power unless reasonably certain that the odds are in its favor and that it will not be set upon by other great powers, but this, obviously, does not mean that a great power need hesitate to attack an inferior great power or to jump on a small nation unless it has reason to fear that such an attack by it will invite counter-attack by one or more great powers. Following a balance of power policy will not prevent a nation great or small from being attacked by an equal or superior power. Balance-of-power considerations merely tend to discourage great powers from venturing upon what for them are doubtful wars. In the case of Germany in 1939, however, these considerations were not a restraining factor for the simple reason that Germany felt sure of Russian cooperation and both Japanese and Italian neutrality. Balance-of-power considerations in the spring of 1939 should have held back Britain and France from guaranteeing Poland but should not have been expected to restrain Germany from moving against Poland.

Those who say that it is collective security or else subjugation of the entire world by one aggressor nation or by several aggressor nations do not recognize that it is just as hard for the bad as for the good nations to dominate the entire world. The unity of the bad is just as unattainable as the unity of the good. The supremacy of the wicked is just as impossible as the supremacy of the good. This, of course, does not mean that a big bad nation may not gobble up one or more small nations just as the big good nations, Britain, the United States and France have done in the past. But once a single bad nation goes far on the path of conquest it runs afoul of other bad nations of equal power. The more a great power expands beyond a certain point, which varies according to the circumstances of the given power, the weaker it becomes. The British Empire is now a perfect case in point. It probably cannot now be defended over the long run without the aid of the United States. Those who threaten us with subjugation by Germany or Japan completely overlook the weakness of bigness when, as Britain has done, it undertakes too much. There is, of course, no formula to prevent aggression or to preserve peace and the status quo. Balance-of-power policy merely tends to avert wars which neither side can hope to win.

Stated somewhat differently, the ideal of the internationalists is to create paper bulwarks against aggression, calling them law and treaties. Obviously, there is only one bulwark against force and that is force. Law is a bulwark only to the extent it has force behind it, and to the extent such force is greater than that opposed to it. Every war is an international lawsuit which is always won by the side having the greater force. The balance-of-power policy reckons that the best possible check to one aggressor is another aggressor. It is not always possible to invoke that check. Finland and Poland could not invoke Germany against Russia, for example. British stupidity in vainly trying to encircle Germany with an Anglo-Russian-French alliance had made that impossible for poor Poland and Finland. A policy which declares war on all aggressors, as does collective security, can never utilize the force of one aggressor or would-be aggressor against another. Collective security makes the assumption basic to all law, namely, that the good or law-abiding members of the community greatly outnumber the bad or the lawbreakers. In the international community the assumption is false as regards any possible body of rules. If the three good and great powers, Britain, France and the United States undertake to make war on every bad great power making an aggression, they, thereby, tend to unite all potential aggressors who would never otherwise be united. If half the international community is disposed to break what the other half considers law, why unite the lawbreakers, when united they are nearly invincible?

It is a sound rule of experience that wickedness does not unite any more than goodness. But, attacking simultaneously in the name of righteousness two or more great powers pronounced bad cannot fail to unite them, at least for the duration of the attack by the good. This is why an attack by the good on the bad is rational only if calculated to result in the achievement by the good of a monopoly of power. If this is clearly impossible or most improbable, then the only rational policy is to encourage the rascals to fall out and fight among themselves, which experience shows they always end up by doing. Why send good Englishmen to kill bad Germans when there are so many bad Russians available to do the same thing if only given a chance? Why send good Americans to kill wicked Japanese when there are so many wicked Russians available for this good purpose if only given a chance? Anglo-American policy is calculated to unite aggressor nations in a way they could not possibly attain unity if left to their own devices.

The main trouble, of course, with following a balance-of-power policy within the framework of democracy is that it involves a degree of realism which a popularity-seeking politician or publicist dares not expound or defend. And that is democracy's funeral. The new revolution will not end war any more than did the capitalist revolution. In its youth capitalism made a rational use of war as an instrument of national policy. In its senility it makes an impotent use of war as a means to unattainable ends. The new revolution will mark a return to rationality in the use of war. Briefly, men will kill, not for the kingdom of heaven, but for something on earth or not at all. This will mean less killing by reason of the elimination of futile killing for righteousness' sake. In so far as the new revolution is a revolt against religion it will be largely a revolt against religion or other worldly values as motives for worldly wars. It will be a gain for humanity to whatever extent war for the unattainable is discouraged since such warfare is always over and above warfare for the attainable which will always go on as long as there are things to be attained by war and human wills so to attain them.

CHAPTER XV
The Bloody Futility of Frustrating the Strong

A necessary part of the new revolution is a recasting of most of the world into four or five power zones to be dominated by as many of the greatest of the great powers. One of these, naturally, is the United States, commanding the Western Hemisphere; another is Japan, commanding how much of the Orient one cannot accurately foretell; another is Russia, commanding within her present borders nearly a sixth of the world's territory; a fourth is Germany, destined either to control a large part of Europe or to be destroyed in the attempt; and a fifth is Britain, dominating how much of her present empire in the near future no one can foresee. Possibly, Italy and France with their populations of around forty million each, or less than half the populations of the five great powers just named, may be able to dominate permanently considerable empires. Whatever the final distribution resulting from the present war may turn out to be, it is fairly certain that it will be drastically changed.

The internationalists say that America must join the Allies in an attempt to prevent redistribution by force. Before following this counsel, Americans should reflect that territorial redistribution and world unification have always in the past conformed to the new patterns of force factors. The status quo is always doomed, in some places sooner than others. Those who link their survival with the maintenance of the status quo everywhere doom themselves to an early destruction, or to destruction as soon as the status quo is changed anywhere. For the first time in her long history Britain has made her survival conditional on the maintenance of the status quo all over Europe and Asia, a fatal error of impotent senility. Americans should reflect that the current processes of change of the territorial status quo by violence are taking place wholly outside this hemisphere and hold no imminent menace for us.

A great deal of futile verbiage has been wasted on the question whether the dissatisfied nations are justified in their resentment against the status quo and in their efforts to change it. There is little point to holding court on the grievances, real or fancied, of the dynamic Have-nots, since the verdict would be determined more by the interests and bias of the jury than by the evidence or any relevant rules of law or justice. Indeed, there are no rules of law or justice relevant to the adjudication of the claims of the Have-nots. Publicists with a bent for statistics and economics like Sir Norman Angell make merry showing to their own entire satisfaction the hollowness of the complaint of the dissatisfied nations that they lack access to food and raw materials. It is pointed out how raw material and food prices have fallen since 1929 and how the Haves have been more eager to sell than customers have been to buy. The obvious insincerity of this argument inheres in its failure to recognize that, to buy from the Haves, the Have-nots must be able to sell to the Haves, which they are seriously limited in doing by reason of the high protectionist policies of the Haves. The liberals are impotent in liberalizing the trade policies of the Haves towards the Have-nots in time of peace, but terribly effective in inflaming the Haves against the Have-nots in time of war.

It is not any normative view of the claims of the Have-nots or counterclaims of the Haves which will determine redistribution in the future. It will be rather the play of the force factors. Here we must consider mainly the point of view of the other fellow and his war potential. All races are not equal. No peoples are more given to acting on this generalization than are the Americans and the British. If there are superior races, it is obvious that the Germans and the Japanese belong in that class. Yet it is a first principle of British policy that the Germans shall be kept down and of American policy that the Japanese shall be denied not only equal rights with whites in this country but also equal rights with the British to expand in the Far East. The United States stands for the closed door to the Japanese in America and the open door to the Americans in China. This Anglo-American policy of frustrating the Germans and the Japanese may be most persuasively rationalized as the defense of the rights of small nations. For this rationalization the support of a specious doctrine of equality of all nations may be invoked.

Actually, if Europe and Asia were divided up into myriad small states all guaranteed equality one with the other and all dominated by the money power of London and New York, there would be great joy and rejoicing in capitalist and idealist circles in the democracies, but there would be felt widely throughout the world the heavy hand of economic exploitation and the sting of gross personal and class inequalities. A legal system in which the Albanians would be in every way equal to the Germans and the Rumanians to the Russians could be nothing but a hollow sham. A system of world finance and trade, idealized by our internationalists, free traders and bankers, and exploited by London and New York constitutes a very real instrument of exploitation and oppression of human beings. It is precisely for that reason the system is being wrecked the world over by current measures of socialism and economic nationalism. Such a system may be rationalized and defended as a noble ideal. Be that as it may, some four hundred million Germans, Russians, Japanese and Italians are determined not to submit to it. If they did not have such a determination, they would be lacking in intelligence and courage. And that they probably are not.

In terms of realism the major population factors in every power equation are numbers and quality. In both respects the Germans yield to no other people in western Europe. In quantity they are second only to the Russians in all Europe. In 1939 the total number of German births in Germany was over one million six hundred thousand or three hundred thousand more than total births in Great Britain and France. In numbers, the Germans, the Russians and the Japanese, respectively, each exceed the white inhabitants of the British Empire. In the qualities that determine industrial and military superiority the Germans and the Japanese are fully the equals of the British or any other people. The issue of redistribution of territory and resources is one which has ultimately to be determined by power, quantity and quality of people being the two most important coefficients of power. To attempt to resolve problems of distribution in terms of ethics which contradict the dictates of power is futile since power always changes ethics.

The essential difficulty with Anglo-American ethics of distribution is that they assume that certain races like the Germans and Japanese can be treated as we Americans treat the negroes or as the British treat the darker races under their rule. It is as easy to rationalize an Anglo-French regime for Germany as it is to rationalize our regime for our negroes. The only trouble is that the Germans are not negroes. Germans who try to be liberals are as naive as Mississippi negroes who try to vote in democratic elections. Germans can no more enjoy equality of opportunity in a liberal, capitalistic Anglo-Saxon world order than negroes can enjoy equality in white America. The negroes cannot do much about discrimination by Anglo-Saxon democracy but the Germans can. The present war is another British bid to Americans to come over to Europe to help the British and the French to put and keep the Germans in their place, which is the doghouse.

No matter how many times we enable the British and French to defeat the Germans we shall never succeed in rendering the Germans amenable to the status of a conquered, punished and inferior people. The Germans just are not an inferior or second-class people and will not be so treated.

The moral case of the Allies is morally strongest and most hypocritical when it pleads for equality for the small nations. A Europe unified by a few great powers will naturally for a long time be rife with the frustrations of small nationalities. But whoever writes the ticket and however it is written, there will be injustice, dissatisfaction and grievances. Of that we may be sure. It so happens, however, that it is good form in America to be indignant over the frustrations of European minorities and to ignore or deny the frustrations of the American unemployed or farm minorities. We cannot tolerate in Europe oppression of minorities but we have never been without it in America from the day the first African slave was landed and the first Indian aborigine was murdered for his land by the white man. And with our ten million jobless Americans we have one of the largest oppressed minorities in Christendom.

If exclusively European force factors are allowed to determine the European distribution pattern, or who gets what, when and how, it seems likely that the distribution pattern will last longer and be accepted with easier accommodations than any possible distribution pattern imposed by a preponderance of non-European force. To allow the rule of the stronger is a more humane course than to attempt to impose the rule of the weaker or to frustrate the stronger. Two reasons based on long experience seem sufficient to support this generalization: The first is that any prolonged attempt to keep the stronger down and the weaker on top is certain to be incalculably costly in human lives and resources expended in battle as well as ultimately to fail. The second reason is that the rule of the stronger is normally calculated to yield a more efficient organization of society and utilization of resources than the rule of the weaker. The most serious objection on social or humane grounds to the Balkanization of Europe is that, to whatever extent it is effected and perpetuated, it renders impossible an efficient economic organization of Europe and utilization of its resources for the maximum social dividend. The very same objection would hold against any division of the United States into a score of sovereign small states.

If after granting full national status to every small national or subracial group in Europe demanding it, the victors of a new holy war could insure complete equality of opportunity for all persons, free trade, free migration and maximum utilization of resources for the good of all Europe, the moral case of the Allies for a new European order would be much stronger than it is in the light of past experience. But the Allies have already demonstrated their utter incompetence to do anything of the sort. They cannot even work out decent solutions for their own depression problems. Yet they ask us to help them save and remake the world by slaying Germans.

The new revolution must everywhere meet the imperatives of modern industrialism and the machine age. This capitalism everywhere has failed to do. These new imperatives call for larger integration as well as better distribution, for large political units exactly as they demand large productive units in industry. In the simple economy of the pre-factory days of the eighteenth century, President Wilson's ideals of self-determination for racial and cultural minorities were not impractical or inhumane. Applied in modern Europe, those principles cannot fail to work out badly for human welfare or to result in complete breakdown. In the eighteenth century and earlier, a village was usually an economically self-sufficient unit. Economic decentralization then made practical political decentralization. Since the end of the eighteenth century the trend has been towards economic centralization and integration, which has necessarily meant an equal trend towards political centralization and integration. None have carried forward these processes more rapidly or aggressively than the United States and Great Britain. We have gone further in industrial concentration than any other country. Yet it is now proposed that we join forces with the British in an armed crusade in Europe to impose upon that continent a reversal of the trend towards centralization of the past century and a half, at least, and now in flood tide.

Aside from the bloodshed involved in an attempt again to impose a new allied dictate on the strongest military power in Europe, there is to consider the implications for welfare through productive efficiency of any attempt to shackle the only advanced large-scale industrial nation in Europe. The harshness of the rule of the strong over the newly subjugated may be, usually is, mitigated with time. The economic losses resulting from the substitution of a lower industrial culture for a higher one may be both incalculable and irretrievable.

The new revolution everywhere stands for redistribution and

reorganization in line with the technological imperatives of the machine age. The cause of the Allies is that of counter-revolution. It upholds the status quo and opposes redistribution according to the indications of need, capacity for efficient utilization of resources and social convenience. It seeks to reverse in Europe the dominant trends, technological and political, of the past century and, more particularly, of the past two or three decades. The democracies have displayed their inability to utilize their resources in a way to end unemployment. But they now propose a crusade in the name of moral absolutes to prevent world-wide redistribution of raw materials and economic opportunities. The real issue before America may be stated as being one of achieving redistribution at home or fighting it abroad. The plutocracy that opposes redistribution at home is all for fighting it abroad. And the underprivileged masses who need redistribution in America are dumb enough to die fighting to prevent it abroad. The probabilities are that we shall have to come to the solution of the domestic problem of distribution through a futile crusade to prevent redistribution abroad. If it so happens, it will prove the final nail in the coffin of democracy in this country. And it should call for a terrible postwar vengeance on those responsible for this great tragedy of the American people.

The world wide and intra- as well as inter-national conflict over distribution is made out by the propaganda of the Haves to be a fight for western civilization. The argument equates this unimpeachable abstraction with the maintenance of the status quo or the concrete interests of the Haves. What is this thing called western civilization which we are told we must fight the Have-nots to preserve? Obviously, the phrase is broad enough to cover any and every current reality known to human experience. But those who use it in the general call to a holy war against the Have-nots mean by it, for purposes of argument, all, and only, the good things in the present social order. Aside from the absurdity of using a phrase like western civilization merely to denote everything one likes in the present social order, the argument has the following weakness: It disregards the fact that a civilization takes its character from its dynamic qualities, whatever these may be, and that, in the case of what is now being called western civilization, these are its vices, namely private greed and public wars of successful aggrandizement, rather than its virtues, the existence of which no reasonable person would deny.

To define a culture solely in terms of its parasitic virtues and to refuse to discuss it in terms of its dynamic vices, is to make rational discourse about it impossible. The endearing young charms of western civilization of the nineteenth century such as liberty, tolerance, education and rising living standards were all parasitic growths on the flourishing trees of greed and war. Parasitic growths can be extremely beautiful, as, for examples, orchids, Renaissance art or nineteenth century capitalistic liberties, opportunities, living standards or tolerance. *But the parasitic is never dynamic.* John D. Rockefeller and Cecil Rhodes, in their old age, became famous philanthropists. It was, however, as money-makers, not philanthropists, that they took their characters for dynamic and historical purposes. What is more, had they not been money-makers in their predatory youth, they could not possibly have been philanthropists in their benign senility.

It would be arrant nonsense to say "Let us have more philanthropists like the Rockefellers and the Rhodes, but let us have no more fortunes made as theirs were made." Most liberal reformers today want to preserve the beautiful orchids of a capitalist culture, which they call western civilization, while, at the same time, cutting down the ugly trees of greed and war on which these fair flowers have parasitically bloomed. The present war, civil and international, the world over, of the Haves versus the Have-nots is not really being fought over whether there shall be any more orchids. It is a war to see who gets the orchids and, also, over what kind of a tree the orchids shall be grown on.

Wars are fought between peoples, not isms or abstract ideas. Isms and ideas help to make people fight. The Haves are not fighting for an ism; they are fighting for their possessions, which happen, also, to be exactly what the Have-nots are fighting for. If the Haves will not share their wealth voluntarily, it will be taken from them violently. But it cannot fairly be said that the Nazis, the Fascists or the Russian Communists are devotees of a cult of destruction. Of late, they have been maintaining full employment through the creation of new capital goods while the Democracies have been maintaining large-scale unemployment by a reason of an inadequacy of new capital investment.

It is not the beauties but the inequalities of western civilization which are now in dispute. In so far as western civilization means this particular pattern of inequality, it is doomed. The reasons are matters of might rather than right. Present inequalities in distribution dissatisfy individuals and nations too numerous and too powerful to allow of the perpetuation of this pattern of distribution. A new pattern of inequality will, therefore, emerge from the current revolt of the Have-nots and the world-wide triumph of national socialism. But, for some time to come, it will correspond better than the present pattern of distribution to the actual and new force pattern, all of which amounts to saying that it will constitute social justice.

So far as civilization is concerned, the following observations seem in order: First, there is more to civilization than a given pattern of distribution. Hence most civilized values of the present can survive drastic changes in distribution. Civilization in polite terms, of course, is always a monopoly of the ins, the outs always being, by definition, barbarians. But it is always possible for the outs to get in and for the ins to he kicked out. Second, changing the elite does not mean ending a civilization, though it may mean changing it. The preservation of anything against change is impossible. Change is inevitable, but no given pattern of change is inevitable, however much the theorists of liberal capitalism may have believed the contrary. Third, civilization, itself, is nothing so much as a pattern of change. The current revolution, so far as civilization is concerned, is essentially a matter of changing the pattern of change. The people at the top will henceforth get there by different means or techniques from those used by the successful in a middle class civilization. This is not a revolt against civilization or against reason, as is so commonly alleged. It is a revolt against reasons for, and means of, keeping the present ins in and the present outs out.

CHAPTER XVI
After War, Pyramid Building

After our sentimental masses have been led by a politically calculating President and an economically miscalculating plutocracy into a second war in one generation to save the world from foreign sin, it will be necessary for us to take up permanently pyramid building to create work for the demobilized soldiers and the discharged war workers. It is, therefore, important at this time to give thought to the social function of pyramid building. There is, of course, nothing to pyramid building of almost any magnitude as an engineering performance. It is much easier to build pyramids today with steam shovels than in the days of Pharaoh with slave labor. All there is to pyramid building really is having the will to decide what to build and to enforce the necessary discipline, organization and administration. The choice of pyramids is also relatively unimportant. What the people need is not so much the pyramids as the work of building them. Pyramid building is for social order what physical exercise is for personal health. All that matters about exercise is getting one of several suitable varieties and the right amount for the given person. The end of exercise is not what is done but the doing of it.

By pyramids I mean any kind of public works, housing or long-term capital investments by the state which would never be created by private capital and enterprise for a profit or for interest. In other words, I mean public investments which are strictly nonproductive or nonreproductive in a capitalistic sense. I expressly use the word pyramid building though I well know that the term and the idea are most unpopular. Many protagonists of increased public investment as a necessary part of any remedy for stagnation try to deflect from their pet projects popular objection to pyramid building by denying that their proposals are pyramid building or nonproductive. By a type of casuistry worthy of the traditional Philadelphia lawyer, these special pleaders seek to justify building better homes for workers than the workers can afford as being really productive and both financially and economically sound within the framework of the capitalist system. Such sophistry is intellectually dishonest and easily shown up for what it really is by any one who understands the first thing about public and private finance and accounting principles. It is, however, in the best tradition of democracy to get things done by deluding people as they wish to be deluded. This chapter is written to explain not to sell pyramid building. This being true, I have no interest in misrepresenting it or calling the thing by another name. The phrase "pyramid building" is more descriptive than the phrase "capitalistically nonproductive" which, in more technical terms, is what is meant.

The reason we have stagnation in peace under capitalism today is that there are not enough inducements to private capital and enterprise to build or create sufficient long-term investments for a profit. Many people consider this situation highly abnormal and think it must disappear as soon as we get back to normal, by which they mean the nineteenth century. The fact of the matter is that we are getting back to normal and that that is precisely why we shall have to start building pyramids. Egypt in the days of the Pharaohs was far more nearly normal in any long perspective of history than frontier America. Egyptian pyramid building went on over a thousand years. Frontier capitalism played out in a little over one century.

In any economy of comparative abundance, that is to say, one in which the food supply is easily obtained and abundant, pyramid building is a social necessity if there are not enough foreign wars or a sufficiently rapid industrialization in progress to create work for all. Of course, one of the fallacies of capitalism is the notion that industrialization can go on forever. Obviously, as we have already seen, industrialization, starting from the basis of a wholly unindustrialized community and accompanied by rapid population growth, can go on until the saturation point in industrialization and the peak of population growth are reached. Egypt had no industrialization and not enough foreign wars. In addition it had, for the period, an exceptionally productive agriculture, thanks to a semi-scientific use of irrigation and the periodic enrichment of the Nile Valley soil by reason of the river's overflowing its banks. Our industrialization is over, our population growth has turned down and we have a surplus of food. We, therefore, have only war as an alternative to pyramid building. And between wars we shall have to build pyramids.

In preparation for the coming American pyramid building, we need a revolutionary change in ideology and values. The philosophy of capitalism, the frontier, Puritanism and expansion is at variance with pyramid building. Our social philosophy makes pyramid building appear a waste. Under capitalism any capital expenditure not made for interest or profit or one of a few capitalistically tolerated public purposes like police, defense, education and sanitation is waste. Schools eventually came, after considerable early nineteenth century opposition by sound liberals like Herbert Spencer, to be accepted as proper public investments, along with warships. The underlying theory of capitalism assumed that there was a perpetual scarcity of capital goods on which interest or profit could be earned. The fact that a return could be earned on an investment proved that it was good. Investments which were nonproductive of interest or profit, with certain exceptions already noted, as for schools and warships, were presumed to be wasteful and wicked. In the first place, it was taken for granted that the ability of an investment to earn a return in money was the final criterion of its utility and desirability. In the second place, it was considered evil to pay for nonproductive investments either out of taxes or public loans. Taxation was a necessary evil to be avoided as much as possible and the public debt was another evil to be kept as small as possible. Individuals should not be deprived of savings by taxation for public investment when they could, themselves, make a much better use of such savings through private investment.

By this time it will have occurred to many readers familiar with the writings of Stuart Chase, the more radical New Dealers and the utopian socialists to ask why our now redundant industrial capacity cannot be devoted to producing more consumer goods to raise living standards rather than to pyramid building. The answer is to say: first, pyramids may yield consumer goods and raise the standard of living. Pyramids may or may not be great temples to a cult or monuments to a ruler. They may be houses for the working classes which they cannot afford to pay for if building has to be done on a sound business basis. Second, the production of pyramids can be planned. It can be stabilized and temporarily expanded or contracted as may be deemed expedient in the given economic phase of the moment to help iron out an industrial fluctuation. Here it has to be explained, somewhat theoretically and I fear abstrusely, that under any socialized or collectivist economy, control and planning by one central state-planning authority are indispensable, the chief social problem today being that of maintaining full and steady employment, which is to say, order—order of a kind capitalism cannot maintain, as demonstrated over the past ten years.

If the people were given by a supposedly benign socialist state enough purchasing power to pay for the full industrial output, less what it might be necessary to retain for government operating expenses and for new industrial capital to keep the productive plant intact, there would soon develop, even under socialism, the most awful industrial fluctuations and economic upsets. The reason is that the vagaries of consumer taste and demand are such that an economy geared mainly to their satisfaction cannot achieve stability. In an expanding capitalism, a continuous shortage of housing for a growing population and of railroads and capital goods for the opening up of new territory, always compensated for the faults and failings of unsteady consumer demand. And, as has already been pointed out, consumer demand for bread, shelter and clothes is a far more stable factor than consumer demand for automobiles, electric iceboxes and luxury goods generally. Whether all goods are produced by socialized plants, whether a mixed system of government and private enterprise prevails, or whether all enterprise is privately owned and managed, it may be said that the more free consumer spending there is, the more instability there will be in production because the more unpredictability there will be as to future demand. And the larger the percentage of luxury goods consumed, the greater will be this unpredictability and the greater the consequent disorders in industrial production.

Now there are, broadly speaking, just two ways to meet this difficulty: The one is rationing and the other pyramid building. Of the two, pyramid building seems by far the lesser evil or the greater good. Some reasons follow. For one thing, pyramid building can be used in conjunction with a large measure of consumer freedom in a free production sector of the economy, thus avoiding the necessity for rationing which must always meet with strong psychological resistance as a bureaucratic tyranny over taste. A system of rationing would undertake to prevent industrial fluctuations and facilitate planning by making payment of all wages and salaries in fifty or a hundred different kinds of coupons which would entitle the bearer to given quantities of given classes of goods.

Pyramid building would mean regimentation in the matter of housing, thus denying to the poor their present democratic freedom to pick their own slum hovel. But regimentation in housing would seem less apparent or oppressive than regimentation in the rationing of consumer articles. Pyramid building would also permit the making available of a large quantity and range of free or nearly free goods which every one needs and in respect of which there is not much choice, as in milk, to name only one example. In the selection of ice cream, there is flavor, color and packaging to choose. In the selection of milk, there is just good, medium and bad milk to choose, with every one preferring good milk if he can afford it.

Americans are apt to think of welfare exclusively in terms of money income and the availability of things that money will buy. It is easy to show how many forms of individual, family and group enjoyment can be made available by public investments of a nonproductive character. Members of a family living in a city like New York on an income of less than two thousand dollars a year can buy comparatively few luxuries, little recreation and little medical and dental service. If liberty be proportionate to opportunity to use it, they have very little economic freedom or choice. They would obviously be better off if five hundred dollars a year of their money income were retained and spent for them by the state in a way to yield them satisfactions which they could not buy the equivalent of for one thousand dollars a year. Such satisfactions would have to result mainly from pyramid building such as housing, amusement and recreation buildings and parks, medical and dental clinics, milk-distribution plants and equipment to make this standard commodity available to the masses at less than cost, and so forth. One has only to compare the old Coney Island with the new state reservation at Jones Beach, New York, the latter being a perfect example of pyramid building, to get an idea of what a paternalistic state can do in the way of adding to the real income of the people in the way of recreation.

Of course, it will be necessary to educate the people to the use of public facilities for recreation and to the enjoyment of luxuries like a state-subsidized theater, opera, physical culture, adult education, and recreation center for each large community. Persons with incomes above five thousand dollars a year need not worry about getting homes outside of the slums, medical care, or recreation, since they are able to take care of these needs fairly well by shopping around for themselves in the free, commercial market. But the poorest third of the population, who have nearly two thirds of all the children, have little real freedom of choice or ability to satisfy their elementary needs in the free commercial market.

Pyramid building can and must be carried over into the supplying of standard types and grades of food, raw material like coal, and services like heat, light and transportation. These economic goods can be made nearly free or sold way below cost if the plants used in their production are treated as pyramids and built by the state out of a reserved part of the national income. The point here is that the production and distribution, gratis or nearly gratis, of economic goods through pyramid building would not be done primarily with the view of raising living standards and certainly not of catering to the vagaries of popular taste, but with an eye single to stabilizing maximum production and employment. These objectives of order can be achieved by having men dig holes and fill them up again, by war or by building structures and creating industrial capital capable of yielding public satisfactions. But if the left-motif in public investment is not public order, public order will not be a result. This means that public investment must be integrated with a totalitarian scheme of things and not done in the good democratic way of log rolling as public investment is now done in this country. If an attempt is made to give the people what they want, it will inevitably break down, because their several wants will not add up to a feasible program and rhythm of integrated and stabilized production and distribution. Certain strategically situated minorities will get more and other weaker minorities will get less than should be coming to them under any rational scheme of social justice. And the resulting pattern of production will break down because of bottlenecks in some branches and overproduction in others. We cannot have social order with pressure-group economic planning and interventions as at present under democracy.

Our farms have excess productive capacity. They are the most important area for raising our citizens of tomorrow. And they cannot operate on a free-market basis. The people need more milk but cannot pay for more milk under the present system. The state can spend hundreds of millions of dollars endowing the milk industry with productive capital to effect distribution of milk below cost. The idea will not be to give people with large families or a taste for milk something for nothing. The idea will be simply to create greater social stability by subsidizing agriculture, and, for this purpose, it will be found preferable to give away milk rather than to pay farmers for killing hogs.

Pyramid building would unquestionably increase regimentation just as the building of several new bridges and tunnels by which to enter New York has increased the regimentation of New York traffic. How much less regimented was the Indian's way of paddling his own

After War, Pyramid Building

canoe to any part of the island he chose to visit a few centuries ago! Most of the talk nowadays against regimentation is nonsensical or intellectually dishonest. Those who do most of this talking are the well to do or the rich who have least ground to complain about regimentation. The rich do not need to ride in the subways, though their chauffeurs must submit to the regimentation of traffic lights and policemen. The rich do not need to live in congested areas, but can enjoy the luxury of an individual country estate, though as a matter of fact most of them prefer to occupy an expensive apartment in the city. Such apartments, incidentally, so far as regimentation is concerned, are not greatly different from the nearby abodes of the poor except as to the amplitude of space and the facilities enjoyed. There is no more individuality to a row of Park Avenue apartments than there is to an East Side slum, in fact there is less because the architecture on Park Avenue is more standardized. The truth is that neither the rich nor the poor really mind regimentation as such. The best proof is to be found in any expensive and overcrowded night club whither the rich repair for amusement rather than to the wide-open spaces where they might enjoy freedom from regimentation and opportunity for the expansion of an individual personality which none of them have or desire. The regimentation the rich really oppose is the regimentation by government which curtails the power of money, usually to exploit the weakness of others. Obviously the poor do not mind such regimentation, as it does not affect the man who has no money.

The welfare problem, so far as the masses are concerned, is not to reduce regimentation but to improve it. The new revolution cannot give every laborer an automobile and chauffeur to free him from the regimentation of the subway, but it can improve the subways. It cannot give him a country estate to free him from the regimentation of the city but it can give him a slumless city. All this can be done only on the basis of pyramid building. Razing the city slums of the democracies would be a wholly nonproductive expenditure. British and American democracy arose with urban slums and must disappear with them. Democracy cannot eradicate slums. The only forces that can wipe out the slums will also wipe out democracy and capitalism.

The cry of our rich lovers of democracy and freedom against regimentation is never more strident than when raised against socialized medicine, plant and equipment for which come under the head of pyramids, because nonreproductive. To say that saving or prolonging life and conserving health for the poor by means of facilities they cannot afford to pay for, is capitalistically productive is all nonsense. Capitalistically considered, the lives of the poor are not worth saving since the higher birth rate of the poor takes care of their higher death rate. Capitalists who oppose socialized medicine are on sound capitalistic grounds. Only, if we are to practise capitalism, we should be much more ruthless than we now are and allow sickness and death among the poor to operate unchecked by charity, thus saving considerable money for the taxpayers. Under chattel slavery, of course, capitalism should practise socialized medicine, but under democracy the capitalists, not owning the workers and having an unlimited supply available, should not waste any of their money on the health of the workers except, of course, for measures of quarantine and isolation of infectious or contagious diseases which might menace the wealthy. Nothing could be more hypocritical than the criticism of socialized medicine made by the higher-ups of the American Medical Association, among our most ardent believers in democracy, whose fees put their services beyond the means of the poor, or by the wealthy whose yearly expenditures on medical attention exceed the total income of the average factory worker's family.

The bad faith of the attack on socialized medicine is best seen in its continuously repeated charge that socialized medicine would deprive the individual of his liberty of choice in the obtaining of a doctor. The charge, of course, is absurdly untrue as no contemplated or practiced scheme of socialized medicine anywhere leaves those with means to pay for private medical attention without opportunity to select their own doctor. Even in communist Russia, where socialized medicine has been carried to its logical extreme, the well-paid higher officials of the Soviet regime hire medical experts for special attendance outside of their official state employment hours and pay them extra for such attendance. All that socialized medicine would mean in a mixed economy, combining private and public enterprise, would be the availability to millions of people, as a matter of right and not of charity, of medical and dental service they cannot now afford and do not enjoy. Actually, of course, the majority of laymen have no knowledge which permits them to make an intelligent choice of a doctor to treat their particular ailment. As a practical matter, most persons if seriously ill will call the nearest doctor or one they happen to know and not to have selected on the basis of expert knowledge, information or comparison. They will then leave it to this doctor to select for them another or other medical experts according to his opinion of their needs and his acquaintance with and knowledge of available experts. The same thing happens under socialized medicine or in an army infirmary. The right of the individual to choose his own doctor, no matter how rich he may be, is largely a meaningless right. His choice is usually determined by the accidents of location and casual acquaintance and by the decisions of doctors who know more about other doctors than he does.

There is another and subtler consideration which favors, if not actually imposes, pyramid building under any nonexpanding collectivism, and that is the need for the enforcement of Spartan discipline to avert demoralization. In an expanding society and a fast growing population, with the industrial revolution in full swing, scarcity alone suffices to enforce a healthy social discipline and to prevent a deterioration of mass morale. A fully industrialized static economy, in which the population curve has flattened out, cannot have discipline enforced by need or scarcity as in the early days of capitalism. If the static economy is in the last phase of capitalist collapse there may be plenty of need by individuals who cannot find jobs or obtain remunerative prices for farm output. But this need is not the result of scarcity and, most important of all, it does not impose discipline. This need is due to unemployment. Such need, therefore, causes the ruling classes to mitigate it with relief. Work for the needy disciplines; unemployed relief for the needy demoralizes. The morale, discipline and character of a nation cannot be maintained with a third of the population directly or indirectly on relief. Capitalism can no longer maintain the discipline of work. It can only prolong its decline by relief which demoralizes instead of disciplining. The succeeding socialist state must keep the people fully employed in order to maintain social discipline and morale. Yet it will not have in highly industrialized and raw-material rich countries like the United States the disciplining force of scarcity. Therefore, it must go in continuously for pyramids or wars to insure scarcity.

The economists and political scientists of democracy and capitalism, whose thinking has been done in the unrealistic terms of hedonism and Benthamism, have tended to overlook the social necessity of discipline. Consequently, they have failed to see how democracy depended for its discipline on the transient coercions of scarcity, need and national defense operative in the era of the frontier, empire building, rapid population growth and industrialization. This discipline was made effective partly by the hunger of the masses and partly by the greed of profit seekers. Today agricultural surpluses and relief eliminate the discipline of hunger for the masses; and lack of opportunity to make large profits eliminates the discipline of greed for the capitalists. The masses are growing soft and demoralized on relief and a lack of work, and the capitalists are growing soft and demoralized on tax-exempt government bonds and a lack of new business ventures. The theorists of capitalism and democracy never foresaw the day when their system would lack discipline any more than they foresaw the day when it would lack dynamism. The socialist state must rely largely on war and pyramid building for discipline, without which no society can long maintain a higher order of culture or perpetuate itself.

Many of the socialists of the utopian schools as well as most present-day New Dealers think that the big social problem is how to achieve greater abundance. The problem is not that at all. Abundance without dynamism or discipline may be called the cause of our trouble. The problem is not how to get abundance, but how to get on in spite of it. For, if we cannot work out a formula for preserving dynamism and discipline with abundance, we shall have to get rid of abundance in order to recover dynamism and discipline. This we shall do in going to war, and this is about the only plausible rationalization for our going to war.

Abundance, if permanently compatible with dynamism and discipline, which remains to be proved, must be a by-product of better social order, organization, management and morale and not the main social objective. A socialist state in which a painless and nearly effortless abundance of material goods and services was enjoyed by everyone would quickly disintegrate and soon perish. It did not take Russian communism, which started out with free love and free abortions, long to find out that all that nonsense had to be stopped and the stern virtues of the family and the workshop had to be restored. Interestingly enough, during the past ten years of depression, communist Russia, Fascist Italy and Nazi Germany have been tightening up on discipline and democratic America, England and France have been relaxing on discipline.

An economy of easy abundance would create no spiritual values to give life dignity and meaning. Five million middle-class American homes with shiny bathtubs and chromium-plated mechanical gadgets do not in their entirety contain the spiritual values to be found in one medieval Gothic cathedral. There is no need to denounce a business civilization. It contains the seeds of its own destruction. Its smug prigs grow too comfortable and selfish to breed. The rest is natural history and jungle law.

A civilization must exalt a tradition of heroism. This it may do in war or pyramid building. Liberalism never glorified heroism in theory but, in its frontier empire-building days, it exemplified heroism in its practice. Now that the frontier and empire building are over for the democracies, the communities dominated by capitalism and democracy face the problem of developing a new design for living heroically. The Utopian socialists and New Dealers would build pyramids only for the greater ease of the masses. Pyramids, of whatever the type, must be built for the greater glory of the larger community, call it race, nation or cult as you like. Pyramids must express heroism and sacrifice, not hedonism and ease.

It must not be forgotten, of course, that the culture of capitalism inherited many dynamic taste factors from the preceding culture of medieval Catholicism and feudalism. It inherited tastes which are still aesthetically normative but no longer sufficiently dynamic to create full employment. As long as the rich kept on growing richer on the rising prosperity of an expanding capitalism, tastes surviving from Renaissance and pre-Renaissance days caused rich men to produce the counterparts of pyramids in the great mansions and country estates which the newly arrived vulgarians of trade built all over England and our eastern seaboard. The lavish expenditures by the eighteenth and nineteenth century plutocracy on mansions fulfilled almost every requirement of pyramids except that of socially convenient periodicity. They were built when times were good rather than when they were most needed, during hard times. Now that the rich everywhere are on the greased skids of taxation, inflation and hard times, they can no longer build many pyramids. And even many of the rich who can still afford to build pyramids lack the noblesse oblige or confidence to do so, preferring the shoddy ease of expensive city apartments, which are indistinguishable from office buildings or warehouses, to the state which should go with their wealth. They are economizing to compensate for the drop in interest rates on their tax-exempt bonds.

As indicated at the outset, the undertaking in this chapter has been to plant a few seminal ideas about the social function of pyramid building as a key to an understanding of the near future rather than to outline a program of pyramids to build. The thing for the elite now to understand about pyramid building is the why rather than the what or the how. Our problem in respect to production is to find ways of spending more money so as to permit of the most efficient public control and the best social order. Our ideas of economy belong to the eighteenth and nineteenth centuries and neither to the thousands of years that preceded them nor to the years immediately to come. It has always been the function of a ruling class to spend money unproductively, except during that brief era of expanding capitalism when they could invest money at high rates of return. We are now getting back to normal. We must get rid of the concept that a nation can live beyond its income. Whatever a nation consumes it has to produce. With our productive capacity and labor underemployed, our main problem is to spend and consume more so as to bring our production and employment up to capacity. In doing this, the idea is not to achieve abundance, though that may be a tolerable by-product, but to achieve full employment with order and freedom from present industrial fluctuations.

The defenders of democracy and capitalism who really know what it is all about frankly admit that unemployment is necessary for their system and prefer it to a loss of individual liberty or an increase of state control. This is not an issue which can be debated since it is, fundamentally, an issue of ultimate values. *De gustibus non est disputandum.* The issue will have to be resolved by force and not persuasion. The force may be only the pressure of events and strong minority group demands for better public order. Be that as it may, if large scale unemployment proves inconsistent with public order, as this book argues, those who prefer freedom with unemployment to regimentation with order will just have to be ploughed under in the chaos which their beloved freedom brings on and in the ensuing revolutionary steps to restore order.

To sum up the discussion of pyramid building. If the new revolution succeeds and does not land us in permanent chaos, it will probably develop a mixed economy. As regards private and public ownership and enterprise, this economy will consist of two sectors: one of small-scale enterprise in which private initiative will operate and one of large-scale enterprise in which public ownership and initiative will prevail. As regards the allotment of the productive factors, this economy will be divisible into a free sector in which consumer preference will govern and another sector in which the state will determine production. The goods produced in the free sector will have to be paid for by individuals. The goods produced in the controlled or planned sector will be paid for collectively and distributed free or below cost, such goods consisting in large part of the satisfactions individuals will receive from roads, public works, parks and cultural and recreational facilities of every sort provided by the state. In the free sector governed largely by consumer preference, of course, the state will constantly intervene to prevent or correct serious miscalculations and maladjustments. Industries losing consumer demand will have to be promptly readapted to other lines of production without the slow, costly and socially disruptive processes of failure, bankruptcy, idleness and reorganization peculiar to free enterprise. In the controlled or pyramid-building sector, the central objective will be the maintenance of order or full production and employment. This will mean using state demand and production in this sector to compensate for excesses or deficiencies in the sector ruled by consumer preference and industrial calculation to meet such preference. It will also mean the use of public investment as a general instrument of social policy, actual uses made of the instrument naturally being determined in every case largely by the changing objectives of social policy. Presumably the maintenance of full production and employment will be a fairly constant objective of social policy in any rationally conducted society. Preparation for war, preparation for greater economic self-sufficiency or a simple raising of living standards are special objectives which, in addition to that of order, may influence and guide the use of the pyramid instrument in given countries at different times.

The chief essential for the success of economic planning and social order is the suppression of what we now know as democracy or the parliamentary—i.e. log rolling, pressure group—form of government. This will probably have to be learned in war when the anarchy of parliamentary government becomes intolerable from the point of view of defense, the demands of which carry more weight with the people than the peacetime demands of welfare which democracy relegates to the secondary order of charity. Charity is only a Christian virtue while defense is a national virtue. Therefore, socialism must be inaugurated by national war (duly blessed by the Christian Church) and not by Christian influences which are so obviously secondary in our culture.

Chapter XVII
We Stagnate Because There Is No Common Will to Action

Activity, stability and order are the essential objectives of the new revolution the world over. They are being pursued everywhere with different means peculiar to different local situations. Everywhere this pursuit of order is being accompanied by a curtailment of individual economic liberty, i.e., the power of the moneyed few, and a continuous extension of social control, with increasing stress on individual duties and diminishing emphasis on individual rights. The terms communism (referring to the revolution in Russia), Fascism (referring to the revolution in Italy), Nazism (referring to the revolution in Germany) and the New Deal (referring to the revolution in America) now appear clearly to be each just a local —*ism.* Looking at the entire world situation, one may now say that there is just one revolution and just one significant *ism:* socialism. Everywhere it is a socialist revolution, differences being largely local peculiarities of different situations.

The new revolution is not the discovery of new means, but of new social ends. Democracy was the escape of the individual. The new socialism is the emergence of new folk communities. It is not the escape of peoples to Utopia. Individuals formerly could escape to America or to the upper classes. Peoples in mass cannot escape any longer anywhere. They have to stick it out more or less where they are. Japan may be able to do some considerable settlement of its people in Manchukuo and it may be able to export large numbers of people in imperialistic projects in the Far East. But, for western Europe and the United States, large-scale shifts in population are no solution, not even for Germany and Italy, except that large scale migration from the British Isles is indicated. The problem, then, is not discovering a place to go or finding a means of getting there. The problem of peoples everywhere is essentially one of staying where they are and developing there a community will to face the necessities and frustrations of the given situation. This means trying to change the situation by community effort. It is no longer feasible individually or collectively to flee from a bad situation to a better one as did the founders of the American colonies who came from Europe to this Promised Land. The tradition of democracy being escape, the tradition of most humanitarian and liberal varieties of socialism has been flight from reality to Utopia, usually by means of some panacea or series of panaceas.

The underlying assumption of all reformers and most socialists under democracy has been that the main problem in getting a better social order is one of finding and acquainting the people with the right means. This is the basic assumption of the New Deal as well as of the leaders of the Republican party. Actually, this assumption is wholly wrong. It cannot fairly be said that there has been a failure to find means to end stagnation, simply because there has been no collective will or effort to find such means. What has been lacking has been the collective will to end stagnation.

The preceding statement may come as a surprise to many who have thought of the New Deal as having received two distinct mandates from the people to end the depression and bring about recovery. That interpretation of those elections is an easy or plausible view to take of events. But it is not one which will bear searching analysis. Actually, the people making up the majorities which elected four New Deal Congresses and gave Mr. Roosevelt two terms voted as they did for a variety of reasons. Their several motives in voting did not add up to a single mandate to end unemployment and bring about full production. He has fulfilled partially or wholly some expectations and disappointed others. The farmers wanted higher prices and did not care about unemployment. They have got somewhat better prices but not enough better to satisfy them or to relieve the government of the necessity of giving them around a billion dollars a year as a straight dole. The unemployed wanted jobs and did not care about farm prices. Unemployment has been reduced from fifteen to eight to ten million, according to the phase of the business cycle, but this reduction in unemployment has not been enough to dispense with the need for at least a couple billion dollars a year for unemployment relief. Certain rich speculators in late 1932 wanted Mr. Roosevelt to devalue the dollar and raise the price of gold and silver so they could make a killing speculating in these and other commodities. He did as they wished, not, of course, merely because they so desired. In consequence, they made their killing. Those speculators who made this particular turn on Mr. Roosevelt's first important monetary policy came nearest to getting exactly what they wanted of any important group of Roosevelt backers. But those capitalists who voted for the New Deal for a restoration of business prosperity have, on the whole, been as little satisfied as the farmers with the results.

It cannot be said that the American people as a whole have ever wanted full employment and full production or voted for Mr. Roosevelt or anyone else to bring about these desiderata. No one, of course, is opposed to these boons and everyone will say that he wants them. Yet it is his own immediate interests that the voter in a democracy votes for. He cannot vote for full recovery because there is no candidate or party committed to achieving full recovery. Of course, it may be said that he also votes to have the Constitution upheld and so forth, but the Constitution does not give a man a right to a job or food for his wife and children, nor does it give a farmer a right to a fair price for his product. Hence the irrelevancy of the Constitution.

It is, of course, quite as it should be in a democracy that individuals and minorities should be concerned over their self-interest rather than that they should be obsessed with a passion for some ideal of collective interest such as putting the unemployed to work, raising the standard of living of all the people or stabilizing full production. One assumption of democracy is that politics is a game in which individual and minority group self-interest must enjoy free play under the rules of law and the umpiring of the courts. If order does not result from the playing of this game, the game has to be called off, notwithstanding the protests of the still satisfied winners who cannot see anything wrong with the game.

At no time since 1929 has the executive or legislative branch of the federal or state governments ever had a real mandate to create full employment. They have had mandates to do and undo specific things, mandates which have been partly carried out and partly unfulfilled. Consider the difference when the nation goes to war. Although there is not a plebiscite on the declaration of war, war is never made unless the people are as a whole in favor of it. The people, of course, can always be lined up behind a war once it is declared, even though they voted only a short time previously against going to war, as occurred in this country in 1916-1917. Once the nation is at war, the people want the war prosecuted with the utmost vigor. There is a definite mandate from the people to the government to win the war. Consequently it does not happen that a modern nation goes about winning a war or trying to win it as ineffectually as the American government has gone about trying to end unemployment. The Germans lost the last war, but it cannot be said that they or any of the belligerents at any time during the course of the war failed to try to win it. The people everywhere wanted to win the war, once they were in it. The proof is the sacrifices and efforts they made to win it. But the American people at no time since 1929 have really wanted, as a whole, to end unemployment. The proof is the lack of sacrifice and concentrated effort to end it. Billions have been spent to help victims of the depression but not to end it.

Every intelligent person knows perfectly well that it would be an easy matter, technically considered, to end unemployment in the United States within six months, just as it would be for the United States to mobilize the entire nation for war within the same period. But there is no national will to mobilize America to end stagnation. Why? Essentially the reason is that recovery or the mere ending of stagnation and unemployment are not sufficient as ultimate values to inspire the necessary faith and create the necessary national will to carry out any recovery program. Under democracy, recovery has to be a by-product of the pursuit by individuals and minorities of self-interest or like pursuit of victory by the nation at war. Whatever national will we now have is united only on the maintenance of this game. If playing of the game does not yield the by-product of recovery, that is just too bad for the unemployed. Individuals want jobs for themselves, but do not care about jobs for others. That is good liberalism, good democracy and good capitalism. Why should an individual suffer a loss in his liberty or pay taxes because the other fellow fails to find a job? An affirmative answer to this question is not possible within the framework of democracy.

The chief mistake of New Dealers like Stuart Chase, Rexford Tugwell and Mordecai Ezekiel, etc., has been in not seeing that full production and employment are not, in themselves, spiritual values or ultimate objectives for which any people, as a whole, are ever willing to fight and die. There is no problem to finding ways of ending unemployment any more than there would be to finding ways of waging war. The only real recovery problem is to find things the people want done, the doing of which would suffice to end unemployment and maintain full activity. At present these things have not been found for the American people.

The orthodox assumption of democracy that needs and desires are insatiable and dynamic is all nonsense. Under democracy and capitalism it is greed, not need which is insatiable and dynamic. What is wrong today is that greed is no longer sufficiently stimulated by opportunity or unfettered by taxation and regulation to furnish the necessary dynamism to end stagnation. It is the greedy, not the needy, who run things under democracy or socialism. Under democracy the greedy of profits run things; under socialism the greedy of power run things. Under no system is there a government of the needy, by the needy and for the needy. The most needy people in this or any other community are the least dynamic. The needy have never yet led a revolution. If the needy masses really felt an inordinate desire for more goods, they could quickly and easily take the necessary steps of organization and action to satisfy such desire, exactly as frontier communities a few generations ago took collective action to rid themselves of Indians, horse thieves and other undesirables.

Revolutions are not the work of people looking for unemployment relief, old age pensions or farm doles, or of businessmen looking for government subsidies, freedom and lower taxes. Revolutions are made by people of strong will who are looking for power and action, not Utopia. They are made by the dissatisfied elite who are angry and frustrated rather than hungry and oppressed. Of course, the growth of the "gimme" groups tends to create in time of peace a revolutionary situation by reason of the disorder caused by trying to meet their demands. Similarly, the failure of those ordinarily greedy for profits to find enough incentives to stimulate them to activity contributes to the creation of a revolutionary situation. But the reaction to stagnation will have to come from the frustrated and angry elite who will want action and power to restore order. The new revolution will be a reaction of the will and not a discovery of new means.

It is not President Roosevelt's fault that he cannot create a will to end stagnation. If he had tried to do so, he would not have become President. Nor is he to be blamed for not telling the people the truth about the necessity for large deficits to keep unemployment down. If he did not promise to try to balance the budget as soon as possible, he would not continue to command popular support. And if he did not break that promise by dishing out money to the "gimme" groups he would not have been reelected either. No politician can be elected to an important office in America today who does not conceal the truth from the people about the relation of fiscal policy to economic stability and make false and insincere promises. This is a reflection, not on successful politicians but on democracy which makes the delusion of the people a condition of success for a politician. There is, of course, no public will to balance the budget either. There is neither a will to sound finance in the orthodox sense nor to a realistic use of public finance for economic order.

Achieving full production and employment is not dramatic and has no sufficient appeal to the masses. Fighting Hitler or the Japanese would be dramatic and could be sold to the American people. Full production and employment would be a by-product. It is easy to arouse a will to war but impossible to create a will just to full production, full employment and a high standard of living for all.

Chapter XVIII
Out of War A New Revolutionary Folk Unity

While the Department of Justice has been rounding up adolescent nonentities for conspiring to overthrow the government of the United States and while the Dies Committee has been investigating crackpots charged with similarly dangerous designs, the only really serious preparations under way in this country for the substitution of a totalitarian dictatorship for the American system, by force and violence (legalized, of course), have been those connected with the Industrial Mobilization Plan for the event of war. This plan is being worked on jointly by the War and Navy Departments in cooperation with the nation's leading industrialists. Incidentally, these officials preparing for war and what they are to do in this event have more confidence (and more reason for it) in the imminent occurrence of that expected event than any leaders or members of subversive groups have in the immediacy of their hoped-for revolution. As the plan of the War and Navy Departments to replace the traditional American system with a totalitarian dictatorship by the Chief Executive in the exercise of his war powers is both legal and highly patriotic, I cannot possibly be prosecuted, investigated or even criticized for applauding it with all the enthusiasm of one who sincerely hopes for the revolutionary achievement of the new order which this plan and its governmental agents are eminently well suited to initiate under the smoke screen of a war to preserve the American system and check the march of dictatorship abroad.

As for the hunting down of subversive movements, juveniles, rowdies and crackpots by Messrs. Dies and Hoover, together with their own and other governmental agencies, I can only observe with interest that we are already getting warmed up for our totalitarian Gestapo or Ogpu and with some sadness that this feature of totalitarian socialism is the one which already seems clearly indicated to enjoy the greatest popularity with the American masses. This I naturally find not at all surprising. It fully confirms my pessimistic views of democracy which are as depressing as these substantiating indications. To understand democracy, it is essential not to believe in it. To believe in it, is usually not to understand it. The people everywhere understand and both enthusiastically and blindly approve of minority repression and persecution. They could not be made to understand the implications of the Industrial Mobilization Plan. And they would not approve of the plan if they did understand its implications. Hence official Washington plays it down, and the press give Messrs. Dies and Hoover the headlines. The stuff to give the masses in preparation for war is denunciation of dictators abroad and subversive minorities at home—any minority that is small and picturesque will do. This hate stuff creates the right emotional climate for war and the essential dynamism for revolutionary social change. It also diverts the thinking of the masses away from the real revolutionary changes implicit in our going to war.

The function of this war for us will be to facilitate the socialization of American industry under the war powers of the President, just as the function of the Civil War was to permit the liquidation of slavery by an executive proclamation of emancipation. We have a good American precedent for resort to war to effectuate a revolutionary change which we have not the social intelligence or folk unity to bring about without war. In the next war industrial and financial control by private capital will be liquidated by the war powers of the President as a necessity in a war emergency just as slavery was so ended during the Civil War. What could be sweeter for the national socialist leaders of tomorrow than to have the army and navy do most of the dirty work of the revolution while all possible opponents are at war salute to the martial strains of the "Star Spangled Banner?"

At some stage of the game it will be the task of a new elite to take over the new revolution made by the President as a war dictator with the aid of his war powers and War and Navy Department officials. This new elite must be prepared to rationalize the new revolution and to give it the dynamic ideology and leadership it will need to keep going as every revolution must do if it is to be a success. It is for the guidance of that new elite that this book has been written.

The new leaders must understand in advance at least two things about the war and the revolution: The first is that there is not going to be any return to a prewar normal as the Industrial Mobilization Plan (Page 27 Draft of 1936) promises "The controls and functions under discussion are not and should not be exercised in peace. The emergency would automatically terminate after the war." (The emergency created by the last war has not terminated yet. It is now just becoming really acute.) The second thing to understand is that this is a new revolution and neither a peacetime wave of reform nor a wartime emergency phase. This is a permanent new revolution as a successor to the capitalist revolution now over. Its chief functions are to preserve order and end stagnation. It cannot perform the one without performing the other. The only imperative the leaders of the new revolution really need to understand and respect is that they must keep the revolution going. If they do not slip up on this, they can learn all they need to know by experience or trial and error and correct all their errors as they go along.

Order and activity versus anarchy and stagnation are the issues, not democracy and liberty versus dictatorship and regimentation. Justice, as ever, will be the interest of the stronger, in this case the majority. And this interest will center around the major objectives of order and activity. Up until recently Moscow talked democracy here to spread communism while the American plutocracy talked democracy to get lower taxes and less government regulation. Mr. Roosevelt has talked democracy to keep war against Hitler as an ever available ace up his sleeve to win a third term. Americans out of work or living on the margin of despair do not think or talk democracy or liberty. They think in terms of jobs, ham and eggs and individual security. These require order and activity of a degree democracy cannot achieve.

As a term, a concept or a pattern of institutions and ways, democracy is of no real interest or importance today. The world is not trying to get back to the democracy of the slave-owning Greeks or the slave-owning founders of this republic. The world is trying to find dynamism for the machine age. If a workable formula is found, it can and probably will, in this country, be called a democracy. And the term will be quite as applicable to it as to the slave-owning democracies of Athens or tidewater Virginia. Whatever form of government and society the people get will, by virtue of their definition, be democratic, if they like the word at the time. The solution of the problem of stagnation through a new social dynamism and folk unity will have to be worked out in action rather than on paper. As already seen, the first major phase of the action or gestation of the new revolution is likely to be world war, unnecessary and unfortunate as it is for us so to bring about here the new revolution.

The new folk unity must be spiritual rather than contractual. That is to say, contrary to Rousseau, it must be felt in men's hearts rather than defined on paper, as in a constitution or some written document.

Seven years of the New Deal phase of the new revolution in America have failed to develop either a new dynamism or a new folk unity. The explanation is simple: A national electoral majority of "gimme" groups does not add up to a national unity. Mr. Roosevelt's only success in national unification for the purposes of dynamism has been in the realm of foreign policy, where he has united the plutocratic critics of his social policy with the masses, those on relief sharing the same sentiments as the plutocracy as to the necessity of putting an end to the wicked foreign *isms*. All this merely proves that the American people are united over European and not over American problems. The explanation is simple: The solution of our own problems calls for a quality of folk unity which we lack, whereas an attempted solution of Europe's problems calls only for a hate of Hitler, Stalin and the Japanese, which we do not lack. A solution for America's problems would require folk unity, which we lack. A solution for Europe's problems, namely hating Hitler and killing Germans, calls only for moral unity which we have to burn.

We lack folk unity but have plenty of moral unity for the cause of the Allies, and sundry small nations as well as the Chinese who are far from being a small nation. A moral unity for war, or a unity which was not a true folk unity, has at least twice before been the bane of American democracy. In our Civil War and the late World War we were morally united for wars which were not over interests of the whole people. Had the American people in 1860 had a folk unity, they would have imposed on the industrial interests of the North and the planter slavery interests of the South a compromise settlement involving the liquidation of slavery with indemnification to avert a needless war. But, alas, not being united as a people, Americans in 1860 easily allowed themselves to be morally united for war and emotionally barnstormed into it, one section against another, by the machinations of dominant economic interests of the two respective sections. Scarcely one per cent of the people owned slaves in the South or factories in the North. A thousand different formulas for peace on the basis of compromise between the factory and slavery interests could have been worked out, any one of which would have been better m every way for the interests of the American people than was the Civil War. But there was no folk unity to impose such an approach to the problem and such a solution for it. That this was true, was typical of democracy. In a democracy powerful minority interests always determine events and no single folk interest ever imposes itself to bring about a solution for the general welfare. If the conflict of minority interests is sufficiently big, as it was are united over European and not over American problems. The explanation is simple: The solution of our own problems calls for a quality of folk unity which we lack, whereas an attempted solution of Europe's problems calls only for a hate of Hitler, Stalin and the Japanese, which we do not lack. A solution for America's problems would require folk unity, which we lack. A solution for Europe's problems, namely hating Hitler and killing Germans, calls only for moral unity which we have to burn.

We lack folk unity but have plenty of moral unity for the cause of the Allies, and sundry small nations as well as the Chinese who are far from being a small nation. A moral unity for war, or a unity which was not a true folk unity, has at least twice before been the bane of American democracy. In our Civil War and the late World War we were morally united for wars which were not over interests of the whole people. Had the American people in 1860 had a folk unity, they would have imposed on the industrial interests of the North and the planter slavery interests of the South a compromise settlement involving the liquidation of slavery with indemnification to avert a needless war. But, alas, not being united as a people, Americans in 1860 easily allowed themselves to be morally united for war and emotionally barnstormed into it, one section against another, by the machinations of dominant economic interests of the two respective sections. Scarcely one per cent of the people owned slaves in the South or factories in the North. A thousand different formulas for peace on the basis of compromise between the factory and slavery interests could have been worked out, any one of which would have been better in every way for the interests of the American people than was the Civil War. But there was no folk unity to impose such an approach to the problem and such a solution for it. That this was true, was typical of democracy. In a democracy powerful minority interests always determine events and no single folk interest ever imposes itself to bring about a solution for the general welfare. If the conflict of minority interests is sufficiently big, as it was in 1860, the people simply line up on the sides of the two contending minority interests to fight a wholly unnecessary war. Of course, minority interests caused the Mexican and the Spanish-American Wars, but these wars might intelligently have been fought by a united folk interest since they both added to the patrimony of the whole people something which probably could not have been got otherwise. But the Civil War added nothing to our patrimony which a united people could not have achieved without the war. The Civil War gave us the liquidation of slavery and a more perfect political union, but a folk unity would have given us both without such a war. As for the World War it gave us literally nothing of value to the whole people. It did not even teach us anything, which is one compensation which national suffering should afford.

A healthy folk unity has to be grounded in the self-interest, self-defense and self-aggrandizement of one folk. A unity of a people grounded in abstract, absolute or universal morality is an unmitigated disaster since it can be a dynamic factor only in the promotion of a war over interests other than their own or interests which are not those of the whole people. This is a truth which Americans find great difficulty in grasping. To them it seems cynicism, wickedness or a paradox to say that a war for pure morality is worse than a war for pure national selfishness. Yet it is true. When the American people or any other people fight for moral absolutes or universal abstractions and not for their own selfish interests they are almost certain to be fighting either for the wholly unattainable, such as world peace and collective security, or for the selfish interests of some other nation. Wars for national selfishness there will always be. The humane thing is to keep them as small and make them as infrequent as possible. If Americans always fight for the selfish interests of Britain and France, they thereby merely make such wars larger and more frequent than they would otherwise be. If Americans fight for unattainable ideals, they thereby merely add to that amount of fighting for attainable material objectives which is inevitable a wholly unnecessary amount of additional fighting. The American people, having been conditioned or habituated to wars for moral purposes wholly apart from folk interest, are easy marks for Anglo-French propaganda exactly as they were in 1860 for northern industrial and southern planter propaganda.

Our trouble is that we think and feel, not as Americans but as moralists, religionists, legalists, capitalists and, last but not least, as loyal British colonials. We love moral abstractions, not American blood which we are ready to spill in torrents for moral abstractions. We are loyal to freedom for the Finns or the Poles or to justice for the Chinese, but not to employment for Americans. Employment is not a moral abstraction. A White House Conference on Children in Democracy reported on January 18, 1940, the finding that two children out of every three in America live in homes where income is inadequate for a decent standard of living. This, of course, is largely due to the fact that the poor have most of the children in a democracy. Does that state of affairs excite any wave of moral indignation in America as does the plight of the Chinese, the Poles, the Finns or the Abyssinians? Obviously not. Our elder statesmen, our Mr. Hoovers, go into action and morally mobilize America for relief of the Belgians or the Finns, but not for the ending of the unemployment of ten million Americans.

The British have had through several centuries, and still have today, the advantage over us of being fairly united as a people over British interests, not moral abstractions. At the same time they are past-masters in the manipulation of the moral symbols by which the American people can be moved like puppets into war. This superiority to us in folk unity is mainly a result of a different historical development. What has contributed most to British unity has been the elementary fact, comprehensible to the dullest English wit, that they are all in the same boat, the empire, and that all else is the sea; that they must live by their loot or perish without it.

For folk unity, a people must feel a consciousness of a common danger and a common destiny. This, the British have in a fighting. The American people, having been conditioned or habituated to wars for moral purposes wholly apart from folk interest, are easy marks for Anglo-French propaganda exactly as they were in 1860 for northern industrial and southern planter propaganda.

Our trouble is that we think and feel, not as Americans but as moralists, religionists, legalists, capitalists and, last but not least, as loyal British colonials. We love moral abstractions, not American blood which we are ready to spill in torrents for moral abstractions. We are loyal to freedom for the Finns or the Poles or to justice for the Chinese, but not to employment for Americans. Employment is not a moral abstraction. A White House Conference on Children in Democracy reported on January 18, 1940, the finding that two children out of every three in America live in homes where income is inadequate for a decent standard of living. This, of course, is largely due to the fact that the poor have most of the children in a democracy. Does that state of affairs excite any wave of moral indignation in America as does the plight of the Chinese, the Poles, the Finns or the Abyssinians? Obviously not. Our elder statesmen, our Mr. Hoovers, go into action and morally mobilize America for relief of the Belgians or the Finns, but not for the ending of the unemployment of ten million Americans.

The British have had through several centuries, and still have today, the advantage over us of being fairly united as a people over British interests, not moral abstractions. At the same time they are past-masters in the manipulation of the moral symbols by which the American people can be moved like puppets into war. This superiority to us in folk unity is mainly a result of a different historical development. What has contributed most to British unity has been the elementary fact, comprehensible to the dullest English wit, that they are all in the same boat, the empire, and that all else is the sea; that they must live by their loot or perish without it.

For folk unity, a people must feel a consciousness of a common danger and a common destiny. This, the British have in a higher degree than we Americans because of their abject dependence on sea power for food and on the empire for income. We have been taught to revere the Constitution and the British to revere the fleet as a national bulwark. There is a lot more realism to a sixteen-inch gun than a Supreme Court decision. And there is a lot more folk unity in national defense than in constitutional law. Now that we have long since virtually exterminated the Indians and ended that frontier menace, we have had for generations no consciousness of a foreign danger. The Civil War ended a secession and secured the formal framework of our national unity, but it added nothing to our feeling of folk unity. Rather, for a long time it worked against the development of such a sentiment. Then, shortly after the Civil War our feeling of folk unity suffered by reason of a radical change in the composition of our immigration from the Anglo-Saxon and Germanic Protestant stocks of northern Europe which were racially and culturally cognate with our own to the southern European and Russian stocks which were racially, religiously and culturally far removed from the dominant white native American stock. America thus came to mean an opportunity rather than a nation. Americanism to most people here and abroad meant the personal success story of an Andrew Carnegie rather than the tradition of a Nelson. "England expects every man to do his duty" is not the same tradition as "America expects everybody to make money." A nation is a nation by reason of what its citizens have done for it rather than because of what it has done for them.

The first requisite of the new revolution in America will be a shift in emphasis from success to sacrifice—for America. America as a big opportunity to write a personal success story is over. America as a unified great nation is about to be born—in war, travail, disillusionment and grim determination. Let the elite catch now, in advance of events, the vision of a new America the keystone of which will be the people and not the person. One will hear less about the rights of man and more about the duties of men and the rights of the American people.

Made in United States
Orlando, FL
21 December 2023

41537045R00137